This book focuses on the extent to ... ...res across Egypt, Libya and Tunisia affected Britis... ...campaign in North Africa during the Second World W... ... the work analyses the terrain from the operational and tactica... ... argues that the landscape features heavily influenced British operati... ...uld now be considered alongside other standard military factors. The wor... ...rs from previous studies in that it considers these additional factors for the entire campaign until the Axis surrender in May 1943. Until now it has been widely assumed that much of the Western Desert coastal plateau was a broadly level, open region in which mobile armoured operations were paramount. However this work concentrates on the British operations to show they were driven by the need to capture and hold key features across each successive battlefield. At the operational level planning was also led by the need to hold key ground across Libya and especially the province of Cyrenaica during the crucial middle period of the campaign.

A secondary theme of the work argues that British forces began to improvise certain tactical doctrines, which altered the early practice of combined arms assaults into one of Infantry and Armoured formations fighting largely separated battles until the autumn of 1942. Other developments in doctrine which were affected by the terrain included the practice of unit dispersal to hold key ground and the use of temporary units such as Jock columns to harass and engage the enemy. The two themes are interlinked and contribute fresh insights to the debate on British methods of warfare.

The author has consulted key documents, reports, war diaries and published memoirs, from major UK archives and compared these with the campaign historiography to develop the main themes of the work. These include the National Archives, the Churchill Archives Centre, the Liddell-Hart Centre for Military History, the National Army Museum, John Rylands Centre, Imperial War Museum at London and Duxford and London and the Tank Museum Archives at Bovington. The sources include many of the key published and some unpublished memoirs. His text is supported by a large number of specially-commissioned colour maps.

Neal Dando has been interested in the study of military history from an early age. He followed this with an Army scholarship and subsequent training. Before returning to academic study, Neal Dando worked as a retail manager for various national companies. He then completed his PhD in March 2014 at Plymouth University, where his research focussed on the North African campaign, 1940-1943. He has been an Associate Lecturer at Plymouth and is currently an Associate Lecturer at the University of Exeter, and also taught for two years at an Independent School in Devon. His current research continues to focus on the development of tactical doctrine, training and command amongst Divisions of the British Army and the Empire, during the early period of the Second World War. He is married and lives in Devon.

FROM TOBRUK TO TUNIS

From Tobruk to Tunis

The Impact of Terrain on British Operations and Doctrine in North Africa, 1940-1943

Wolverhampton Military Studies No.38

Neal Dando

Helion & Company Limited

Helion & Company Limited
Unit 8 Amherst Business Centre
Budbrooke Road
Warwick
CV34 5WE
England
Tel. 01926 499 619
Email: info@helion.co.uk
Website: www.helion.co.uk
Twitter: @helionbooks
Visit our blog http://blog.helion.co.uk/

Published by Helion & Company 2016. Reprinted in paperback 2023
Designed and typeset by Mach 3 Solutions Ltd (www.mach3solutions.co.uk)
Cover designed by Paul Hewitt, Battlefield Design (www.battlefield-design.co.uk)

Text © Neal Dando 2016
Maps drawn by George Anderson © Helion & Company Ltd 2016

Every reasonable effort has been made to trace copyright holders and to obtain their
permission for the use of copyright material. The author and publisher apologize
for any errors or omissions in this work, and would be grateful if notified of any
corrections that should be incorporated in future reprints or editions of this book.

ISBN 978-1-804512-45-6

British Library Cataloguing-in-Publication Data.
A catalogue record for this book is available from the British Library.

All rights reserved. No part of this publication may be reproduced, stored in
a retrieval system, or transmitted, in any form, or by any means, electronic,
mechanical, photocopying, recording or otherwise, without the express written
consent of Helion & Company Limited.

For details of other military history titles published by Helion & Company Limited
contact the above address, or visit our website: http://www.helion.co.uk.

We always welcome receiving book proposals from prospective authors.

Contents

List of Maps

Glossary

---

1. Local Names and Terms

Deirs – Crater-like and often large depressions with edges raised about ground level; the edges offered a defensive position and often overlooked the surrounding lower terrain. Some were over a mile wide and therefore offered useful forming up places for formations.

Escarpments – Low limestone ridges, either sharply defined to one side, or broader in width. They were stony covered or with a thin layer of gravel/sand which proved difficult to dig into. They offered important artillery observation places and from which the surrounding ground could be dominated and were therefore the key features over which many of the battles were fought.

Trighs – Desert tracks, often up to 100 yards wide, which rapidly turned to fine dust or winter mud due to the sheet volume of vehicles using them.

Wadis – ditches or a wide river bed, mostly dry but often flooded by winter rains.

2. Military Glossary

AGRA – Army Group Royal Artillery; a group of Regiments of Artillery, designed to give large concentrations of fire where needed.

Anti-tank gun – weapon designed to engage armour.

B-echelon – these were the British supply units for each Regiment. They moved constantly between the frontline units and the Field Supply Depots.

Barrage – Massed Artillery fire which targets an enemy position or unit.

Battalion – Army Infantry unit, usually of four companies and an HQ, averaging 400-700 men.

Battery – Artillery unit of 4-8 guns, often three to an Artillery Regiment, 250 men each.

Brigade – Army unit, usually of two to four Battalions or Regiments of Armour.

CinC – Commander-in-Chief Middle East. Successively held by Generals Wavell, Auchinleck and Alexander through the campaign.

CO – Commanding Officer, usually of a Regiment, Infantry Battalion or Brigade.

Corps – Army formation, usually off two or more Divisions and attached Brigades.

COS – Chiefs of Staff: The three Service Commanders-in-Chief for the Army, RAF and Royal Navy in London. They advised on plans and operations with the CinC Middle East.

Crusader – British tank of various marks with 2pdr gun

Division – tactical Army unit, usually consisting of two or three Brigades, and supporting units of Artillery, Engineers, Signals and Supply units.

Flash-spotting – method of observation of enemy gunfire by Artillery spotters

Forward Supply Depots (FSDs) – British supply depots sited in the desert.

GHQ – General Headquarters, based in Cairo, for British Middle East forces. This developed into numerous departments with hundreds of personnel.

Heavy machine guns – Infantry weapon designed for maximum firepower in defensive positions.

Jock Columns – formed by Lieutenant-Colonel J.C. Campbell in 1940, to utilize his artillery batteries more offensively against Axis positions, whilst holding a front-line position. They usually consisted of one battery of Artillery, protected by up to one company of Infantry, and single platoons of 3 anti-tank-guns and 3 Bofors AA guns, plus detachments of signals and engineers. A full discussion of their influence on the campaign is made in Chapter nine.

LRDG – Long Range Desert Group; formation originally set up by Major Ralph Bagnold for reconnaissance and raiding duties behind the lines. It used the more inland deeper Oaises of the great Sand Seas to traverse to its operations.

Matilda – British Infantry or 'I' tank, slow moving Infantry Support tank with a 2pdr gun and thick 78mm frontal armour.

2nd NZ – New Zealand; The 2nd New Zealand Division, or elements of – which became one of the leading Dominion formations of Eighth Army, along with the 9th Australian Division.

Patrolling – doctrine of sending out small units to watch or engage enemy positions

Recce'd- short or slang for reconnoitred or unit which made a reconnaissance of the ground or an enemy position.

Reconnaissance in force – a powerful raid into enemy territory often designed to destroy supply dumps or individual positions and gain intelligence intentions.

Royal Horse Artillery (RHA) – British Artillery Regiment, with three batteries of eight guns.

RTR – Royal Tank Regiment. British Armoured Regiment consisting of numerous units. Each one – designated 1st/ 2nd RTR, etc was classed as a 'battalion' of the regiment. Each of which had three squadron structure, like the Cavalry Regiments some of which had only recently been converted to armour.

Squadrons – Armoured Unit of 13-17 tanks, or Armoured Cars. RAF unit of 12 aircraft.

WDAF – 'Western Desert' Air Force; The frontline RAF unit in Egypt and Libya, although 'Western' was hardly used, it was referred to as the Desert Air Force. Other RAF formations also contributed to the air support provided throughout the campaign.

Western Desert Force – **WDF**, the original British frontline Corps which invaded Libya in 1941. The first British Corps formation which held the frontline in 1940 and became 13th Corps from January 1941.

3. Axis Formations and Terms

Deutsches Afrika Korps (DAK) – the first German units sent to North Africa. The force became a Panzergruppe **in 1941 and part of** Panzerarmee Afrika **from January 1942.**

5th Light Division – The First German Division which arrived in February 1941, with only one battalion of tanks plus other supporting arms. This converted to the 21st Panzer Division in 1941.

15th Panzer Division – The second German Division to arrive by May 1941, and together with the 5th Light Division formed the Afrika Korps.

90th Light Division – This unit originated from a mixed group of regiments and became the *Zur Besonderen Verfügung* (*z.b.V.*, i.e. a division at special disposal of the commander) Division during Crusader, before being named 90th Light Division from 15 December 1941, see Chapter 6.

Luftwaffe – German Air Force

Panzer Division – the three deployed in North Africa were the 15th, 21st and later the 10th Panzer Divisions. They consisted of two battalions of Panzers, each of 60-72 tanks, and supporting Infantry, anti-tank and artillery units.

Panzergruppe – Axis forces designated an Armoured Corps in 1941.

Panzerarmee – Axis forces designated an Army from January 1942.

Raggruppamento – Italian Armoured Group in 1940.

Italian Divisions: Ariete was the first Armoured Division, **Trieste** was a Motorised Division and the remainder were other Infantry Divisions. In mid-late 1942 reinforcements included the **Folgore** Parachute Brigade and **Littorio** Armoured Divisions.

The Wolverhampton Military Studies Series
Series Editor's Preface

As series editor, it is my great pleasure to introduce the *Wolverhampton Military Studies Series* to you. Our intention is that in this series of books you will find military history that is new and innovative, and academically rigorous with a strong basis in fact and in analytical research, but also is the kind of military history that is for all readers, whatever their particular interests, or their level of interest in the subject. To paraphrase an old aphorism: a military history book is not less important just because it is popular, and it is not more scholarly just because it is dull. With every one of our publications we want to bring you the kind of military history that you will want to read simply because it is a good and well-written book, as well as bringing new light, new perspectives, and new factual evidence to its subject.

In devising the *Wolverhampton Military Studies Series*, we gave much thought to the series title: this is a *military* series. We take the view that history is everything except the things that have not happened yet, and even then a good book about the military aspects of the future would find its way into this series. We are not bound to any particular time period or cut-off date. Writing military history often divides quite sharply into eras, from the modern through the early modern to the mediaeval and ancient; and into regions or continents, with a division between western military history and the military history of other countries and cultures being particularly marked. Inevitably, we have had to start somewhere, and the first books of the series deal with British military topics and events of the twentieth century and later nineteenth century. But this series is open to any book that challenges received and accepted ideas about any aspect of military history, and does so in a way that encourages its readers to enjoy the discovery.

In the same way, this series is not limited to being about wars, or about grand strategy, or wider defence matters, or the sociology of armed forces as institutions, or civilian society and culture at war. None of these are specifically excluded, and in some cases they play an important part in the books that comprise our series. But there are already many books in existence, some of them of the highest scholarly standards, which cater to these particular approaches. The main theme of the *Wolverhampton Military Studies Series* is the military aspects of wars, the preparation for wars or their prevention, and their aftermath. This includes some books whose main theme is the technical details of how armed forces have worked, some books on wars and battles, and some books that re-examine the evidence about the existing stories, to show in a different light what everyone thought they already knew and understood.

As series editor, together with my fellow editorial board members, and our publisher Duncan Rogers of Helion, I have found that we have known immediately and almost by instinct the kind of books that fit within this series. They are very much the kind of well-written and challenging books that my students at the University of Wolverhampton would want to read. They are books which enhance knowledge, and offer new perspectives. Also, they are books for anyone with an interest in military history and events, from expert scholars to occasional readers. One of the great benefits of the study of military history is that it includes a large and often committed section of the wider population, who want to read the best military history that they can find; our aim for this series is to provide it.

Stephen Badsey
University of Wolverhampton

Preface

This volume is an analysis of the significant impact of the physical terrain on the outcome of the British operations throughout the campaign in North Africa. It will consider this from a strategic, operational and tactical perspective and show that it also influenced certain improvised tactics which in turn, delayed a successful outcome and forced a prolonged campaign where units learnt by a steady progression of experience. This study's contribution to knowledge clearly shows that terrain heavily influenced planning, command decisions and tactics in operations. The thesis is different from previous studies of the campaign because it considers the importance of terrain and the subsidiary effect this had on tactical doctrine, from the opening phases of the Italian declaration of war in 1940, through to the final surrender at Tunis on the 13 May 1943. By consulting key primary documents, reports, war diaries and published memoirs, the impact of terrain has been considered alongside more commonly established military criteria.

Until now it has been widely assumed that much of the North African coastal sector was a relatively flat, open region in which mobile operations proliferated. However this work focusses on areas where terrain influenced the three layers of military operations. Firstly that strategic planning was dominated by the Libyan province of Cyrenaica, secondly that operations included the capture of key ground. Finally at the tactical level, the thesis concentrates on key features of ground which quite often turned the tactical battle. The terrain features include the importance of strategic ports through areas of operational importance to the tactically important features including high ground and depressions which remained key unit objectives. Commanders often based their operational tactical decisions not only on unit strengths and remaining armour or guns, but on whether the important ground had been gained or lost, which influenced the viability of continuing the action or exploiting any successes.

A secondary theme of the study argues that British forces began to improvise certain tactics, which became more standardized and widespread as the campaign progressed. These included vital practices of unit dispersal when formations moved but also temporary units known as Jock columns, which became a common feature and also heavily influenced the outcome of certain key battles. The two themes are inter-linked and contribute fresh insights to the debate on British methods of warfare. The methodology was based on archival material from an extensive range of major UK archives, including the Bovington Archives, Churchill Archives Centre, the Liddell-Hart Centre for Military History, the National Army Museum, John Rylands Centre, Imperial War Museum at Duxford and London and the National Archives. Sources included unit diaries, after action reports, Army and RAF files, along with published and unpublished memoirs. The analysis of these two themes will show that key terrain features were a significant influence upon all levels of military planning and operations throughout the campaign.

Acknowledgements

For their ever present support and unstinting patience I would like to thank my supervisors Dr. Harry (G.H.) Bennett and Professor Kevin Jefferys, throughout the development of the original thesis on which this study is based. Also, I would like to thank other members of staff from the Schools of Humanities and Library at Plymouth University, for their advice and encouragement. This book would not have been possible without the amazing support and guidance of the team at Helion and Company, owner Duncan Rogers, the Commissioning Editor Michael LoCicero, and the excellent drafting skills of George Anderson, who brought my rough sketches and basic ideas to life by creating some outstanding maps. I should also like to thank the staff of the following archives for their helpful guidance in making documents, maps and papers available: The National Archives at Kew, the Imperial War Museums at London and Duxford, the National Army Museum in Chelsea, the Liddell Hart Centre for Military History at King's College London, the John Rylands Library at Manchester University, the Churchill Archives Centre, Churchill College Cambridge and the Archives at Bovington Tank Museum. Finally the work would not have been possible without the support of my parents Hazel and William and also from Mary and Mike, who helped me to begin the whole process of studying again.

1

Introduction

This study sets out to consider the impact of terrain on British land operations throughout the whole campaign in North Africa. Previous studies have broadly followed the campaign narrative in terms of standard military factors such as command, supply equipment and training issues, often for both sides but concentrating on British forces.[1] They have also considered the importance of the air and sea war in terms of the battle to close the Axis supply routes to Libya. Yet in most of these studies, the effect of terrain on operations has always been treated as a relatively minor factor in comparison. This study re-assesses the effect of terrain at both the operational level and the tactical level, from a British perspective, throughout the campaign between June 1940 and May 1943, and will show that the outcome of the key battles also depended upon the possession of essential terrain features or vital areas of land which enabled them to dominate or outflank the enemy. Secondly, the nature of dispersal of forces throughout the landscape also heavily influenced a degree of improvisation in British tactical doctrine. The combination of these two influences meant that British methods of fighting evolved through a series of stages which will be discussed in relation to the tactical battles and the impact of the natural landscape.

This research found that numerous primary documents, reports and war diaries often had clear evidence that terrain heavily influenced planning, command decisions and the tactics used. Units made continuous operational moves to capture and hold high ground or other features in order to gain an advantage over the enemy, whilst commanders at various levels made tactical decisions based on the success or failure of gaining these features as well as targeting the destruction of enemy units. They also planned subsequent moves based on their unit's ability to hold key ground, whilst taking into account regular, military factors of remaining unit strength, morale, cohesion and supply of their formations. It was a heartening confirmation that at a symposium in Birmingham in April 2011, a roundtable discussion by leading military

---

1 For ease of reference, the multi-national units and divisions which fought as part of the British Ground Forces are referred to as the British Army or British forces in this study.

historians noted that terrain was one of the numerous but important topics which had yet to be fully analysed in relation to British Army operations during the Second World War.[2] The main battle chapters seek to assess how well the British forces approached each major action and briefly assess problems they faced. The central aim then considers how far the terrain features impacted on the battle and doctrine, what the outcomes were and how the formations learnt and developed doctrine from the combat experience.

In North Africa, the British Army faced a range of desert environments; the coastal terrain of Egypt, commonly referred to as the Western Desert, was a mixture of soft sand, depressions, low stony ridges and escarpments. As they reached eastern Libya, this contrasted with a hard stony limestone plateau across much of the province of Cyrenaica, also divided by ridges and escarpments. The northern coast of Cyrenaica was almost a peninsula of ground jutting westwards into the Mediterranean, most of which was dominated by the high ground of the Djebel Akhdar. This has a maritime coastal climate along its north and western sea facing slopes and through which the Italians built their via Balbia coast road connecting westwards to the capital at Tripoli. There were many places in the hills which offered both sides suitable defensive positions, but all of this high ground was largely outflanked to the south by more passable terrain of the deeper Libyan plateau, although even this desert short cut towards the Tobruk sector, had its difficult and slow going sections.

Western Libya included the coastal regions of Tripolitania and which included a number of key defensives sites, but which again were largely outflanked by more passable desert routes which undermined any serious defence near the coast. Eighth Army would took advantage of these during its long advance to Tripoli by January 1943. Finally, when Eighth Army advanced into Tunisia, the relief features became much more substantial and provided the Axis with some impressive defences. These required a series of new and developing alternative assault doctrines by Allied formations in order for them to be captured or by-passed. By this time Eighth Army had become a well-tuned fighting force with excellent supporting units, including HQs which actively analysed ground and the best routes across them.

There were other limiting factors which greatly affected British operations throughout much of the campaign, for instance from the early days, British forces had limited manpower and equipment, at least until the major Crusader offensive of November 1941. Further powerful reinforcements arrived for Gazala in the spring of 1942, many of whom were then lost during that battle or at Tobruk. Churchill's involvement from August 1942, brought in a third wave of fresh formations of men and materiel which carried Eighth Army through to Tunisia. This early problem of a lack of units and equipment contributed to limiting the offensives in terms of

2   Symposium: 'Revisiting Churchill's Army: New Directions in the Study of the British Army in the Second World War', University of Birmingham, Friday 14 September 2012. Roundtable Discussion: *New Directions*.

formations committed and the tactical doctrine used during operations. Yet it was also the impact of the tactical terrain, and at the operational level, trying to hold whole regions such as Cyrenaica, with limited resources which influenced events.

Tactical terrain often influenced the flow of battle as the numerous features were often developed into serious defensive positions by Axis forces and meant that the fewer British units were spread even more thinly trying to capture them. If a 'middle period' of the campaign can be defined, – broadly from Crusader to Gazala – even the large, well-equipped and supplied Eighth Army was again dissipated across widely dispersed terrain objectives. By the final battles in Tunisia, the final offensives were constantly limited by a lack of available Infantry particularly after the heavy losses at Second Alamein, and Eighth Army needed to combine with First Army Divisions to finally break the Axis defence.

In doctrinal terms, in late 1940- to early 1941, British units won a series of battles using a successful doctrine of combined arms in both attack and defence, where it inflicted a major defeat on the Italian 10th Army. During the next phase of the campaign British doctrine changed sharply with fewer units fighting mostly separated actions without combined arms support. The exception to this was the defence of Tobruk against the early Axis assaults. This period also saw extensive use of formations including Jock Columns. These were meant to be an improvised tactic to hold large areas of ground using small groups of Infantry and Artillery just to harass the enemy. Their use developed and continued through the middle phases of the campaign during 1941 and into the late summer of 1942. British doctrine was transformed again following the arrival of General Montgomery in the autumn 1942, and this contributed heavily to tactical success at Second Alamein. The final phases of the advance through Libya and Tunisia saw Army doctrine evolve in both attack and defence. This pattern suggests that overall British doctrine was a steadily improving one, with a sort of 'stumble' during the middle period of the campaign. After Second Alamein it enabled British forces to be more flexible in attack and defence, to combine both ground and air units, so that the Army became a formidable fighting force once again.

This work contributes a study which argues that the importance of terrain should be looked at equally, alongside other military factors. Therefore its aim is to complement other studies, such as Niall Barr's *Pendulum of War*, David Rolf's *Bloody Road to Tunis* and Jonathan Fennell's *Combat and Morale*, which are all highly detailed studies but which have concentrated on specific issues or time periods of the Army and its performance in North Africa.[3] This work is noticeably different to previous efforts in that it considers the impact of terrain on British operations and doctrine throughout the whole campaign.

---

3   David Rolf, *The Bloody Road To Tunis* (London: Greenhill Books, 2001), Niall Barr, *Pendulum of War. The Three Battles of Alamein* (Woodstock: The Overlook Press, 2004), and Jonathan Fennell, *Combat and Morale in the North African Campaign. The Eighth Army and the Path to El Alamein* (Cambridge: Cambridge University Press, 2011).

Background to the British involvement in North Africa

From 1882 Britain had retained an administrative hold over Egypt, and later used it as a military base for numerous campaigns before and during the First World War. After this, Egypt became the 'veiled protectorate' for the next twenty four years, with detachments of the Army watching over the vital Suez Canal route to India and the Far East.[4] The capture of neighbouring Libya by the Italians in 1932 increased the Fascist threat to British Egypt and the Middle East in general and raised the importance of the Mediterranean theatre in British defence planning as war approached. Throughout the late 1930s Mussolini tended to dominate Mediterranean politics, successfully dividing the British and French moves, as they tried to appease him. Mussolini viewed the Royal Naval bases at Malta and Gibraltar as 'bars' blocking his fleets from pushing into the Atlantic and the Red Sea and he impatiently awaited the chance to take control of the North African coastline to create a new 'Roman Empire.'[5] As pre-war crises developed in Europe, Britain increased its forces in Egypt in response to Mussolini's threats and enabled the Army to train and begin understand operating in the unforgiving desert conditions.

Following the French defeat and surrender in June 1940, Mussolini began his 'parallel war'. It was his chance to defeat Britain and takeover the North African territories he had always coveted.[6] Unfortunately for Italy, his armies were rapidly defeated in Libya and Egypt by the smaller but better trained British forces and the Italian retreat in early 1941 forced Hitler to send German forces to prop up the subdued Italian troops in Libya. Suddenly Britain was faced with a renewed Axis effort to regain both eastern Libya and Egypt. The subsequent 'pendulum of war' would see the campaign traverse the coastal desert region for two more years and see an expansion of the British war effort which finally brought in other Allied Armies to defeat the combined Axis forces by May 1943.

For Britain, the North African campaign had initially been one of just defending Egypt, to protect the Suez Canal and the land route to the oil producing centres in Iraq. However Prime Minister, Winston Churchill also saw the campaign as a means of defeating Italy first and diverting Axis forces from other fronts. The campaign also provided the British Army with the opportunity to engage the more professional German forces from 1941. Therefore victory in North Africa became the focus of British strategy which drew in her main ally, the United States, who initially had just supplied equipment to British forces there but later committed powerful ground and

---

4   Artemis Cooper, *Cairo In The War 1939-1945* (London: Penguin, 1995), pp.11-13.
5   Reynolds M. Salerno, *Vital Crossroads. Mediterranean Origins of the Second World War, 1935-1940* (New York: Cornell University Press, 2002), pp.11-13.
6   Douglas Porch, *Hitler's Mediterranean Gamble. The North African and the Mediterranean Campaigns in World War II* (London: Weidenfeld& Nicolson, 2004), p.40.

Air forces directly to the region. The allies believed this would weaken the Axis alliance and provide lines of attack on Germany itself through southern Europe.

Research focus and methodology

This study raises a number of questions about how far terrain impacted on British operations and looks to answer these by consulting primary military documents, unit diaries and anecdotal evidence from private and published memoirs. Each of the major engagements is considered chronologically using terrain as the particular focus, and its impact on unit planning, and battle outcome. For those wanting to read blow by blow accounts of the actual fighting, other works cover the major battles in meticulous detail which does not need repeating here.

The second chapter starts with an discussion of the landscape in which the campaign took place, focussing on the coastal sector across Egypt, Libya and Tunisia, whilst Chapters 3 to 10 provide a detailed analysis of the battles in nearly chronological order, with more of a focus on the impact of the tactical terrain. The battles have been summarised to avoid revisiting the detailed narratives of previous works and the discussion remains centred on the effects of terrain and doctrine. For the most part the campaign chronology is maintained, with the exception of the retreats from Cyrenaica which are considered together as they were so similar and are discussed in terms of the defence of the province. The final chapter briefly considers the other military factors in order to show the equality of their influence on the campaign.

The archives provided some key documents which contributed to the thesis; the National Archives provided the bulk of the series WO 201 and WO 169 documents which covered the campaign. Other Individual papers of personnel or units which served in the campaign were found at Churchill College Cambridge, the National Army Museum, the Imperial War Museum (IWM) in London and the John Rylands Library in Manchester. The IWM Archive at Duxford included some useful translations of operational documents from the Afrika Korps, while the Bovington Archives provided key regimental war diaries and battle reports of the various British Armoured Regiments involved.

The primary sources

The main group of documents which proved most useful were the WO 201 series held at the National Archives. Although these cover the North African campaign from a variety of topics, the main focus was to extract information specifically relating to commentary on the impact of terrain features either at the operational and the tactical level. The most telling folder was WO 201/578 on the Topography of Tunisia and showed how far the Eighth Army HQ had developed in calling for a full appraisal of the upcoming terrain by the final stages of the campaign. Earlier reports on either Libya or Egypt tended to be much less detailed and part of Intelligence summaries within command files or post action reports (e.g. WO 201/2691 Lessons of Cyrenaica).

Many of the higher level reports on the need to capture supply bases or key airfields were found amongst the command and planning folders, (WO 201/156, and WO 201/421), whereas reports relating to the impact of terrain at the tactical level came mainly from 'after-action' reports submitted by Regimental Officers who wanted to pass on their knowledge. Many of these post battle summaries were found either in the files referring to individual battle reports, such as (WO 201/539A) on the 150th Brigade Box at Gazala in 1942, or from within Regimental files such as the 1st Worcester's Regiment, (WO 169/5074) from the WO 169 series.

Most of the unit War Diaries are in the WO 169/series, which give a range of data from weekly unit strengths to movement and position information and occasional reports on actions. One minor difficulty with this series was to pinpoint when a Regiment was actually involved in the campaign because each year has a different file for each Regiment or Brigade. Equally useful were the Battle reports, (e.g. WO 201/2692 Gazala report) and the larger unit folders, (e.g. WO 201/530B Guards Brigade at Agedabia). These provided a lot of tactical detail relating to the key features, although there was not one for every action or unit involved. Some reports were just listed as Eighth Army Tunisia (WO 201/598) and offered a basic overview of events.

Other important WO 201 documents included the telegrams between the current CinC and London, (WO 201/401) which gave useful detail on their thoughts and plans based on the information they held at the time. The third group of this series were those dealing with the arms of service topics such as Signals (WO 201/369), which are highly detailed and offer lots of analysis on their operations and show how they were influenced by terrain. A final group of folders which provided useful supporting evidence were the AIR and Admiralty series, (e.g. ADM 199/414) which note support for Army operations by the fleet. Other RAF support folders are found within the WO 201 series, (e.g. WO 201/363, the RAF during Crusader).

Other archives also provided important evidence about the impact of terrain on the campaign. The Royal Tank Regiment documents at the Bovington Tank Museum Archives contributed numerous after action reports and letters by soldiers who wished to explain what had occurred in the battles in which they fought. The War Diaries added in details of movements and timings to these reports. Regimental diaries which proved most helpful included 3rd RTR, 6th RTR and 44th RTR. It was interesting to note that certain months were missing especially those of May-June 1942 when so many Regiments were shattered at Gazala and this may have been because of the disruption caused by the battle and subsequent retreat. Similar useful reports were found amongst the papers of various officers and men, deposited at other archives. For example, the papers of Tom Corbett at Churchill College Cambridge provided many details on the training and planning by 4th Indian Division relating to formations in the wider terrain. Both the Liddle Hart Centre and the Imperial War Museum included participants such as Brigadier Ray Briggs from the 1st Armoured Division, while the National Army Museum gave Eric Dorman-Smith's report and maps from June 1942 which offered a fascinating insight into his thinking after the debacle of Gazala. The John Rylands Archive contains Auchinleck's papers which were again useful for the controversial middle period of the British campaign, despite their heavily censored approach to releasing documents. The primary documents therefore provided the bulk of the evidence and were supported by the memoirs, studies and narrative histories which are discussed next.

Literary review

The importance of terrain in military history was clearly noted by writers as early as Sun Tzu, who argued that terrain was one of the five structural 'estimations' for any commander.[7] Most of the more recent military studies tend to place the importance of the impact of terrain on military operations in a separate description of the ground, or as a minor part of the narrative rather than showing its influence on the battle and outcome.

The more tangible military factors such as the quality of command, training, doctrine and weaponry of the campaign are always more paramount to most military writers, perhaps because many of the principles of doctrine involve a separation of the military formation to continue to function, no matter what the environment. For example the armoured doctrine booklets of mid-1942 discuss attack and defence but terrain is not discussed. Historians may well have followed on from this mindset, so that most works on modern conflicts tend to consider the impact of the more usual military factors such as command, intelligence, weapons and equipment, leaving the terrain often only as a background description linked to environment factors. There are the exceptions to the rule , such as Christopher Duffy's excellent study on the campaigns of Frederick the Great, which contributes a important chapter on the terrain features and how they influenced Prussian operations both in operational manoeuvres and at the tactical level.[8]

Published sources most useful for details about terrain and doctrine

Many of the memoirs provide useful details about the campaign, along with some beneficial references about the impact of tactical ground on operations, whilst other texts give more detail about the narrative of battle, and tactics, as well as the merits of equipment, training and life in general in the desert. War reporters such as Alan Moorehead and Alexander Clifford, published just after the events and these accounts have a nearness untainted by later histories and also present an outsiders' view of the campaign.[9] There are excellent memoirs by soldiers from British Armoured

---

7   Ralph D. Sawyer, *Sun Tzu. Art of War* (Oxford: Westview Press, 1994), p.167, describing ground as being, 'difficult or easy, expansive or confined, fatal or tenable,'
8   Christopher Duffy, *Frederick the Great, A Military Life* (London: Routledge Keegan & Paul, 1985).
9   Alan Moorehead, *African Trilogy* (London: Hamish Hamilton, 1946), and Alexander Clifford, *Crusader* (London: George Harrap, 1942).

Regiments; two of the most important being Cyril Joly's account of his part in the campaign, whilst equally detailed is Robert Crisp's account of 3rd RTR during Operation Crusader. Again there are more recently published armoured memoirs, but these again have an immediacy of post-war publishing but also they are important for noting the use of terrain and for details on tactics and operations.[10]

Some of the more patriotic wartime published volumes still offer useful examples of tactical doctrine including works such as *With Pennants Flying,* which contains first-hand accounts of Beda Fomm and Tobruk,[11] and John Verney's poignant account of a Yeomanry Regiment at Gazala and Alamein.[12] They have been rarely consulted since publication and can be compared with Keith Douglas's more often quoted memoir, which also notes the starched regimental characters he found within Yeomanry Regiments by 1942, and covers the tactical battle during Second Alamein and the pursuit to Tunisia.[13] Roy Farran served with the 3rd Hussars from pre-war and early campaign and his is an important memoir full of tactical detail of this period.[14] Rea Leakey discusses his pre-war desert training and some of the early operations up to the siege of Tobruk.[15] Jake Wardrop's diary usefully covers 5th Royal Tank's campaign from the soldiers' perspective.[16]

Other arms of service also provide some details of the tactical battle, such as life within a Jock Column in 1941 are covered by both R.L. Crimp and H.J. Griffin along with an unpublished account by Gerald Jackson which gives useful detail on armoured tactics and Jock Column operations.[17] Dan Billany's *The Trap* is an almost unknown wartime account of the 150th Infantry Brigade at Gazala, little referred to these days.[18] Many Divisional histories were written in the immediate post-war era, and included numerous first-hand accounts by returning officers which provided important details on landscape features and doctrine, one example being the Fiftieth

10   Cyril Joly, *Take These Men* (London: Constable, 1955), and Robert Crisp, R, *Brazen Chariots. An Account of tank warfare in the Western Desert, November–December 1941* (London: Frederick Muller, 1959).
11   David Masters, *With Pennants Flying. The Immortal Deeds of the Royal Armoured Corps* (London: Eyre & Spottiswoode, 1943).
12   John Verney, *Going to the Wars* (London: The Reprint Society, 1955).
13   Keith Douglas, *Alamein To Zem Zem* (London: Bantam Books, 1985).
14   Roy Farran, *Winged Dagger. Adventures on Special Service* (London: Cassell, 1999).
15   Rea Leakey, *Leakey's Luck, A Tank Commander with Nine Lives* (Stroud: Sutton, 1999).
16   George Forty (ed.), *Tanks Across the Desert. The War Diary of Jake Wardrop* (London: William Kimber, 1981).
17   R.L. Crimp, The Diary of a Desert Rat (London: Pan, 1974), and H.J. Griffin, *An Eighth Army Odyssey* (Pentland Press,1997), and Gerald Jackson, *A Long Parting* (undated, unpublished).
18   Dan Billany, *The Trap* (London: Panther, 1964).

Division history provides excellent detail from the battle of Gazala to the end of the campaign.[19]

The Tunisian campaign is covered by wartime published memoirs such as John D'Arcy Dawson, who argued that the First Army units 'materially' contributed to the final victory,[20] and A.D. Divine's work.[21] John Frost's account of the First Parachute battalion,[22] and one of his Engineer officers, Peter Stainforth, both relate the tenacious battles for the important high ground made by these First Army units.[23] The Infantryman's battle for key terrain at Longstop hill is well recorded by John Kenneally.[24] Memoirs from HQ personnel include Freddie de Guingand, who served under Auchinleck and Montgomery, and usefully compared their different styles of command.[25] David Hunt, an Intelligence officer at 13th Corps HQ, is good for both command and Intelligence matters,[26] while Bernard Fergusson served as Wavell's ADC so gives another insight into the first CinC and GHQ in 1941.[27] Denis Falvey served with the 64th Medium Artillery Regiment and covers the later campaign from their perspective.[28]

The army was made up of Empire and Commonwealth formations and these memoirs complement those of British soldiers; Howard Kippenburger gives an important and detailed account of the campaign as a battalion commander and later Brigadier in the 2nd New Zealand Division from Crusader to Tunis.[29] The biography of Captain Charles Upham VC adds detail on the tactical battles as he served in Kippenburger's 20th Battalion at First Alamein.[30] Brigadier Clifton also provides useful details of First Alamein and Alam Halfa in which he was captured.[31] Geoffrey Cox produced an important memoir of his time as Intelligence Officer, perhaps the only published account which referred to the importance of the escarpments near Tobruk and their impact on battle at Crusader.[32] An Australian Infantryman's view

19   W. Clay, *The Path of the 50th. The Story of the 50th Northumbrian Division in the Second World War, 1939-1945* (Aldershot, Gale &Polden, 1950).
20   John D'Arcy Dawson, *Tunisian Battle* (London: Macdonald & Co, 1944).
21   A.D. Devine, *Road to Tunis* (London: Collins, 1944), 78th Division, the Guards Brigade and 6th Armoured Division.
22   John Frost, *A Drop Too Many* (London: Sphere Books, 1983).
23   Peter Stainforth, *Wings Of The Wind. Active Service with the 1st Parachute Brigade* (London: Grafton Books, 1988).
24   John Kenneally, *The Honour And The Shame* (London: Headline Review, 2007).
25   Francis de Guingand, *Operation Victory* (London: Hodder & Stoughton, 1947).
26   David Hunt, *A Don At War* (London: Frank Cass, 1990).
27   Bernard Fergusson, *The Trumpet in the Hall* (London: Collins, 1970).
28   Denis Falvey, *A Well Known Excellence. British Artillery and an Artilleryman in World War Two* (London: Brassey's, 2002).
29   Howard Kippenburger, *Infantry Brigadier* (Oxford: Oxford University Press, 1961).
30   Kenneth Sandford, *Mark of the Lion* (London: Hutchinson, 1962). Upham won a bar to his VC at Ruweisat Ridge and was captured there.
31   George Clifton, *The Happy Hunted* (London: Panther, 1952).
32   Geoffrey Cox, *A Tale of Two Battles* (London: William Kimber, 1987).

is provided by Herb Ashby who offered a compelling account of his battles at Tobruk and Second Alamein with the Australian 2/48th battalion and the importance of the heights which his unit fought for.[33] The letters of Lieutenant-General George Brink are an important defence of his record as commander of the ill-fated 5th South African Brigade during Crusader.[34] Kaushik Roy offers some key insights into Indian Army commanders brought over by Auchinleck.[35] The wartime published account of the 4th and 5th Indian Divisions entitled *The Tiger Kills,* offers some useful detail on the impact of terrain and complements the official histories of both Divisions which are full of tactical details.[36] Many veterans have also written useful histories about specific battles. Michael Carver served throughout the campaign as a staff Officer, and has provided detailed histories of three key battles. His work on Second Alamein made some discussion of terrain impact but emphasized issues about British equipment and command failures.[37] The *Dilemmas of the Desert War* focussed more on defending Ritchie's leadership at Gazala in May-June 1942.[38]

Narrative histories provide structure and often make use of less well known first-hand accounts; Barrie Pitt, an Infantry veteran, wrote three detailed volumes highlighting the Infantry role in a campaign supposedly dominated by armoured warfare.[39] John Strawson served there as a young officer and produced an early one volume history.[40] The siege of Tobruk has become a popular subject for analysis recently with studies by William Buckingham and Robert Lyman, who both argue it was the decisive battle which saved the British desert campaign.[41] The only issue with such an argument is that each stage of the campaign could also make that claim; Wavell's first counter-offensive which saw off the Italian invasion of Egypt, the defence of Tobruk, Crusader, Gazala and First Alamein and so on. Nevertheless they contribute to the debate on the dramatic events at Tobruk. Frank Harrison showed the contribution

33   Peter Dornan, *Last Man Standing, Herb Ashby and the Battle of El Alamein* (Crows Nest NSW, Allan & Unwin, 2006).
34   Carel Birkby, *Uncle George. The Boer Boyhood, Letters and battles of Lieutenant-General George Edwin Brink* (Johannesburg: Jonathan Ball, 1987).
35   Kaushik Roy, *War and Society in Colonial India* (Oxford: Oxford University Press, 2006).
36   HMSO, *The Tiger Kills* (London: HMSO, 1944) and G.R. Stevens, *Fourth Indian Division* (Uckfield: Naval & Military Press, 2011) and Antony Brett-James, *Ball of Fire. The Fifth Indian Division in the Second World War* (Aldershot: Gale & Polden, 1951) now accessed at: http://www.ourstory.info/library/4-ww2/Ball/fireTC.html
37   Michael Carver, *El Alamein* (London: B.T. Batsford, 1964), and *Tobruk* (London: B.T. Batsford, 1963).
38   Michael Carver, *Dilemmas Of The Desert War. The Libyan Campaign 1940-1942* (Staplehurst: Spellmount, 2002).
39   Barrie Pitt, *The Crucible Of War.* 3 volumes (London: Cassell, 2001).
40   John Strawson, *The Battle for North Africa* (New York: Charles Scribner's, 1969), and Roger Parkinson, *The War In The Desert* (London: BCA, 1976).
41   William F. Buckingham, *Tobruk. The Great Siege 1941-2* (Stroud: Tempus, 2008), and Robert Lyman, *The Longest Siege. Tobruk the battle that saved North Africa* (London: Macmillan, 2009).

of the British 70th Division in breaking the siege during Crusader.[42] The fight for Bir Hacheim was covered by Richard Holmes and is a useful analysis of Free French forces showing the diversity of forces within the Eighth Army.[43] Peter Bates, a New Zealand veteran captured at First Alamein, argues this battles importance over the more famous victory later that October.[44]

The Second battle of Alamein is the perhaps the most studied battle of the whole campaign. It made Montgomery's reputation and began a new phase in the development of British doctrine for future operations. Jon Latimer and Niall Barr have written two of the more detailed recent assessments, with Barr defining changes in Eighth Army doctrines in this period.[45] Other narratives, such as those by John Strawson and Fred Majdalany are useful for some analysis of the terrain and for details by veterans who served there.[46] Michael Carver's history includes an analysis of alternative plans.[47] Richard Doherty's study adds some valuable analysis of the battle's place in military history, [48] while Richard Holmes argued that the victory was important for the army[49] while Paddy Griffiths considered the important 'Snipe Action' which defined Second Alamein as an example of the changing nature of doctrine and how improved weaponry created an 'empty battlefield'.[50] Bryn Hammond has provided the most recent detailed study of the battle, re-assessing Montgomery's planning and operational to the battle.[51]

The long advance from Second Alamein is less well studied but *Exit Rommel* details the tactical battles of the Axis retreat and Tunisian battles.[52] The works by Gregory Blaxland, David Rolf and Rick Atkinson have confirmed the importance of the Tunisian campaign as a separate stage of the campaign and not just a footnote to the Eighth Army's long march towards Tunis. Gregory Blaxland defends the First Army's experiences despite the difficulties faced but David Rolf's work is a more

42   Frank Harrison, *Tobruk the Birth Of A Legend* (London: Cassell, 2003).
43   Richard Holmes, *Bir Hacheim. Desert Citadel* (London: Pan Ballantine, 1971).
44   Peter Bates, *Dance Of War. The Story of the Battle of Egypt* (London: Leo Cooper, 1992).
45   Jon Latimer, *Alamein* (London: John Murray, 2002), and Barr, *Pendulum of War* (Woodstock: Overlook, 2005).
46   John Strawson, *El Alamein. Desert Victory* (London: Sphere Books. 1982), and Fred Majdalany, *The Battle of El Alamein. Fortress in the Sand* (University of Pennsylvania Press. 2003).
47   Michael Carver, *El Alamein* (London: B.T.Batsford, 1963).
48   Richard Doherty, *The Sound Of History. El Alamein 1942* (Staplehurst: Spellmount, 2002).
49   Richard Holmes, *Battlefields of the Second World War* (London: BBC, 2003).
50   Paddy Griffiths, *Forward into Battle. Fighting Tactics from Waterloo to Vietnam* (Chichester: Anthony Bird, 1981).
51   Bryn Hammond, *El Alamein: The Battle that Turned the Tide of the Second World War* (Oxford: Osprey Publishing, 2012).
52   Bruce A. Watson, *Exit Rommel. The Tunisian Campaign, 1942-43* (Mechanicsburg: Stackpole, 2007).

recent reassessment and a detailed operational study and draws similar conclusions.[53] American authors have taken more interest in their own formations and the impact of the Torch landings on the campaign, Orr Kelly's work gives an overview of Torch and the US battles in Tunisia.[54] Dominic Graham combined his own experiences with a history of the campaign.[55]

Historians such as Robin Neillands have used numerous veterans' accounts for their studies on the Eighth Army and 7th Armoured Division, which are important when adding weight to regimental diaries.[56] Richard Doherty's works on the Eighth Army and the 51st Highland Division are more patriotic in tone, but also offer useful primary accounts.[57] His later work on the Royal Artillery is based compliments the official Artillery history.[58] The recent regimental history of the South Notts Hussars used many first-hand accounts for Tobruk and Gazala.[59] The final battles of the Eighth Army have been less well covered. Barry Barnes used many veteran accounts on the battle for the Wadi Akirit (6 April 1943). Ken Ford has recently written a series of brief battle histories which include Crusader, Gazala, Second Alamein and Mareth (March 1943) which offer useful context, orders of battle also.[60] David Fraser wrote a Divisional level history of the British Army which gives a general officer's view on Divisional effectiveness during the campaign.[61]

Journal articles covering the campaign are less common. There are a few which include an early analysis of Libya which was published by the Royal Geographical Society in 1940 and should have been of great interest to British forces in North

53 G, Blaxland, *The Plain Cook and the Showman. The First and Eighth Armies in North Africa* (Abingdon: BCA, 1977), and David Rolf, *The Bloody Road To Tunis* (London: Greenhill Books, 2001).

54 Orr Kelly, *Meeting the Fox. The Allied Invasion of Africa, from Operation Torch to Victory in Tunisia* (New York: John Wiley, 2002).

55 Dominic Graham, *Against Odds: reflections on the experiences of the British Army, 1914-45* (London: Macmillan, 1999).

56 Robin Neillands, *Eighth Army* (Woodstock: The Overlook Press, 2004), and *The Desert Rats, 7th Armoured Division 1940-1945* (London: Weidenfeld& Nicholson, 1991).

57 Richard Doherty, *None Bolder. The History Of The 51stHighland Division In The Second World War* (Staplehurst: Spellmount, 2006), and Richard Doherty, *A Noble Crusade. The History Of Eighth Army 1941-1945* (Staplehurst: Spellmount, 1999).

58 Richard Doherty, *Ubique. The Royal Artillery in the Second World War* (Stoud: History Press, 2008), and Martin Farndale, *History of the Royal Regiment of Artillery. The Years of Defeat, 1939-1941* (London: Brassey's, 1996).

59 Peter Hart, *The South Notts Hussars: The Western Desert 1940-1942* (Barnsley: Pen & Sword, 2010).

60 Barry S. Barnes, *Operation Scipio. The Eighth Army at the Battle of the Wadi Akirit, 6th April 1943* (Market Weighton: Sentinel, 2007), and Ken Ford, *The Mareth Line 1943* (Botley: Osprey, 2012).

61 David Fraser, *And We Shall Shock Them. The British Army in the Second World War* (London:Cassell, 2002).

Africa.[62] There were some later discussions by members of the LRDG on their role in the desert in 1945, which related more to the deeper Sand Seas than the coastal sector.[63] Articles relating to doctrine include a brief study about Wavell's first Offensive in Libya from 1956 while John Buckley's more recent study noted that British Armoured doctrine tried to adapt to changes to combat better Axis equipment and doctrine[64] while other factors included the Air Battle for Malta and the importance of US aid to Britain in 1940.[65] Brad W. Gladman's recent study on how far Intelligence aided the improvement of RAF doctrine in the Western Desert is useful and a precursor to his later book.[66] These few articles represent the majority of past journal studies on the campaign, however there is a great deal of forthcoming new research on the British and Indian Army which should hopefully redress the balance.[67]

Studies on other military factors

There are many studies which cover the various other military factors which also contributed to the performance of British forces in the campaign. These are briefly discussed here to coincide with the final chapter which offers some examples about where these factors directly influenced the campaign; the reasons for the British presence in Egypt and her Mediterranean strategy to 1942 is assessed by Steven Morewood.[68] Studies on the British Army provide useful insights into doctrine and training and include David French's work which notes the development of command and control.[69] Harris and Toase make a useful assessment of problems in the development of armoured doctrine.[70] whilst Azar Gat's revisionist work argues that military

---

62   K.S. Sandford, 'Libyan Frontiers', *The Geographical Journal*, Vol.96, No.6, pp.377-388.
63   R.A. Bagnold, 'Early Days of the Long Range Desert Group', *The Geographical Journal*, Vol.5, No.1/2, pp.30-42.
64   Buckley, J, 'Tackling the Tiger: The Development of British Armoured Doctrine for Normandy 1944'. *Journal of Military History*. Vol 74 (4). pp1161-1184. p1165, and Hafiz, 'The Offensive in Libya: December 1940-February 1941,' *Journal of the Royal United Services Institute for Defence Studies*, Vol.101 (602), pp.206-216.
65   Michael J. Budden, 'Defending the Indefensible? The Air Defence of Malta, *1936-1940.' War in History*. 1999. Vol 6 (4), pp.447-467, p.448, and Haglung,D.G., 'George C.Marshall and the Question of Military Aid to England, May-June 1940', *Journal of Contemporary History*, Vol.15(4), pp.745-760.
66   Brad W. Gladman, 'Air power and intelligence in the western desert campaign, 1940–43', Journal of Intelligence and National Security, Vol. 13, (4) 1998, pages 144-162.
67   Conference: 'Revisiting Churchill's Army: New Directions in the Study of the British Army in the Second World War', University of Birmingham, Friday 14 September 2012. Various papers given on the Campaign.
68   Steven Morewood, *The British Defence of Egypt 1935-1940: Conflict and Crisis in the Eastern Mediterranean* (London: Frank Cass, 2005).
69   David French, Raising Churchill's Army. The British Army and the War against Germany 1919-1945 (Oxford: Oxford University Press, 2001).
70   J.P. Harris, & F.H. Toase, (eds.), *Armoured Warfare* (London: Batsford Ltd, 1990).

thinkers like Liddell Hart was actually a strong influence on German thinking and contributed to the development of Axis armoured doctrine while British doctrine was struggling for clarity.[71] David Fletcher argued that poor pre-war British tank manufacture contributed to the poor performance of British Armoured Divisions in combat and led to poor quality of armoured vehicles being sent to the desert.[72]

Certain histories describe the terrain at battlefields such as El Alamein, but the narrative always returns to the impact of other military factors. Niall Barr analyses the theory of the pendulum effect of war on armies; this argues that the effectiveness of an Army declines the further it moves away from its main supply base and into enemy territory. Taking this theory beyond Alamein British operations included an objective area they hoped to advance into effectively created a 'mini-pendulum' effect for the Army. In 1940, British forces were only expected to get beyond the Libyan frontier or at least only to Tobruk. In 1941 for Crusader, the main objectives included Tobruk and the western airfields, whilst in 1942 the planned advance from the Gazala line was only planned to reach to Benghazi. Finally in 1943, the advance into Tunisia was only made when Libya was secure.

Bidwell & Graham offer an Artillery perspective on operations and offer some more controversial arguments about the effectiveness of certain British Commanders.[73] The fictionalized accounts written by veterans often talk of other factors include George Greenfield's *Desert Episode* which recounted a typical Infantry attack at Second Alamein, based on his own experiences. His later memoir is a useful comparison of this earlier novel,[74] whilst *Men of Alamein* described the signallers role in the same battle.[75] Joan Beaumont details the operations of the Australian Divisions which were used at the beginning of the campaign and later at Alamein.[76] Winston Churchill directly influenced the campaign at key moments and his wartime career has been closely scrutinized by numerous studies, the latest of which is by Carlo d'Este.[77] The strategic move to support Greece vitally altered the North African campaign in 1941 and Churchill's role in this decision has been analysed in Sheila Lawlor's work.[78] His influence on successive commanders is best covered by their individual biographies,

71   Azar Gat, *British Armour Theory and the Rise of the Panzer Arm. Revising the Revisionists* (London: Macmillan, 2000). Liddell-Hart had been discredited by earlier revisionists for overstating his influence.

72   David Fletcher, *The Great British Tank Scandal. British Armour in the Second World War. Part 1* (London: HMSO, 1999).

73   Shelford Bidwell, & Dominic Graham, *Firepower. The British Army Weapons & Theories of War 1904-1945* (London: Pen & Sword, 2004).

74   George Greenfield, *Desert Episode* (London: Panther, 1955), written in 1944, and *Chasing the Beast* (London, Richard Cohen, 1998).

75   C.P.S. Young, *Men of Alamein* (Stevenage: Spa Books, 1987).

76   Joan Beaumont, *Australia's War 1939-1945* (Sydney: Allen & Unwin, 1996).

77   Carlo D'Este, *Warlord. A Life of Churchill at War, 1874-1945* (London: Allen Lane, 2009).

78   Sheila Lawlor, *Churchill and the Politics of War, 1940-1941* (Cambridge: Cambridge University Press, 1994).

including John Connell's hagiography of Auchinleck and Victoria Schofield's more balanced account of Wavell.[79]

The most detailed study on the impact of airpower during the campaign is by B.W. Gladman, although perhaps being an air historian, he overstates his argument that the Allied Air-forces alone were the, 'single greatest factor' for victory, an argument which this work must refute.[80] Tedder's own biography gives his biased view on Army operations while a typical air battle account is given by Humphrey Wynn who used the diaries of two pilots to recount the air battles at First Alamein.[81] A.J. Levine has made an important study of the development and effectiveness of the Allied Air Forces which deployed in Tunisia and enabled air superiority to complete the final defeat of Axis forces.[82] Perhaps the most important primary study of the Axis forces during the campaign is that by Martin Kitchen which shows the other side of each battle.[83] Other useful works include James Lucas's study of Afrika Korps veterans along with the memoirs by F.W. von Mellenthin and Heinz W. Schmidt, which give valuable details of the Axis views on British operations as well as their planning, operations and doctrine.[84] The impact of Malta and the Royal Navy on the campaign has been extensively covered in major studies and narrative histories. These include both naval and air aspects such as Tony Spooner's *Supreme Gallantry* about the impact of Malta on the Mediterranean campaign and James Holland's detailed study about the defence of the island.[85]

Conclusion

Overall this study will argue that during the North African campaign from 1940-1943, British operations were also influenced by the impact of the key terrain features both at the operational and at the tactical level. Secondly, it contends that these impacts should be considered alongside other standard military factors, as they had

79   John Connell, *Auchinleck* (London: Cassell, 1959) and Victoria Schofield, *Wavell, Soldier &*
     Statesmen, (London: John Murray, 2006).
80   Brad William Gladman, Intelligence and Anglo-American Air Support in World War
     Two. The Western Desert and Tunisia,1940-1943 (Basingstoke: Palgrave Macmillan,
     2009).
81   Lord Tedder, *With Prejudice* (London: Cassell, 1966) and Humphrey Wynn, *Desert Eagles*
     (Shrewsbury: AirLife, 2001).
82   A.J. Levine, *The War Against Rommel's Supply Lines, 1942-1943* (Westport:Praeger, 1999).
83   Martin Kitchen, *Rommel's Desert War. Waging World War Two in North Africa,1941-1943*
     (Cambridge: Cambridge University Press, 2009).
84   James Lucas, *Panzer Army Afrika* (London: Macdonald and Jane's, 1977), F.W. von
     Mellenthin, *Panzer Battles*, (Stroud: Tempus, 2001) and H.W. Schmidt, *With Rommel in*
     the Desert (New York: Bantam, 1979).
85   Tony Spooner, Supreme Gallantry. Malta's Role in the Allied Victory 1939-1945
     (London: John Murray, 1996), James Holland, *Fortress Malta. An Island Under Siege 1940-*
     1943 (London: Phoenix, 2004).

such a major influence of the outcome of each battle, especially in relation to the Army's use of improvised doctrine, which developed slowly throughout the campaign. The research uses a range of primary documents including command papers, intelligence summaries, battle reports and unit War Diaries, along with numerous personal accounts to prove how far the key landscape features was important. The thesis has also consulted a large range of the published historiography. These works remain firmly focussed on the impact of other military factors contributing more to the outcome of the campaign but rarely or fail to mention the equal importance of terrain in the same way.

2

Terrain

The campaign was mainly fought along the North African coastline, from El Alamein in Egypt, through Libya and ending at the Tunis-Bizerte bay. This chapter is an assessment of both the geography of the coastal sector from a strategic perspective and an analysis of each of the major areas of ground from a tactical level. British operations along the coastal sector were influenced by the strategic impact of each sector, which directly affected decisions about the placement of vital supply bases and possession of several airfields in western Cyrenaica. These will be discussed, along with an evaluation of how far the areas of tactical terrain influenced each of the key battles.

This study is the first to make a full assessment of the ground conditions throughout the entire campaign, whereas other studies only offer a brief description and define its parameters and combine it with the well documented problems faced by troops living in desert conditions; climate, disease and survival in such a difficult arena. The desert environment demanded coastal supply bases which made the few available ports into important operational and strategic targets. The geography of the various coastal ports played a significant role in the development of British strategy. The need to supply the Army across North Africa was affected by the position and distances of the key ports and was a priority for GHQ. It believed that the coastal terrain was considered to be, 'well suited to mechanized movement and…strategically there was great scope for offensive manoeuvre.'[1] There was also an additional requirement to protect the sea convoy routes to Malta. These issues focussed British planners' attention on the importance of capturing the few ports along the coast, but also the vital air requirement to capture and hold the coastal airfields which were positioned near the ports and stretched north around the Cyrenaican peninsula.

---

1   TNA WO 201/2692. Operational Reports: first Cyrenaican Campaign. METP No 10, Lessons of Cyrenaica Campaign, Dec 1940-Feb 1941, p.39.

Egypt: strategic perspective

Egypt was an obvious communications hub for the British from which to mobilize Divisions from the Empire, gathering them in the Delta bases for despatch elsewhere. Supply routes were directed towards Port Said at the northern end of the Suez Canal, whilst Port Suez on the Red Sea was the safest supply base for the majority of the campaign. The outbreak of war with Italy forced most British convoys to use the safer but longer route, travelling 12,000 miles around the Cape of Good Hope to Port Suez. Alexandria had become the main British naval base after Malta and became a target for Axis air attacks. From Alexandria there were numerous road and rail networks linking military bases near Cairo and to the oil terminal at Haifa in Palestine. This whole area had become of prime importance to the British war effort and could not be given up lightly. Beyond this vital communications and supply 'hub', in the west lay the Western Desert, which stretched for up to fifty miles inland to the Great Sand Seas, although only reconnaissance units operated in these more inland desert areas.

One of the main transport issues facing British forces was the single metalled road which ran for nearly 400 miles from Alexandria to Sollum on the Libyan frontier. Military doctrine recommended that a major supply base was needed at least every 200 miles so this dictated that the forward supply base was sited at Mersa-Matruh, where the road and single railway ended in 1940 and which carried all supplies and units forward. This distance from the Delta limited the size and number of units which could be maintained on the frontier, which was another 140 miles beyond Mersa. British forces ideally needed another forward base nearer the border, but this would be immediately vulnerable to enemy air and possible ground attack as the Italian base at Bardia was only just across the Libyan border. Therefore the Army remained on a stretched supply route back to Mersa and the Delta.

The railway had been hurriedly completed and even by late 1940 it was rapidly becoming an overworked supply route leading to an over-crowded railhead which was hemmed in too near the coast at Mersa by the closeness of the escarpment. This natural feature meant there was no land available to increase the supply base capacity. A new railhead had to be built at Quesaba, fifteen miles behind the front, but which only increased overall journey time to the front.[2] Further railheads were developed in 1941 and the railway was extended forward to Mischiefa near the frontier for Operation Crusader,[3] so therefore British operations were hampered throughout 1941 because of the lengthy strategic distances from its main bases in the delta to the frontlines. In 1942 the railway was extended to Belhamed near Tobruk in early 1942 and became a major supply base for Eighth Army linking with Tobruk. It was captured and used

---

2   Peter W. Rainier, *Pipeline to Battle. An Engineer's adventures with the British Eighth Army* (New York: Random House, 1943).
3   TNA WO 201/418. Cyrenaica campaign: planning, 1941 Nov.-1942, p.3.

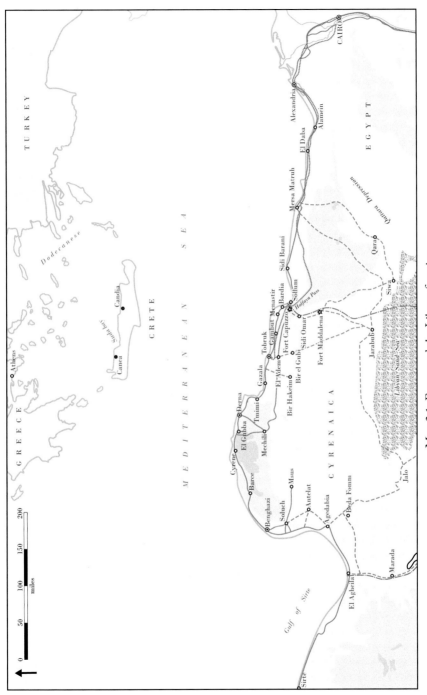

Map 2:1 Egypt and the Libyan frontier.

with limited success by the Axis, running supplies back into Egypt, though the track and trains were vulnerable and remained under constant RAF attacks.

Libya: strategic perspective

The border with Libya was an important sector for both sides and became a tactical battlefield during 1940-1941. Across the border, the eastern province of Cyrenaica became the central arena of the campaign during much of 1941 and 1942 and consequently became the focus of much British attention by GHQ. The problem with defending the province is discussed in Chapter 4 but overall the scale of the province remained the biggest problem affecting British operations. The major port in western Libya was Tripoli, which remained the main Axis supply base until January 1943. Further east Benghazi and Tobruk were major port bases in Cyrenaica, and both repeatedly changed hands throughout the campaign. Bardia was a smaller port, a few miles inside the Libyan border, which was used as an intermediary base to prevent overstretching supply lines to Tobruk 80 miles in the rear whilst in Axis hands.

Tobruk was a deep water port delivering an average of 20,000 tons of supplies per month.[4] It became an operational target for both sides because of its position and the location of airfields nearby. The Italians had built major air bases outside the perimeter defences; at El Adem, Gambut and Sidi Rezegh. This group of airfield facilities became important to cover the airspace over the border sector and into Egypt as well as the sea routes to Malta. As already mentioned the Djebel Akhdar hills to the west formed the strategic high ground of the Peninsula. Amongst the hills was the small port of Derna. Tactically the town had a deep wadi on its eastern side which offered, 'a naturally strong position if…not encircled via MECHILI,' and was one of the best sites for defence in covering the coast road.[5] These hills provided numerous strong defensive positions which could block the road. The weakness was that the entire Djebel area was outflanked by difficult but still passable desert routes to the south, rendering any coastal defence as near useless. The north-western coast of the bulge was additionally strategically important due to the group of air bases sited there. These included Martuba near Derna and Benini at Benghazi, from which aircraft could target the sea routes to Malta and Tripoli.

Distances again became important but also the need to capture a functioning port in the forward battle area. Benghazi was over 400 miles from Tripoli and 170 beyond Tobruk and became a forward Axis port, delivering an average of 30,000 tons of supplies per month. British forces captured it twice, to make it a forward British port; first after Beda Fomm in January 1941 and later after Operation Crusader in

---

4   Bungay, *Alamein*, p.44. It had capacity for 40,000 tons but in 1942, RAF air attacks limited this level of unloading supplies.
5   TNA WO 201/2692. Operational Reports: first Cyrenaican Campaign. METP No 10, p.26.

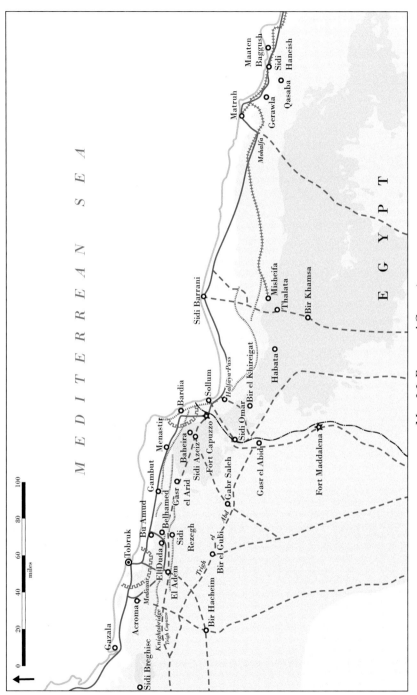

Map 2:2 Egypt and Cyrenaica.

December 1941.[6] However, they only held it for two short periods, (February–March 1941 and December–January 1942), and on both occasions it was limited as a supply base because air attacks from Tripoli and Sicily denied its full use. Later, when under Axis control, the RAF also made it a priority target and effectively reduced its supply capacity for the Axis.

Despite having the two main ports in the centre of the campaign arena, Cyrenaica remained logistically weak for British supplies because the ports and coast road were vulnerable to air attack. The more direct inland route to Tobruk ran south of the Djebel hills, then east-west across desert Trighs (trackways), via colonial forts at Mechili and Msus. The Trighs re-joined the coast road west at Benghazi and south-west to Mersa-Brega.

South and west of Brega the coastline turns north-west at the Gulf of Sirte and continues another 435 miles to Tripoli. This sector of coastal area had fewer defensive sites for the Axis following Alamein and even these were outflanked by British units moving inland. Tripolitania is considered in less detail here because the Axis retreat did not halt here for a variety of reasons, until it reached the Mareth line in southern Tunisia. This was the first major defensive site and was based on an old French defensive line built to keep Italian forces from invading Tunisia, it was further developed by Axis engineers to hold Eighth Army in early 1943.

The western province of Tripolitania became important to British forces in the later stages of the campaign, as they advanced towards Tunisia, as it contained Tripoli which was the major port in this sector and any advance into Tunisia, needed the port to be captured. The Eighth Army Commander General Bernard Montgomery remained cautious as he pursued the Panzerarmee, even by this sector of the coastline, because he was short of troops and he feared an Axis riposte as they had done in previous years.

Tunisia: strategic perspective

Tunisia became the battleground for the final six months of the campaign in 1943. Eighth Army HQ was now fully aware of the need to obtain the best analysis of the local terrain through which it would have to advance to reach Tunis-Bizerte, the final Axis held ports. One major intelligence report by a British HQ now focussed on the terrain and what impact it would have on the final advance. It was an in-depth analysis of the approachable routes north and of all features of the ground which would affect operations and was complete with tables of good and poor 'going' for vehicles, route reports, distances and key hill features.[7] This developed from regular updates issued

---

6   Bungay, *Alamein*, p.44. The full capacity was 60,000 tons per month, but RAF bombing reduced this.
7   TNA WO 201/578. Topography of Tunisia. Report by Eighth Army. March 1943.

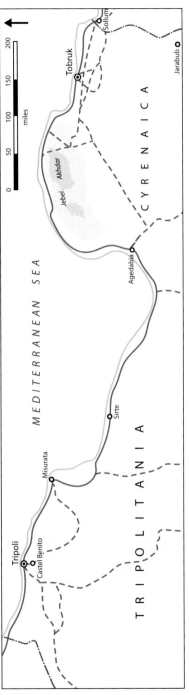

Map 2:3 Tripolitania.

in weekly Intelligence summaries, and was recognition by Army HQ of the need for accurate information about the landscape on which to make operational plans.

The final advance by the Eighth Army first required the capture of ports along the eastern Tunisian coastline for supply, including Sousse and Sfax. In the west the major Torch landings in Algeria and Morocco brought fresh Allied ground forces which developed as First Army, was also heading for Tunis. Their routes led through northern Tunisia and they were held up for six months by the failure to capture two prominent hill features along their two approach roads.

For the First Army approach, the eastern edges of the Atlas Mountains cut across the country from south west to north east, which meant the coast roads from Algiers passed through many gorges and tunnels which were easily blocked.[8] Further south, the Medjez valley provided a more direct route for the First Army from the hills and down onto the plains near Tunis. However these hills were also dominated by some key heights on either side of the Medjez valley and Axis forces delayed the Allies here too for six months.[9] South of the Medjerda valley is the high Dorsale region, a mixture of steep hills and narrow passes. This rugged terrain influenced the winter battles and prevented both sides from gaining a major advantage in their February offensives. This blocking of the First Army's advance meant that the operational initiative was back with the Eighth Army which was coming up from southern Tunisia.

Egypt: tactical features at the El Alamein position

The following tactical level analysis of each battlefield is described following a geographical order rather than chronological one from El Alamein to Tunis. To the west of the Nile delta, the Western Desert stretched forty miles inland from the coast, before reaching the Qattara Depression which is an area of impassable salt marsh. South of this is the Great Sand Sea, another impassable region with huge sand dunes reaching all the way into Libya. Consequently, mechanized operations were confined to the coastal sector mostly due to the nature of the ground surface.

Moving west from the Delta, the first defensive position to have a major impact on the key battles was sited sixty miles west of Alexandria near the railway halt at El Alamein. This sector of the tactical ground has been described in many accounts, with analysis ranging from a brief commentary to more analytical comments by Niall Barr. The main features of ground which influenced the three battles of Alamein were a series of low limestone ridges and deirs (depressions). Each ridge was a few miles long and became higher further south near the Qattara Depression. The ridges are broadly in parallel with the coastline, from south-east to north-east, and the low valleys on either side of them became traversable passing routes for motorised units.

---

8   Alan J. Levine, *The War against Rommel's Supply Lines, 1942-1943* (Westport: Praeger, 1999) p.62.

9   'Longstop Hill' became one of the major Axis defensive positions in the Medjez valley.

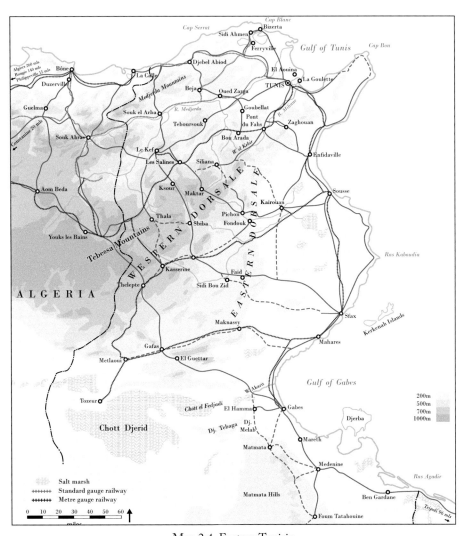

Map 2:4 Eastern Tunisia.

Nearest the shore was the Tel el Eissa feature, traversed by the coast road and which overlooked the Alamein railway halt. Its capture became a vital pre-requisite of the successful armoured break-out during both Alamein battles because it dominated the surrounding ground.[10] Immediately south of here the ground gradually climbed to the higher and much larger Miteiriya ridge which had a long south-westerly slope. The capture of this ridge became the main objective during Operation Lightfoot in October 1942 as it dominated the ground to the west and overlooked Axis positions.

Other features of tactical importance at El Alamein also included the low, hummocky ground near 'Kidney Ridge'; which was covered by scrub bushes and soft sand and lay to the west of the Miteiriya ridge. Paddy Griffiths rightfully noted that this low ground provided good cover for low profile well dug-in anti-tank weapons, and was therefore as defensively important as the higher ridges.[11] South of Miteiriya ridge was a further area of low ground flanked by two deirs. These had high-rimmed perimeters which gave useful observation points similar to a ridgeline. Infantry Lieutenant George Greenfield noted that observation from these was, 'everything' in the desert'.[12] The Deir-el-Shein depression protected Ruweisat ridge from the north-west and the larger El-Mrier depression extended west and across the ridge's southern side. In battle, both of these areas needed to be captured in order to advance onto the Ruweisat itself.

The central sector of the battlefield was dominated by the narrow Ruweisat ridge which ran east-west for 15 miles. It became a forward position for both sides at times during the Alamein battles, and as with any salient position, defending troops were exposed to enemy fire from three sides. The limestone rock made digging-in nearly impossible and required pneumatic drilling equipment or explosives to make it an effective defensive site. This was a re-occurring problem for the units which captured the ridge, as the New Zealanders found out. A feature which became known as 'Stuka Wadi' overlooked the low ground south of Ruweisat before rising to the smaller Alam Nayil ridge. East of Alam Nayil was Bare ridge which ran north-easterly and developed into the much higher Alam Halfa ridge. This line of southerly ridges dominated the traversable desert either side and provided the Axis a route of advance to their objective at Alam Halfa in August 1942. Overall the forty mile stretch of inter-connected low ridges and deirs was the best available defensive position from which British forces could protect their delta bases, and the whole area dominated the fighting from July to October 1942.

---

10   TNA WO 201/424, The October Battle of Alamein and the advance to Tripolitania. Nov-Dec 42. Report Brief Notes on "El Alamein" battle, 23 Oct – 4 Nov 42, map of phases.
11   Griffith, *Forward Into Battle*, p.111, and Paddy Griffiths, *World War II Desert Tactics* (Oxford: Osprey, 2008) p.19.
12   Greenfield, *Desert Episode*, p.51.

Egypt: Tactical features in the Western Desert

Beyond Alamein the important tactical factor was how much traversable desert was available for vehicles to move east-west. This sector widened as the Qattara Depression dropped away to the south, leaving an inland high plateau. Dividing the plateau was the major feature was a desert escarpment which averaged 500 feet in height and had only a small number of routes traversing down to the next level. The passable ground below it ran along an east-west axis and alternated between slower going soft sand and faster hard gravel areas. The central plateau below the escarpment reached to within ten miles of the coast where another escarpment dropped the land level to the coastal plain. In 1940, the Italian 10th Army used numerous higher features in the coastal area to create a series of defensive camps from which they attempted to delay a British advance. Their weakness however, was that the areas of good going enabled motorised units to by-pass the camps altogether.

The forward base at Mersa Matruh was situated 182 miles from Alexandria and was the advance post for British forces. It was only protected by weak minefields but British commanders considered it to be a fortress similar to Tobruk. The main weakness of the base as a defensive position was that it was easily by-passed along the higher plateau, as shown by Axis forces in late June 1942.[13] However, it was a useful supply base and was used as the headquarters by the Western Desert Force. Eighty miles beyond Matruh along the coast was Sidi Barrani. Here the old colonial fort and adjacent inland escarpments provided tactical features which needed to be captured before forces could move further west.

The Libyan border: Tactical features

This Libyan border was dominated by a landscape which could be used defensively by the Axis and easily halt British mobile operations. The main feature was the high escarpment, which curved inland and divided the coast into two sectors. At the border near Sollum Bay, this ridge became a high cliff with unrivalled views eastwards and across the coast road below. East of Sollum the road climbed sharply up the cliff face near the Halfaya Pass with a series of hair-pin bends. In 1941, Axis troops showed that this route could be effectively defended and that the top of the pass was an equally good defensive site due to the lack of cover for approaching forces from across the plateau.

The desert plateau above the cliff was dominated by a series of low hills and small ridges which extended inland for twenty miles. These were noted as important features by British planners in 1940, and were developed by the Axis into a series

---

13   Axis forces used this route going east in late June 1942.

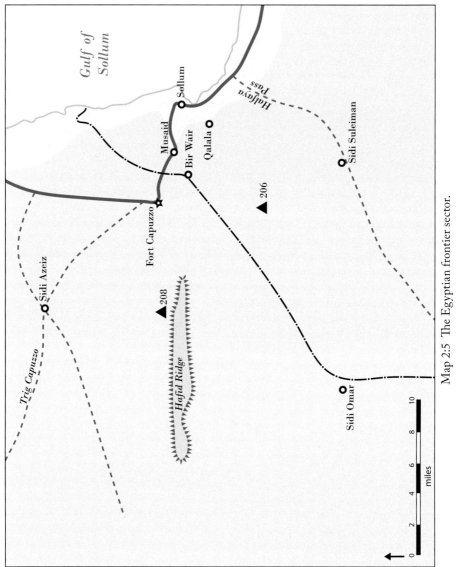

Map 2:5 The Egyptian frontier sector.

of interlocking defensive positions by May 1941.[14] The Italian base at Fort Capuzzo was positioned on one of these high features and dominated the border and coast road. Other key heights included Pt 206 and 208, and further inland was the Hafid ridge feature which consisted of three separate ridges. This group of Axis held positions became the British objectives for both Operations Brevity and Battleaxe in the summer of 1941. The following autumn, Eighth Army simply by-passed them by a 50 mile detour inland before driving into Libya for Operation Crusader. The border south from Capuzzo was marked by a thick barbed wire fence erected by the Italians to prevent the local Senussi tribes moving into Egypt. It was a deep array of up to five layers of wire, which stretched passed the Omar position to Fort Maddalena fifty miles inland. This was the southern-most point where large mechanized forces crossed the border. The Omars were developed into one of the strongest defensive Axis positions along the frontier in 1941.

Cyrenaica: Tactical features

The importance of tactical terrain in Cyrenaica increased as the campaign progressed. By 1942 the Eighth Army HQ began requesting more details from weekly Intelligence reports, for data on relief and the vehicle going across different types of ground.[15] The small port of Bardia was the first key objective for British forces advancing into Cyrenaica. The perimeter defences were situated on the plateau above the port, but these were overlooked by ridges outside the perimeter and divided by a ridge of high ground inside the defences.

Moving west beyond the frontier, much of the traversable landscape now consisted of a hard gravel plateau, with three long escarpments running west to the Djebel Akhdar hills. Along the coast, the next main port was Tobruk which was situated eighty miles west of Bardia. The perimeter defences here stretched for thirty miles, built by the Italians and included two lines of concrete pill-boxes, barbed wire and trenches each protected by minefields and a deep anti-tank ditch. The higher ridges inside the perimeter created additional defence lines facing south for observation and artillery batteries, making it a formidable fortress.[16] The weakest point of the perimeter was in the low ground to the south-east, which was overlooked by a high ridge.[17] The three escarpments south of the port combined to make a complex series of defensive positions which overlooked the Axis by-pass road and Sidi Rezegh Airfield. It was this area which became the focus of British operations during Operation Crusader.

---

14 TNA WO 201/2691.Operational reports: first Cyrenaican campaign, Sept 1940- Feb 1941, p.16.
15 TNA WO 201/539, Eighth Army: Intelligence matters: Topographical Reports, Eighth Army HQ, 9 Feb 42.
16 William F. Buckingham, *Tobruk. The Great Siege 1941–2* (Stroud: Tempus, 2008).
17 The British broke through this sector in 1940, as did Panzerarmee in 1942. Rommel's attacks of April 1941 were hasty and poorly reconnoitred in comparison.

The quadrangle of high ground to its north and west dominated the whole area in that sector.

The western coast of Cyrenaica contained stretches of very poor going with soft sand, which slowed travel and hindered navigation. The inland area south-east of the Djebel hills was a mixture of hard gravelled plateau, deep wadis and larger rocks which slowed movement. The plateau offered a broader stretch of passable going and was crossed by numerous tracks running east-west or north, which provided routes for vehicles and aided navigation. However these were soon ruined by the passage of hundreds of vehicles which ground the surface to a fine dust which clogged air filters and engines. Vehicles parts rapidly wore out which made movement here difficult, but both sides used this shorter route to gain an operational advantage over each other.[18] The Via Balbia continued south from the Djebel hills towards Cyrenaica's second major port of Benghazi. The port was surrounded by a low plain to south, and this plain was bordered in the east by a ridge which was assumed by British commanders to be a good defensive line. However, it proved inadequate after the first Axis advance in March-April 1941, when GHQ noted that it was, 'indefensible from a military point of view.'[19] This whole area of western Cyrenaica proved to be a region too far, as far as British logistics were concerned and many units were lost here trying to defend this wide area of terrain.

Beda Fomm to Tripoli

The coastal plain south of Benghazi was broadly low, undulating ground, which only provided navigation points and landing grounds to hold this large expanse of desert. The notable place in the south was the small settlement of Mersa Brega, with its important coast road and track junction. Near Beda Fomm the coast road crossed over low hills and was often bordered by soft sand dunes which proved impassable to vehicles, especially in bad weather. These features restricted the Italian retreat in February 1941 and heavily contributed to their defeat.

South of Mersa Brega, the passable desert terrain was narrowed to a just few miles by the deep wadi Feragh and some appallingly bad hummocky ground. British forces twice attempted to make this area into a viable defensive position and failed miserably because of a combination of the bad terrain, overlong supplies and poor doctrine. Further west the El Agheila colonial fort was a much more effective position, here the passable terrain was blocked inland by wide salt marshes and was overlooked by high features to the west. This marked the high point of British advance by March 1941 until they advanced again in December 1942, when the defeated Panzerarmee only used it as a delaying position en-route to Tunisia.

---

18   TNA WO 201/2692. Operational Reports: first Cyrenaican Campaign. METP No 10, p.62.
19   Moorehead, *African Trilogy*, p.136. Cairo Communiqué, 3rd April 1941.

The province of Tripolitania had a more broken physical terrain along the coast road sector. It was good defensive ground with numerous deep wadis, and high land mixed in with barrier dunes, ridges and marshy lagoons. It provided some of the strongest defensive positions during the Axis retreat of January 1943. Near Tripoli, a line of hills gave the Axis a chance for a more lengthy defence but they retreated again by the 23 January, although they had succeeded in dramatically slowing the Eighth Army's advance to the Tunisian border which added to its supply problems. Axis commanders decided to make a proper defensive site using the old French Mareth Line in Southern Tunisia, rather than trying to hold the British in Libya.

Tunisia: Tactical view

The need to overcome the terrain became part of the planning process to defeat the Axis bridgehead which now surrounded the ports of Tunis-Bizerte and defended approaches to these from the hills inland. Their air forces operated from all-weather airfields on the plains south of Tunis and effectively countered Allied air superiority during the winter months of 1943. In the south, Eighth Army's approach crossed more undulating desert which was divided by the Djebel Dahar hills running parallel to the coast. To the west was the Great Erg region which had difficult going near to the hills and deep sand dunes further west.[20] Therefore British forces were forced to remain on the eastern side of the Djebel and advance near the coast, both to manoeuvre and maintain supplies more easily.

At Mareth French engineers had built a defensive line of concrete positions from the hills and behind two coastal wadis. By 1943, Axis engineers had adapted these and created new battalion sized defences and numerous heavy anti-tank positions specifically to delay Eighth Army's advance. Its only weakness was a gap in the hills to its rear at the Djebel Tebaga, which led behind the Mareth line. It was reconnaissance by the Long Range Desert Group (LRDG) which discovered a route which led to an outflanking march by the New Zealand Corps which also used new offensive doctrine to overrun the hasty Axis defences in the gap. The Mareth line artificially strengthened a wide coastal wadi and its defence was aided by the wet spring weather which waterlogged the low area.

South of the Dorsale hills were large salt lakes called the Chotts which narrowed movement northwards to a fifteen mile wide Gabes gap from the marshes to the sea. Here the Wadi Akirit and the high ground behind it provided one of the strongest defensive positions on the entire coastline for the Axis to defend.[21] Eighth Army quickly appreciated the problems here, 'the easiest way to take the MARETH line is in the rear and that if ROMMEL'S forces are to [retreat]…the GABES gap must be

---

20   TNA WO 201/578.Topography of Tunisia.p.2.
21   The Gabes gap included the immensely strong wadi Akirit position, considered almost a mini Alamein in terms of a defensive position.

closed.'[22] This was one of the few positions which could not be outflanked, except by strategic movement of forces into the Dorsale uplands, such as an advance by the U.S. 2ndCorps from the east. Southeast of the Chotts undulating dunes were interspersed by extensive wadis which became heavily waterlogged in the winter/spring months. The Gabes gap was divided by the Wadi Akirit and was overlooked by a series of high hill features which combined to make the sector one of the strongest defensive positions in the region but Axis did not have time to make it impregnable. Further north Enfidaville provided an even higher range of hills which did block direct advance by Eighth Army. As well as directly influencing the fighting, the upland nature of Tunisia led to a change in the style of operations, giving the Allies more of a taste of what they might face in southern Europe; and it required strategic co-ordination and tactical cooperation by First and Eighth Armies to overcome this difficult ground.

Therefore the geography and terrain of North Africa directly influenced British operations throughout the campaign. The four hundred miles of Egyptian desert from the Delta bases to the frontier affected operations, while the scale of capturing and then holding Cyrenaica became the overriding problem for British forces over two years. This was partly driven by the need to secure the western airfields needed for the protection of convoys to Malta, but also to deny Benghazi and Tobruk from the Axis. Benghazi and Tobruk remained vulnerable to Axis air attack from Sicily, Tripolitania and Crete, which undermined their operational capacity. The final advance into Tunisia was affected by the location of the more dramatic relief features which delayed or blocked the final advance to Tunis-Bizerte. Tripolitania had more undulating features along the coast which were useful delaying positions but the open desert flank undermined these. Tunisia provided more European relief features which presented British forces with fresh problems of assault doctrine.

At the tactical level features of high ground dominated the landscape, made the best defensive positions and acted as a magnet to one or both sides, showed the need to take and hold this high ground for observation, in their operations to defeat the other. Other features such as deirs or low hummocky ground provided effective deployment positions for anti-tank and Infantry formations and took on an increased tactical importance as they also dominated surrounding areas. Terrain constantly affected operational deployments and battle outcomes alongside the constant environmental factors of living and fighting in desert conditions.

22   TNA WO 201/2156. Intelligence Summaries. Jan-March 1943. Summary No. 420, 29 Jan '43.

3

Operation Compass to Beda Fomm, December 1940-February 1941

The first British campaign against the Italian 10th Army and the subsequent capture of Cyrenaica, highlights the way in which the tactical terrain contributed to British successes in each of the main battles. It also shows that British assault doctrines at this time, were successful and how two the final defensive actions near Beda Fomm benefitted from local ground features. Other historians have rightly noted other factors which also contributed to British successes including Jon Latimer, George Forty and Barrie Pitt and include effective planning by O'Connor, better equipment, training, and the higher morale of British troops.[1] However, most commentators only offer vague references to the importance of the terrain and ignore the real importance of the tactical impact shown here. The more obvious operational level impact of the shorter desert route via Msus cutting the coast road south of Benghazi is well documented, but again the weight of discussion mostly relates to supply issues. Whilst this did contribute to the rapid British advance across Cyrenaica, it was clearly the decisive impact of the tactical terrain which contributed to British successes in each of the main battles which will be discussed.

The Campaign: Opening phases

Following the outbreak of war, British forces defended the Egyptian frontier by carrying out small scale patrols and harassing actions against the Italians. The commander of Western Desert Force, Lieutenant-General Sir Richard O'Connor, initially used the 7th Armoured Division to hold the front by maintaining offensive patrols and with attacks on isolated enemy positions. By mid-September, Mussolini successfully pressured Marshal Graziani to order an advance by the 10th Army, which duly entered Egypt and reached Sidi Barrani, sixty miles beyond the frontier. Here it halted and built a series of defensive camps, awaiting improvements to the coast

---

1   Jon Latimer, *Operation Compass 1940. Wavell's Whirlwind Offensive* (Oxford: Osprey, 2000), George Forty, *The First Victory,* and Barrie Pitt, *Crucible of War, Vol I.*

road and fresh supplies. British forces continued operations with improvised tactics including aggressive patrolling and made best use of the terrain to delaying the Italian advance.[2]

By late October Italy had also invaded Greece, and the Chiefs of Staff (COS) pressured Wavell to send air and ground reinforcements to support the Greek campaign, which would weaken O'Connor's forces in the desert.[3] Wavell therefore ordered O'Connor to plan a short counter-offensive against the Italians with possible further exploitation to capture the Libyan frontier sector and perhaps advance as far as Tobruk. This would then free up British formations for other regions of the Middle East campaigns.[4] Supply was also an issue because maintaining two divisions in the desert would quickly use up all the available reserves.[5] British Intelligence estimated there were elements of six Italian Divisions occupying camps around Sidi Barrani with patrols by, 'columns of infantry and guns…reinforced by tanks,' in between.[6] It was this ground which became vital to British success in the operation which followed.

Compass: Terrain

The land between the two armies was an eighty mile stretch of open desert with areas of good-going for vehicles mixed with poor-going sections of soft sand. The coastal plain was divided by a ridge-escarpment running parallel to the coast with few accessible tracks down it. The Italian camps were situated mostly east and south of Sidi Barrani, some were sited to defend the few escarpment tracks, and each was held by elements of a Division. They were mostly sited on a convenient rise adjacent to the tracks, to defend the obvious routes of advance.[7]

Each camp was protected by an anti-tank ditch outside a low bank of earth or stones, and was strengthened by mines and wire on the eastern faces.[8] Near the coast were the Tummars group and Pt 90 which covered the track to Maktila, the farthest point advance for the Italians. The first British objective was Nibeiwa camp situated five miles from the Tummars and sited to defend the escarpment track at Bir-Enba. The vital gap in the Italian line of camps was twenty-five miles across and lay between Nibeiwa and Rabia, before the next group at Rabia and Sofafi, which were sited on top of the escarpment to prevent any British moves along the higher plateau. This group

---

2   Joly, *Take These Men*, pp.21-37.
3   Butler, *Grand Strategy. Volume II*, p.367.
4   TNA WO 201/2691. Operational Reports: First Cyrenaican Campaign, Sept1940-Feb 1941. Appendix A. These were in East Africa and now Greece.
5   TNA WO 201/2691. Operational Reports: First Cyrenaican Campaign, Sept1940-Feb 1941, p.1.
6   Joly, *Take These Men*, p.48.
7   Moorehead, *African Trilogy*, p.57.
8   TNA WO 201/2691. Operational Reports: First Cyrenaican Campaign, Sept1940-Feb 1941.pp.3-4.

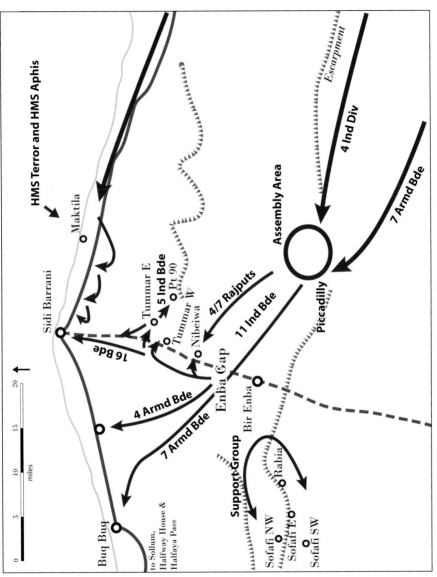

Map 3:1 Operation Compass; the assault on the Italian camps.

was considered too strong for a frontal attack by the limited British units available, so they were screened off by the 7th Support Group Jock Columns.[9]

The ground between Nibeiwa and Rabia was described as, 'flat and featureless, with no vital or commanding ground.'[10] British aggressive patrolling tactics prevented the Italians from establishing another camp on this low ground which provided an opportunity for O'Connor.[11] The localized doctrine of using Jock columns had successfully kept the gap open, and now the two attacking divisions could make their approach march. The going immediately south of Mersa-Matruh was particularly broken terrain, which could have delayed the British advance, so units moved along the upper plateau and then dropped down to the Enba Gap which was still a significant night march of 85 miles. Lieutenant Rea Leakey of 1st RTR noted, 'The upper plateau…was good going for vehicles…The land dropped fifty feet, but there were few tracks down it…the plain was soft sand, wadis and generally bad going.'[12] The British advance to contact was successful because it utilized the better going of the upper plateau, before returning to the softer ground of the plain.

The tactical terrain affected the outcome of Compass and subsequent actions, which led to the defeat and capture of most of the 10th Army. Strategically, the capture of Cyrenaica for the first time eased British naval convoys supplying Malta and protected the Suez Canal sector from aerial bombing. The landscape had an operational impact on planning, because it determined the preparatory moves made by British forces and the first assaults. O'Connor took advantage of the gap between the Italian camps on the escarpment and Nibeiwa camp. later, as is well documented, the pursuit phase across the desert via Msus-Mechili helped to trap the remaining Italian columns at Beda Fomm and Sidi Saleh.

Compass proved that British tactical doctrine at that time was successful, with combined arms assaults made by 4th Indian Division Infantry and the Matildas from 7th Royal Tank Regiment (RTR). The heavy armour had led the break-in through the Italian camp perimeters and the Infantry followed, clearing successive positions. Later on, the 6th Australian Division developed an equally successful 'Infantry-first' variant of these assaults at Bardia and Tobruk. Aggressive British patrolling and the use of Jock columns around the camps had kept Italian units bottled-up inside the camps and reluctant to engage British units beyond their perimeters. The whole process had undermined the Axis desert strongpoints, something the British HQs might have been more aware of during the Gazala campaign of 1942 perhaps.

9   TNA WO 201/2691. Operational Reports: First Cyrenaican Campaign, Sept1940-Feb 1941, p.4.
10   Joly, *Take These Men,* p.48.
11   G.L. Verney, *The Desert Rats, The History of the 7th Armoured Division 1938 to 1945* (London: Greenhill. 1990) p.28.
12   Liddell-Hart Centre for Military Archives (LHCMA) Rea Leakey papers 1/2, pp.20-23.

Compass: Preparations

Operation Compass was the first offensive by Western Desert Force and was to be a five day raid. Fast convoys had provided new vehicles, but these still needed time in the workshops to be prepared for the desert environment while their crews undertook further training.[13] The 7th Armoured Division was strengthened with both Brigades brought up to three regiments, totalling 276 tanks. The 4th Indian Division had two Indian and one British Brigade (nine battalions) with three artillery regiments and divisional support units, the attack force totalled some 25,000 troops. The spearhead of each assault would be led by the Matilda tanks of 7th RTR, supported by four Regiments of Artillery.[14] The Australian 6th Division which arrived in January provided the Infantry force for the later campaign. Briefly, the Italians, in contrast had 75,000 troops in six Divisions, from an estimated 250,000 troops deployed across Libya. The armoured force was General Maletti's Raggruppamento and was considered the most well trained unit, equipped with 120 poor quality tanks and 2,500 Libyan Infantry.[15]

Wavell's order to O'Connor on 2 November, showed the importance of terrain in British planning, 'we are more highly trained…we know the ground and are better accustomed to desert conditions.'[16] Each Division needed a supply dump to cover the sixty mile distance so two Forward Supply Depots (FSDs) were created thirty miles forward of Matruh. The assaults were practised on a full scale replica of Nibeiwa camp built for the purpose in late November. After this some of the tactical plans were altered slightly and this increased the confidence of the participating troops. The RAF committed three fighter squadrons for air cover and ground attacks while six squadrons of bombers targeted aerodromes and communications with the camps being bombed to mask the overnight British approach march.[17]

Compass: Battle summary

The advance was made during the night of 8/9 December, as RAF sorties masked the noise of hundreds of vehicles passing close to Nibeiwa. The first assault began after a brief bombardment, and then two squadrons of Matildas attacked the rear entrance and overran the tank battalion leaguered there. The Matildas were quickly followed by two battalions of Infantry who fanned out to eliminate strong points around the base,

---

13   David Masters, *With Pennants Flying. The Immortal Deeds of the Royal Armoured Corps* (London: Eyre & Spottiswoode, 1943) p.37.
14   Jon Latimer, *Operation Compass*, p.25.
15   Buckingham, *Tobruk*, p.80, 1 battalion each of M11/39 and Light L3/35 tanks.
16   TNA WO 201/2691.METP No.10.Operational Reports: Sept 1940-Feb 1941. Appendix D. 15/12/40.
17   TNA WO 201/2691. Operational Reports: First Cyrenaican Campaign, Sept1940-Feb 1941, pp.1-2.

whilst a diversionary attack was made against the eastern perimeter. It was noted how the Italian Infantry quickly gave up once they had lost their leaders whereas the Italian gunners 'fought like hell,' for over two hours despite being surprised, but by 10.40am the camp was secured.[18] They continued to fight against the imposing Matildas even at close range but could only cause heavy damage to them, which contributed to the collapse of Italian morale and most troops surrendered.[19]

The subsequent assault on the Tummar-West camp was made after a brief replenishment. The lack of surprise and a growing sandstorm made this a much tougher objective to overcome, so only nine Matildas were able to lead a subsequent assault on Tummar-East.[20] The nearby camps were now fully aware of the British attacks and proved to be more difficult to overcome for the British Infantry. The broad pattern of each battle remained the same with aggressive infantry charges against the enemy strongpoints, supported by Matildas. Again, the 'Italian gunners fought to the last,' and again once they were overrun the remaining Infantry quickly surrendered. [21]

Continuing the advance, the larger base at Sidi-Barrani was assaulted the next day by the 16th Infantry Brigade. Using a sandstorm as cover, the eleven remaining serviceable Matildas and other armour led a successful break-in. It was another tough battle and produced the highest casualties for British troops who suffered 250 of the 600 casualties received. The Italians now abandoned the remaining coastal group of camps, 1st Libyan Division withdrew from Maktila and was attacked in the open by Selby Force and surrendered the following day. Operationally, the capture of the coastal group of camps had broken the Italian defensive line and made it untenable. Inland, the Rabia and Sofafi group were also abandoned and the garrisons retreated towards Bardia. Near the coast at Buq-Buq a mass of Italians were caught with their guns and they fought back for a while.

Despite this resistance, the action ended when 1st RTR outflanked and knocked the battery out and took 6,000 prisoners. While the Italian gunners showed some resolve, their Air Force offered only a token resistance, using high level bombing or occasional low level attacks to delay the British advance.[22] The 10th Army had fought back, yet an aggressive doctrine and good use of the terrain had enabled the smaller British forces to outflank and then overcome the defensive line of camps. Minor armoured actions were also affected by terrain as British forces advanced into Libya, with 1st RTR making good tactical use of a ridge to deploy unseen before

18   Peter Cochrane, *Charlie Company. In Service with C Company 2nd Queen's Own Cameron Highlanders 1940-1944* (Stroud: Spellmount, 2007), p.31.

19   Patrick Delaforce, *Monty's Marauders. Black Rat & Red Fox: 4th and 8th Independent Armoured Brigades in WW2* (Brighton: Tom Donovan, 1997) pp.12-15.

20   Pitt, Crucible of War, Vol I, pp.106-107.

21   TNA WO 201/349,"Situation reports on current operations: Operation 'Compass'. 1940 Dec.-1941 Jan. I/1014. 12/12.

22   Farran, *Winged Dagger,* pp.24-25.

advancing onto the flank of a column of twenty Italian M13s.[23] Such aggressive tactics by armour and Infantry strengthened British morale. The Western Desert Force then made a successful pursuit into Libya, but was by now operating at the extremity of its own supply lines and suffering constant shortages of fuel, water and ammunition. The supply situation remained ad-hoc with only essentials being delivered by sea to various small ports along the coast.[24] After the camps were lost, Marshal Graziani wanted to pull back and concentrate his remaining forces near Tobruk and await fresh reinforcements, but Mussolini insisted Bardia was also defended. Wavell countered this plan by blockading each port and then captured them by direct assault, which left Benghazi and the more distance prize of the western airfields as possible objectives after Tobruk.

Bardia: Terrain

The next target to be assaulted was Bardia, which was situated on a cliff top headland overlooking an enclosed small port and was divided from the desert plateau by the Wadi Gefani. The base had a 17 mile perimeter, with the outer line including mine-fields, wire defences and an anti-tank ditch with concreted emplacements every 800 yards for anti-tank guns and heavy machine guns.[25] The interior defences included a secondary line of emplacements, called the 'switch-line', but these were widely spaced which undermined their ability to interlock their fire.[26] The coastal escarpment divided the base on an east-west axis, leaving the northern sector under observation from higher ground and vulnerable to isolation. This main geographical feature there-fore had a direct impact on the defence of the base.

Bardia: Preparations and battle

Bardia needed to be captured by 13th Corps because its garrison could threaten British supply routes if left untouched.[27] There was a three week delay while the 6th Australian Division was brought in to replace 4th Indian: although the newcomers lacked battle experience they were well motivated to assault and capture a major Italian base, if only to prove their fighting capability. The delay in bringing forward the bulk of the Division enabled its HQ to make a more detailed analysis of the defences and identify the key weakness of the 'fortress' and how it might be attacked.[28] They were facing

---

23   Rea Leakey, *Leakey's Luck. A Tank Commander with nine lives* (Stroud: Sutton, 1999), pp.36-37.
24   TNA WO 201/349. Operation Compass: Cipher Messages. 1231/14. 12.14.40
25   Latimer, *Operation Compass*, p.41.
26   Moorehead, *African Trilogy*, p.82.
27   Western Desert Force had been re-named on 1 January 1941.
28   TNA WO 201/2691.METP No.10. Operational Reports: Operations of 13th Corps in Cyrenaica. 12 Dec 1940-7th Feb 1941, p.17.

a garrison which included elements of four Divisions, totalling some 30,000 troops, along with one hundred tanks and over 400 guns.

The key terrain was identified and became a primary objective from which further advances could be made. Sixth Division directed its 16th Brigade towards the high ground, where units were to, 'exploit to an average distance of 1500 yards to the top of the escarpment, thus forming a bridgehead.'[29] The initial break-in would be made by Engineers and Infantry through a narrow front of just four outposts, supported by artillery fire from five regiments to cover the Infantry crossing the open plateau. Only then would 7th RTR's remaining half Regiment of Matildas follow up and help roll up the emplacements either side of the gap. They would also help secure the escarpment to expose the flank and rear of the numerous Italian batteries deployed in the north-east sector.

The assault began early on 3 January with a 25 minute bombardment, following which Engineers cleared wire and mine defences whilst 16th Brigade stormed the frontline positions to be quickly followed by the 'I' tanks and truck mounted anti-tank guns. The Brigade Diary noted that from the beginning, 'hordes of Italians threw down their arms and surrendered…[so] by early afternoon the count had reached 10,000… However other BTYS [batteries] refused to quieten and all day long pounded back at us.'[30] The intensity of the Italian barrage from 400 guns provided the strongest response to the vigorous Australian attacks.

The initial attack successfully divided the Italian defences, which continued to fight on separately at first. The 16th Brigade Infantry secured its objectives and planned for the next day's assault, the battalions used the ridgeline as an enfilade position on the exposed the Italian artillery and gave some protection for the next advance. Heavy naval gunfire support from three battleships helped to break the morale of the remaining defenders and the Italians fought on until the assaulting troops reached them and then most of them surrendered.[31]

The Australian 17th Brigade Infantry assaulted the south-east sector the next day with the last units surrendering in the afternoon of the 5 January. British commanders were surprised by the large numbers of garrison captured and their low morale which the prisoners blamed on a lack of support from Tobruk and their Air Force, who had failed to stop heavy RAF and naval bombardments.[32] This was a second major defeat

29   https://www.awm.gov.au/collection/records/awm52/subclass.asp?levelID=297. AWM 52 8/2/16/6. 16th Infantry Brigade, War Diary. January February 1941, pp.1-2. Accessed 7 February 2012.
30   https://www.awm.gov.au/collection/records/awm52/subclass.asp?levelID=297. AWM 52 8/2/16/6. 16th Infantry Brigade, War Diary. January February 1941. p6. Accessed 13 February 2012.
31   Latimer, *Operation Compass,* pp.-53-54.
32   https://www.awm.gov.au/collection/records/awm52/subclass.asp?levelID=297. AWM 52 8/2/16/6. 16th Infantry Brigade, War Diary. January February 1941, p.30. Accessed 14 February 2012.

for the 10th Army, with over 400 artillery pieces, 127 tanks and 700 trucks being captured along with 38,300 troops. British forces had suffered 500 casualties, with some of the few remaining Matildas receiving further heavy damage from the close range fighting.[33]

The fall of Bardia was a major strategic turning point in the campaign and caused Hitler to decide to intervene with German forces deployed to the theatre to prop up the Italians. The first units of the Afrika Korps (DAK) were dispatched to Tripoli as a blocking force and a Luftwaffe Air Corps of 200 aircraft was sent to Sicily. This unit was to act offensively against the Royal Navy in the central Mediterranean and to attack ports and bases in western Cyrenaica.[34] The first air attacks on the Navy heavily damaged the carrier *Illustrious* on 10 January, which considerably weakened the Royal Navy's capacity to provide air cover in future operations, while Army units in Cyrenaica were constantly attacked.

In Cyrenaica these air attacks were noted by the 11th Hussars diary on the 23 January, just after Tobruk had been captured from the Italians.[35] These also directly influenced the dispersal of British formations and vehicle movement by supply columns, British forces had to face three more months of determined air attacks before any contact with the Afrika Korps. The 6th Australian Division HQ insisted that dispersal discipline was re-established after Bardia, as they feared a loss of trucks would affect their already limited ability to bring forward supplies.[36] At the tactical level, both Bardia and Tobruk capitulated once Commonwealth units had occupied the dominating ridges within their defences. The terrain on the frontier offered a line of defensive positions which forced O'Connor to drive his pursuing units rapidly forward to prevent any Italian consolidation along the frontier.

Tobruk: Terrain and battle summary

The main Italian base at Tobruk had a well-constructed defensive perimeter, but despite this the garrison commanders had little answer to the British advance and simply awaited encirclement. The perimeter defences at Tobruk ran in a thirty mile arc which stretched eight miles inland from the port. The outer anti-tank ditch was twenty feet wide and had been linked with natural wadis where possible. It was over-looked by more than seventy concrete emplacements which were protected by wire and mines with a second line of emplacements sited 500 yards behind. However, the Australian reconnaissance concluded there was weakness caused by a series of ridges inside the perimeter and also noted incomplete perimeter sections in the south-eastern

33   Latimer, *Operation Compass,* pp.41 and 54.
34   Hugh Trevor-Roper, *Hitler's War Directives 1939-1945* (Edinburgh: Berlin, 2004) p.99.
35   WO169/1690. 11th Hussars War Diary, 21 Jan 1941, p.7.
36   https://www.awm.gov.au/collection/records/awm52/subclass.asp?levelID=297. AWM 52 8/2/16/6. 16th Infantry Brigade, War Diary. January February 1941, p.34.Accessed 14 February 2012.

sector.[37] These escarpments overlooked the perimeter, coast road and harbour and were the main objectives to controlling the base. The Pt 209, Ras-el-Madauer height overlooked the perimeter to the south-west, whilst the Hagiag Chargia ridge overlooked the airfield and included the Italian HQ at Fort Pilastrino. The 6th Division took 12 days to plan and train for the assault on the 21 January, which again included making full scale replicas of the defences for the Australians to practice their assault techniques.

The assault began on the 21 January with the 19th Brigade breaking through at the weakest south-eastern sector and advancing towards the Hagiag ridge which was behind the frontline and divided the defences. Two HQ sites were rapidly captured along with the garrison commander by the end of the first day and the Australian commanders then ordered a general advance the following day when the remaining Italian opposition collapsed. The Italians had suffered a third major defeat which forced the remnant columns of 10th Army to retreat across western Cyrenaica mostly along the via Balbia.

Tobruk: Outcome and effect on British operations

British forces pursued the retreating Italians in two groups with the Australians moving along the coast road and they soon captured Benghazi and the nearby airfields. However being winter, these were affected by bad weather which made them unusable by the RAF. Inland, O'Connor ordered a mixed arms force to move rapidly across the shorter route to Mechili to cut the road south of Benghazi, and block 10th Army's retreat. Trooper Palmer from 2nd RTR remembered the approach march of around 150 miles as a combined force of exhausted men and tanks.[38] It was this force which deployed in two defensive sites along the coast road, south of Benghazi, with just a few hours to spare and who engaged the retreating Italian columns.

Sidi-Saleh: Terrain and battle

At Sidi Saleh the tactical terrain influenced the battle in favour of the British units; the soft ground rendered Italian attacks on British positions ineffectual, by limiting them to narrow frontal assaults along the road. Between the road and the sea there were more soft-going dunes which were impassable for vehicles. The supporting British artillery deployed four miles to the east to give covering fire to the whole area.[39] The

---

37   https://www.awm.gov.au/collection/records/awm52/subclass.asp?levelID=297. AWM 52 8/2/16/6. 16th Infantry Brigade, War Diary. January February 1941, p.31.Accessed 13 February 2012.

38   http://www.bbc.co.uk/ww2peopleswar/stories/94/a2064494.shtml, , Memoir of James Palmer, 2nd RTR. Article ID: A2064494. Accessed 17 June 2011.

39   TNA WO169/1390. 11th Hussars Diary. Jan-Dec 1941.Appendix L. Report on battle at SidiSaleh, 5-7 February 1941, by Col. Combe.

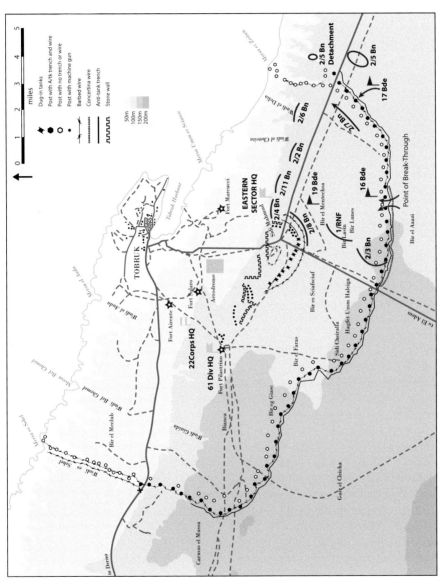

Map 3:2 Italian Defences at Tobruk, January 1941.

Rifle Brigade faced an approaching column of 20,000 Italians with just 2,000 troops, a few armoured cars and eleven anti-tank guns. The British defensive plan was aided by deployment of the Infantry in low, hummocky ground and the ferocity of the defensive fire which stopped the Italian column. The battle continued in darkness with the 7th Hussars breaking up one attempted flank move on the seaward side. The following day three more attacks were repulsed; the last of which penetrated the Rifle Brigade positions, but was stopped at close range by anti-tank and supporting artillery fire.

The British had taken full advantage of the ground to help their defence. The hummocky ground suited the low profile of the 2pdr anti-tank guns and adjacent Infantry positions, which them difficult to locate. There was also close coordination between Lieutenant-Colonel Campbell from 4th Royal Horse Artillery (RHA) and Lieutenant-Colonel Renton from 2nd Rifle Brigade which contributed to the resolute defence battle. An officer observed that just one more determined push by the Italians would have broken through, as they did not realize how incredibly weak the Rifle Brigade position was, with no reserves and little ammunition left.[40]

Beda Fomm: Terrain and battle

The tactical terrain also contributed in a similar way to the final action near Beda Fomm. East of the coast road there was mainly low, undulating ground, where Colonel Combe selected a position to allow the 4th Armoured Brigade to manoeuvre against the flanks of the Italian road columns from cover. A deployment was made by 2nd RTR's CO, who selected two features of high ground from which to fight. The first feature was known as the 'pimple', over which the road passed and to the southeast of this was a further low ridge topped by a mosque, which was used as cover for reserves and supply trucks.

The 'pimple' hill dominated the road west of Beda Fomm while the 2nd RTR used the white mosque hill both as cover to regroup and for hull down positions to repulse numerous frontal armoured attacks.[41] The soft, hummocky ground either side of the road prevented the slower M13s from making any wide outflanking moves. Visibility was hindered by heavy rain squalls and smoke, which enabled British Light armour to attack the columns from the flank. The Italians overestimated the strength of British armour and began to retreat, whilst 2nd RTR made an immediate assault on the main column. After quickly re-arming the fourteen remaining tanks, they moved to attack again. The regiment made good use of hidden ground, using cover and rapid movement to gain maximum surprise.

The initial action lasted about two hours on the first day and developed into two separate defensive actions over the next two days, one by armoured regiments at Beda

---

40   Joly, *Take These Men,* p.86.
41   TNA WO 201/2691. Operational Reports: First Cyrenaican Campaign, Sept1940-Feb 1941.Appendices, maps.

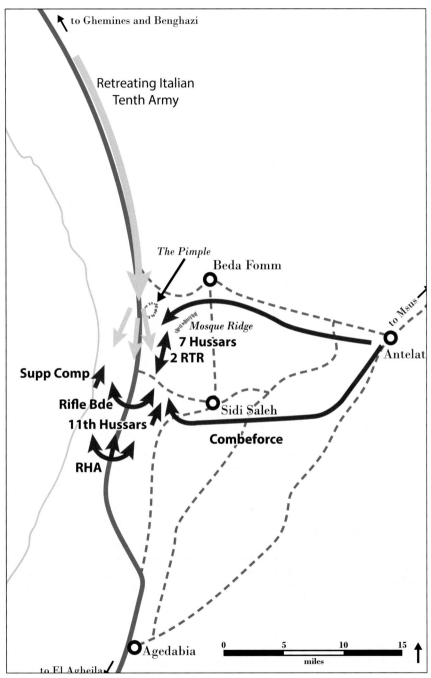

Map 3:3   Sidi Saleh and Beda Fomm, February 1941.

Fomm and the other by Infantry/artillery at Sidi-Saleh. Beda Fomm continued as 'battering rams' of Italian tanks made repeated but uncoordinated attacks against both the pimple and mosque hills.[42] British armour countered the few attempts made to outflank them, which were also blocked by the low dunes and made worse by heavy rain soaking the ground. The supporting artillery also knocked out more than twenty M13s and numerous guns, which enabled the pimple to be retaken and held from late afternoon on the second day.

The actions at Beda Fomm and Sidi-Saleh were both tenacious defence battles which gave O'Connor a close run final victory. The British forces available were minimal but well led by experienced regimental commanders, who made the best use of the available terrain and firepower to defeat the uninspired Italian assaults. Following this defeat the Italians surrendered, giving up a lot of equipment and a further 8,000 troops went into captivity.[43] The Western Desert Force under O'Connor had defeated a larger, better equipped Italian army. The 10th Army had suffered losses of nearly 130,000 troops, many as POWs, 400 tanks and over 800 guns along with ammunition and supplies. British forces had suffered only 2,000 casualties in comparison.

The battles of this first campaign presented the weaker British forces with a series of operational and tactical problems, all of which had been directly influenced by the operational and tactical level terrain. During Compass, O'Connor had used the gap between Nibeiwa and Rabia camps to position his assault force behind the Italians and then carried out a series of well-executed assaults. Similar tactics were used in combined arms attacks on the remaining camps which unlocked the Italian defence line and outflanked the remaining Rabia-Sofafi camps in the advance to Bardia.

The British advance into Libya forced the Italians to abandon the frontier positions at Sollum-Capuzzo and allowed British forces to isolate their supply port-bases. The attacks on Bardia and Tobruk were again well executed by fresh forces using developed doctrines which contributed to the surrender of each port. The attacks were successful in breaking through well defended Axis positions and showed that the doctrine was flexible and could be adapted to changing circumstances. The final battles at Beda Fomm and Sidi-Saleh were improvised defensive engagements by units who made a tenacious defence against difficult odds.

In the next phase of the campaign, the problem of retaining Cyrenaica revolved around the issues of distance and space and the lack of any suitable defensive terrain across the plain surrounding Benghazi and in southern Cyrenaica. British commanders compounded these problems by under-estimating the effectiveness of a more developed German tactical doctrine, especially when commanded by an aggressive and dynamic commander like Lieutenant-General Erwin Rommel.

---

42   TNA WO 169/1390.11th Hussars Diary. Jan-Dec 1941. Appendix L. Report on the battle of Sidi-Saleh, 5-7 February 1941, by Col. Combes.

43   TNA WO 169/1390.11th Hussars Diary. Jan-Dec 1941. 2nd RB, Report on Operations 5th-7th February 1941.

4

The defence of Cyrenaica and the two British retreats, April 1941 and January-February 1942

This chapter considers the defence of Cyrenaica and the two successive British retreats from the Libyan province in April 1941 and January-February 1942. These actions highlight the problems of defending such a huge province at the operational level and also show the impact of a lack of suitable, tactical defensive positions for British forces in southern Cyrenaica. These issues were compounded by an improvised tactical doctrine and changes in British command and orders which resulted in two defeats. British operations also suffered from a lack of troops, equipment and tanks, and an overlong supply line during two successive inhospitable winters.

In February 1941 the War Cabinet in London took the strategic decision to support Greece against a possible Axis invasion. This dramatically reduced British forces in Libya leaving only a few units to successfully defend the front in Cyrenaica. Churchill also mistakenly regarded Benghazi as some sort of, 'strong flank for the…Nile valley and the invaluable aerodromes situated in Cyrenaica,' When the reality was quite different.[1] At GHQ, Wavell viewed the port as having some propaganda value but to him it was of little military importance because the Luftwaffe had made the port almost unusable anyway.[2] The few RAF units in Cyrenaica faced Axis air attacks both from Sicily and from Tripolitania.

Unfortunately for the British, there were simply too few places in western Cyrenaica where a secure defence could be made. In the south, Wavell recognized that Benghazi had less importance as a supply base because of heavy Axis air attacks, yet he still ordered British units much further forward to El Agheila which merely over-stretched the supply capacity through the desert. The passable terrain narrowed at Mersa Brega which created a useful defensible area. The landscape south and east of Benghazi was

---

1   TNA PREM 3/283.WP (41).159. 11 July 1941. Report on the action of the 2nd Armoured Division.
2   TNA PREM 3/283.WP (41).167. 17 July 1941. Minute on the Report on the Action of the 2nd Armoured Division.

too wide open for defence and the coast road continued north across the plain which opened out, with a passable escarpment leading eastwards onto the gravel plains of the higher Libyan plateau. There were numerous tracks eastwards across the plateau but these were almost impossible to block, even along the escarpment. The coast road north was a faster route for supply, and wound its way through the Djebel hills, but was still vulnerable to Axis aircraft, which simply followed the road looking for soft-skinned supply columns. The hills north of the port contained some good defensive sites along the road to Derna, but this upland area was flanked by the passable desert routes to the south, via Msus and Mechili.

This inland route was used by both sides to make a faster crossing of the higher plateau. This route had a series of tracks running northwards through the Djebel hills to outflank any defended position the British might take along the coast road. Axis forces used these tracks northwards in both retreats to manoeuvre British units out of successive positions. The eastern edge of the Djebel hills did create a sector of defensible ground with depth. This was an area which the 4th Indian Division's commander, Major-General Francis Tuker believed could have given British forces a base from which to hold Cyrenaica, west of Tobruk and to counter-attack from.[3] Instead, the British forces in both 1941 and 1942 withdrew further east in both retreats.

At the operational level, the need to defend wide areas of Cyrenaica led to Infantry and Armoured Brigades being spread over a wide area. In both 1941 and 1942 the front lines were too long and held by too few units. A lack of transport and supply issues left other Brigades in the rear and occupying different positions along the coast road, rather than being able to strengthen the frontline. This dispersal of Brigades moved the focus away from a Divisional battle so that they engaged more powerful Axis columns without support and had little choice but to retreat. In both years the battle outcome was to end in an unseemly rapid retreat by numerous units in a state of disorder, as they sought to out-run the fast moving Axis columns across Cyrenaica.

The British defence in both 1941 and 1942 consisted of a frontline initially held by Jock columns supported by a single Armoured Brigade. The need to hold such a wide frontline led to the dispersal of formations to dominate the neutral ground.[4] The harsh nature of the gravel surface of the plateau led to constant wear and tear on the soft-skinned vehicles and contributed to high wastage in tank numbers. By May 1942, after the Second Retreat, Cyrenaica was still a problematic area to defend. By then Eighth Army's new commander, General Ritchie, spread the Infantry Brigades across a forty-five mile long defence 'line' at Gazala, in an attempt to cover both the coast road and more passable sectors of desert to the south. Dispersion was still needed to cover the likely routes of approach from the Djebel hills and tracks south of them. Therefore despite the Army being powerfully reinforced, it was the nature

3   Tuker, *Approach to Battle,* pp.77-78.
4   TNA WO 201/372, 4th Indian Division. Report on Operations.1 -22 January 1942, p38.

of the terrain which was rapidly dissipating it's strength, even before a shot had been fired in the renewed campaign.

The Importance of Tobruk

In 194, the siege of Tobruk was vital to the British defence of Egypt. They had to deny the Axis use of the port which would stretch their supply lines back to Benghazi and Tripoli and deny them the chance to advance east of Tobruk.[5] Axis forces besieged the base from April, and soon the British defence turned from a military necessity into a major political issue. The recent withdrawal from Greece meant that British forces could not be seen to be making further retreats as this might adversely affect morale at home and influence the views of future allies such as the USA. They had to be seen to continue the fighting, even though Wavell doubted the military importance of the base.[6] If the port was abandoned or lost the Axis would regain a forward base from which to threaten further progress into Egypt. The siege has attracted a number of studies which have highlighted its importance to the campaign.[7] Harrison notes the importance of the British 70th Division in the defence and subsequent break-out from Tobruk in December as a turning point for Crusader,[8] whilst Lyman considers it, 'the battle which saved North Africa from the Nazis.'[9]

The ad-hoc garrison, made up of British and Empire units, repulsed a series of hasty assaults. They were opposed by determined defence and counter-attacks made by the 9th Australian Division which were closely coordinated by General Leslie Morshead and led to the first decisive victory against the DAK. In these early attacks, the Axis troops committed too few tanks and infantry and failed to coordinate other diversionary assaults and air attacks. The siege became a major strategic diversion for the Axis over the next eight months while they planned a full scale assault on the port. The attacks made by the RAF and Royal navy on the Axis supply convoys during the autumn created a shipping crisis for the Axis which delayed these plans long enough for Auchinleck's Operation Crusader to begin, which was primarily a major British offensive but also a direct relief of Tobruk. The defence of Tobruk certainly prevented any further advance beyond the frontier by Axis forces and remained a potential thorn to Axis supply routes.

5   Strawson, *The Battle for North Africa,* p.75.
6   Carlo d'Este, *Warlord, A Life of Churchill at War, 1874-1945* (London: Alan Lane, 2008) p.592.
7   Buckingham, *Tobruk,* pp.230-233, the siege last from 10 April to 9 December 1941, a total of 244 days.
8   Harrison, *Tobruk. The Birth of a Legend,*
9   Lyman, *The Longest Siege,* p.xxv.

The First Retreat, April 1941

Operationally, Lieutenant-General Philip Neame, CinC of Cyrenaica Command, had spread his available brigades to cover all the possible approaches available to the Axis. Unfortunately this meant they were too widely dispersed to offer any mutual support. The supply dumps were sited at Msus and Mechili along the desert route and were too far in the rear for the few supply columns to do their job more rapidly, because of the poor terrain between the bases and the front. At the tactical level the British did not deployed enough Jock Columns to hold such a lengthy frontline at El Agheila. Also, the frontline consisted of terrain which was nearly impassable for the truck based units of both the Jock Columns and the supply columns.

Commentators have noted the problems of British dispositions across Cyrenaica.[10] Fraser believed it was a combination of better quality armour and Rommel's aggressive leadership which levered the British out of position and kept up the momentum of the Axis advance but he fails to mention the impact of either Cyrenaica or the tactical ground.[11] Gladman argues that command was the vital factor, with Axis HQs being more efficient while British HQs struggled to control events.[12] The British forces suffered from a number of issues which influenced the outcome of the retreat, including too few and poor quality tanks, and the loss of commanders. In addition they were forced to deploy too widely across the region and frontline units were seriously hampered by the difficult ground.

First Retreat: Terrain

British forces were trying to protect Benghazi from the south which left them deployed in an over-extended position. Tactically, the frontline was moved further forward so that British reconnaissance squadrons could move forward to hold the landing ground at El Agheila. Wavell identified a line of salt marshes after his visit in March which he considered to be a strong defensive position. This feature was located twenty miles west of El Agheila and ran south into the desert but was not used tactically as it was too far for the supply columns. Further east was a vital road junction at Mersa Brega, where the passable terrain was reduced by a sector of hummocky dunes and the wadi Feragh on its eastern desert flank. Another important road junction just north of Brega, was Agedabia, where desert tracks ran eastwards towards the escarpment.[13] These became vital defensive sites amongst the frontline positions.

---

10   Buckingham, *Tobruk*, pp.163-164.
11   Fraser, *And We Shall Shock Them*, p.150.
12   Gladman, *Intelligence and Anglo-American Air Support*, p.59.
13   Kitchen, *Rommel's Desert War*, p.49. Agedabia was the largest town in this part of Cyrenaica.

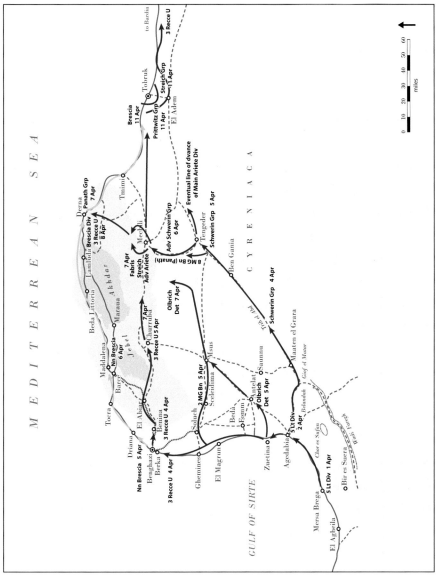

Map 4:1 The First Retreat, April 1941.

North of Agedabia the terrain opened out into an undulating plain with the higher plateau rising beyond the escarpment. The tracks led up sharp defiles running up through the slopes onto the plateau which were defendable places, but the whole escarpment was actually fairly passable by tracked vehicles which meant they were easily outflanked. Once on the plateau, the route to the Msus/Mechili depots had long stretches of difficult going, but later German Engineers began clearing and improving the track through the rocky ground. This route was seen as, 'empty, neutral desert, offering no help or haven...[the choice] was only death by thirst or starvation, or capture by the enemy.'[14] The coast road had few decent defensive positions south of Benghazi once the Mersa Brega gap had been breached, which left the whole of Cyrenaica open. Both routes had to be covered but the coast road remained the quickest back to Tobruk but was also the most vulnerable to air attack.

Preparations

Cyrenaica Command was set up in early February 1941 as a holding force to defend the province. Wavell calculated that German forces would be held back by logistical delays and would not be ready to advance into the province until mid-May or the end of the summer to avoid the intense heat. Churchill had ordered him to make Greece his priority following the victory at Beda Fomm which had diverted many of his best units from Cyrenaica over the previous few weeks, leaving only light forces along the frontline.[15] The commander, Lieutenant-General Philip Neame, was criticized for his poor command and deployment of the remaining units. Neame also had an in-experienced Corps HQ staff equipped with few vehicles or decent radios. The Command had three levels of Corps, Divisional and Brigade HQs in charge of just two frontline Brigades, which made for a top heavy structure and too many delays in orders, when events were fast moving.

The 3rd Armoured Brigade was deployed 40 miles behind the front near Mersa Brega, and contained two units of desert veterans, but their the equipment was inferior and the Brigade under strength; The 3rd Hussars had just 33 Light tanks; the newly arrived 5th RTR had 23 worn out Cruisers while the veteran 6th RTR had just twenty six old Italian M13s, all of which were inferior to the German MkIII Panzers. Wavell later admitted he had not appreciated the poor state of the armour until his belated visit to the front. Both Neame and the Brigade commander had already informed GHQ about the problems but the information did not arrive until after the Axis advance had begun.[16] British plans were for the 3rd Armoured Brigade

---

14   Joly, *Take These Men*, p.93-105.
15   Schofield, *Wavell, Soldier & Statesmen*, p.171.
16   TNA PREM 3/283.WP(41).159. 11 July 1941. Report on the action of the 2nd Armoured Division.

to strike the flank of the Axis columns whilst the infantry and artillery delayed them frontally.

The frontline Infantry were also weak, the 2nd Support Brigade which only had one motor Infantry battalion, one Regiment of Artillery and six anti-tank guns. The reconnaissance was taken over by the King's Dragoon Guards in mid-February who were fresh and faced better armed German reconnaissance vehicles in a new environment for them. They were in daily contact with Axis units from late February, until they withdrew and became part of Tobruk garrison.[17] Behind the front, other Infantry Brigades were dispersed around Cyrenaica at key points. Neame was ordered to maintain a frontline of highly mobile 'covering forces' (Jock columns) to avoid losses, and be prepared to give up ground including Benghazi which Wavell viewed as having propaganda value but was of little military importance by this stage.[18] The 9th Australian Division had one Brigade east of Benghazi and the other at Tocra in the Djebel Akhdar hills, but had few trucks to aid their movement. These units were 150 miles, or two to three days in the rear of the front. The 3rd Indian Motor Brigade arrived in late March without any artillery or support weapons and was deployed in the rear near Martuba to cover routes through the Djebel. The deployment to Greece had also seriously reduced RAF strength leaving four squadrons in direct support.

German units had recently arrived near Agheila and had been designated the Deutsches Afrika Korps (or DAK). The force was based on the experienced 5th Light Division and was led by the aggressive General Erwin Rommel. The Division's main assault unit was the 5th Panzer Regiment, which initially had just 78 tanks supported by Artillery, Panzer-Jager (anti-tank), machinegun and Reconnaissance units. The force was deployed into battlegroups of all arms, which were supported by the Luftwaffe formation, Fliegerführer Afrika, under Major-General Stephan Frölich. This had two groups of Stukas, a fighter squadron and reconnaissance squadron. Rommel was subordinate to the Italian HQ, but in reality had the freedom to operate as an independent command, something which few other commanders had the luxury of.

First Retreat: Battle summary

The flow of this battle was influenced by the poor tactical terrain and by Rommel's aggressive leadership. His reconnaissance and Intelligence showed the weakness of the British deployment, so the leading elements of the 5th Light Division were rushed forward to engage with British patrols and soon captured the important water

17   http://www.qdg.org.uk/pages/WW2-Part-2-73.php, Detailed History of the Kings Dragoon Guards, World War Two – Part 2, El Agheila, Msus, Tobruk, Bir Gubi 1941-1942, accessed 27 July 2012.
18   TNA PREM 3/283.WP(41).167. 17 July 1941. Minute on the Report on the Action of the 2nd Armoured Division.

wells at Agheila by the 24 March. Rommel then ordered the Division to push east and capture Mersa Brega. A further week was spent probing British positions while the Luftwaffe made heavy bombing attacks on British units, denying them freedom of daytime movement. This air superiority also enabled them to counter any British moves near the front.

On the 31 March Axis forces advanced in three powerful battlegroups which assaulted and by-passed the isolated British Motor battalion which was forced to retreat as their position was under constant observation. The single battalion of the 2nd Support Group was deployed along an eight mile front from the coast to Mersa Brega with the 3rd Armoured Brigade on the flank to the south east. Under orders the Armour retired five miles to the north–east; however the Axis battlegroups were able to break through the gap. From the 2 April the retreat north and east of Agedabia was a slow retreating fight with the 3rd Armoured Brigade contesting, 'each ridge and hillock against the superior weight of enemy armour; at other times in a wild flurry of speed and disorder as...we were again being outflanked.'[19] The remnants of the 3rd Armoured Brigade were forced to make a fighting withdrawal to Msus and Mechili over a distance of 160 miles which caused the unit to be annihilated by attrition. The Australian Brigades escaped along the coast road into the Tobruk perimeter to form the garrison with other British units. Other troops retreated beyond the frontier and allowed Axis forces to capture the old frontier positions around Sollum.

First Retreat: Influence of terrain and doctrine

The initial actions had been influenced by British deployment in the difficult land-scape of the frontline sector and by poor doctrine of separated Support Group and Armoured action. The Axis battlegroups assaulted and by-passed the isolated Motor battalion which was forced to retreat as their position was under constant observation. Further back the 3rd Armoured Brigade was deployed in depth, with the armoured cars in front and behind them the 3rd Hussar Light tanks with the remaining two Regiments south-east of Mersa Brega. One 6th RTR Troop leader, Cyril Joly noted the 'draining' effect on his Regiment, which fought daily battles and suffered a steady attrition in tanks and crews, all of which affected their morale and ability to fight on. The Axis Infantry-based battlegroups made similar flanking moves through the coastal dunes near Mersa Brega and past the British armour near Agedabia. The few British units were forced to deploy along a narrow front which enabled the larger Axis columns to outflank the Brigade and force it to retreat.

The key British commanders were later captured by fast moving Axis columns, with Generals Neame, O'Connor and Brigadier Combe all being taken prisoner on 6 April. The capture of Gambier-Parry and his 2nd Division HQ at Mechili a day later completed the dislocation of the British command which compounded

---

19   Joly, *Take These Men*, p.97.

the loss of initiative. The armoured battle highlighted the successful Axis doctrine which defeated the improvised doctrine of the British. Other problems for the British included the early destruction of the supply depot at Msus, which contributed to the rapid demise of the 3rd Armoured Brigade.[20]

First Retreat: Conclusion

The retreat lasted for just over two and a half weeks, with actions fought across much of the province. The constant outflanking moves by the Axis undermined successive British attempts to hold and caused confusion amongst its numerous commanders. Buckingham believes Neame has been unfairly maligned and that Wavell should have accepted more responsibility for the decisions surrounding the initial British deployment. Rommel had surprised Cyrenaica Command and his own superiors by exceeding his instructions and reached the frontier effectively cutting off Tobruk. The loss of Benghazi left a single Australian Brigade defending the coastal route through the Djebel Akhdar hills and the rapidly failing 3rd Armoured Brigade was destroyed along the desert route. British Intelligence Officers, from the 2nd Armoured Division HQ, had made a poor analysis decision about the Axis advance, which destroyed the Msus supply base too soon and completed the destruction of 3rd Armoured Brigade.

The Second Retreat 21 January – 8 February 1942

The Second Retreat of January 1942, was a further attempt by Eighth Army to attempt a defence of a large desert province and prevent an Axis breakthrough towards Egypt. The scale of the distances involved heavily influenced British operational deployment of Brigade groups by causing them to be dispersed across the region once again. At the tactical level the Army struggled to successfully defend sectors of ground which contained too few defensible positions. These problems compounded continuing issues of separated armour and Infantry doctrine which had remained largely unchanged in terms of deployment and defensive tactics. Most commentators attribute the failures to poor command, logistics and weaponry but little mention is made about the impact of terrain or tactics used. Jonathan Fennell argues that the increasing confusion caused by the retreat contributed to a growing morale crisis by the middle of 1942.[21] This may be countered to some degree because of the hard fought nature by many units during the Second Retreat and by the desire of many, not to be overtaken and put, 'in the bag' as prisoners. They were quite happy to continue fighting once the front had been re-established further east.

---

20   TNA PREM 3/283. Report on certain aspects of the GHQ M.E. Report on the Action of the 2nd Armoured Division.
21   Jonathan Fennell, *Combat and Morale in the North African Campaign* (Cambridge: Cambridge University Press, 2011) p.21.

At the tactical level, the frontline Jock Columns struggled to carry out their operations in the very difficult ground south of Mersa Brega. They had specific orders to harass any Axis advance and then to withdraw. The participants commented on the scenes of frustration to which the appalling terrain had contributed amongst the columns.[22] The distances from Benghazi also contributed to an acute shortage in supplies, Benghazi was slowly returning to use as a British base from the 7 January, after months of RAF attacks to deny the Axis its use. The ground in the frontline sector also slowed down the rate at which the B-echelon supply units reached the Jock Columns.

The Second Retreat: Terrain

In Western Cyrenaica, near Agedabia-Antelat, Eighth Army deployed a forward line of Jock Columns. However, this was still a sector of difficult ground and the vehicles could not operate effectively across this landscape. In comparison the Axis Battlegroups contained numerous more tracked vehicles which could overcome the hummocky terrain and took swift advantage of British difficulties and a lack of supporting armour. Major-General Messervy thought it was the only large area of ground where tracked vehicles were actually better suited than wheeled vehicles.[23]

The frontline was situated between Antelat and a narrow strip of passable desert south of Agedabia, where a number of tracks joined the coast road. It was 30 miles long and included further rough going terrain at the eastern edges towards the deeper Wadi Feragh, a natural wadi which blocked movement inland. The area north of Antelat was relatively good going over which vehicles could travel between 50-65 miles per day. South of Antelat, the terrain worsened to particularly bad dunes and hummocks over which travelling were reduced to just 25 miles per day for British columns.

As before, once past this sector, the Benghazi plain was more undulating and offered few defensive positions. It was bordered by the Sclediema escarpment to the east which curved from Antelat north to Benghazi and was crossed by a few tracks which climbed through sharp defiles. Further north, through the Djebel Akhdar hills, the coast road divided and offered numerous defensive sites but all of these were outflanked by the routes to the south. The inland route offered British supply a safer, more direct route to Tobruk from the new frontline and was a mixture of difficult and easier going, with two reinstated supply dumps at Msus and Mechili. Tobruk had become the Eighth Army's main supply port combined with a rail-head depot nearby providing 1,500 tons of supplies per day. B-echelon supply columns took seven days to

---

22   TNA WO 169/4065. 1st Armd Support Group, Jan-Mar 1942. Reconstructed Diary, following capture of original, p.4.

23   TNA WO 169/4065. 1st Armd Support Group, Jan-Mar 1942.

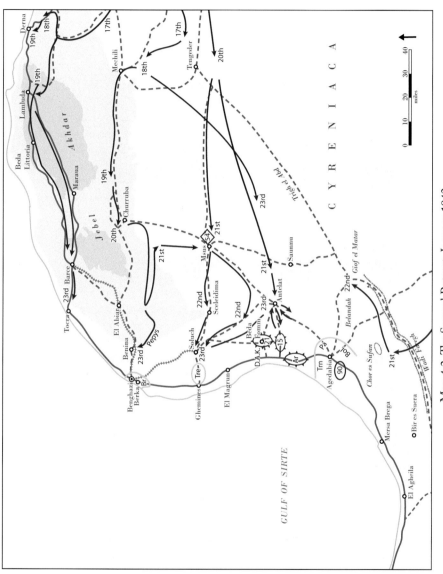

Map 4:2 The Second Retreat, January 1942.

make a return journey to the front via Msus, in comparison the coast road was quicker but had severe bottlenecks which were under constant Axis air attack.[24]

Second Retreat: Preparations

Ritchie had initially intended to resume the advance into Tripolitania, once the Eighth Army had enough supplies and fresh drafts of armour. In comparison to 1941, the front sector was now held by two Support Brigades, although still divided into Jock Columns, and one Brigade from the 1st Armoured Division. The 200th Guards Brigade had two battalions and five batteries covering the coast road while the 1st Support Group was inland, with another two battalions and four batteries. However they had orders to withdraw and not to become entangled with enemy columns.

The armour was to remain free (and separate from the Infantry) to engage the enemy near Antelat, while the Jock columns were designed to harass and delay any advance. Again though, units were newly arrived and unused to either desert conditions or the nature of frontline existence; the 1st Support Group had only taken over on the 19 January just two days before the Axis advance began.[25] Lieutenant-General Godwen-Austen planned for a controlled retreat in case the situation changed rapidly.[26] He also believed that the most defensible position was at Gazala, east of the Djebel hills and not forward at Antelat-Agedabia, but this did not allow for holding western Cyrenaica and its vital airfields. There was more armour though near the front this time, near Antelat, was the newly arrived 2nd Armoured Brigade of three regiments, one motor battalion and five batteries. The RAF had 280 aircraft and but suffered from numerous equipment shortages. Further back, across Cyrenaica the 4th Indian Division had one Brigade at Benghazi with transport, and two others without, at Barce in the Djebel hills and Tobruk. Overall British forces were more powerful than in 1941, but the nature of the province and other factors had led to a wide distribution of the Brigades, few of which were mutually supporting.

For a short period of the winter build up, Panzerarmee was stronger at the front, and could disrupt Eighth Army preparations to advance, by capturing Agedabia and inflicting heavy casualties on them. Rommel again confused British intelligence, by disobeying his orders from OKW and he took the opportunity to advance again whilst the Eighth Army was overstretched along the frontline.[27] The British again thought

---

24   TNA WO 201/370.Major operations Q(P) aspect, 1941 Dec.-Mar.1942. Eighth Army Requirements by Sea and Rail, 11 Jan 1942.
25   TNA WO 169/4065. 1st Armd Support Group, Jan-Mar 1942. P.4 and Reconstructed Diary.
26   TNA WO 201/500. General Auchinleck's despatch on Operation `Crusader'. Brief Survey of Operations between 21 Jan and 5 Feb 1942. By Lt Gen AR Godwen-Austen. He resigned shortly after the retreat.
27   Rommel now had full operational control of Axis forces with the Panzergruppe being renamed Panzerarmee Afrika on the 22 January 1942.

that the Axis formations were too reduced from Crusader to renew operations this quickly, as the three German divisions totalled just 12,500 men and the seven Italian Divisions just 25,000 men. The 13th Corps HQ intelligence thought that numbers must have increased to between 50-70 tanks in the forward areas whilst Ariete Division had another eighty tanks.[28] The Panzer battlegroups now had more powerful MkIII 'specials' supported by a battalion of 30 anti-tank guns. Major-General Messervy at the 1st Armoured HQ noted the build-up of Axis armour but believed they were for reconnaissance only. Axis Air Forces had recovered their strength to nearly 300 serviceable aircraft so had a reasonable advantage over the RAF along the front.

Second Retreat: Battle summary

This battle was hampered by bad winter weather which covered the Axis approach march and caused poor atmospherics which blocked British radio communications at crucial moments. The severe dust storms along the frontline also prevented observation and weak intelligence was compounded by the withdrawal of British Reconnaissance units which left the task to the newly arrived and inexperienced Jock columns. The Axis advanced on the 21 January towards Antelat with two columns thrusting eastwards after a short bombardment of the front line. The supporting 2nd Armoured Brigade was ordered north to engage the enemy armour on the 23 January. It was divided to cover two small villages and was attacked and defeated by more powerful battlegroups. For four days to 30 January, Axis formations remained around Msus whilst the Ariete Division advanced towards Benghazi. German columns were seen on the escarpment at Scelediema advancing north and west to support the Italians on the 30 January.[29]

Ritchie attempted to protect the desert flank of 4th Indian Division to halt the Axis advance, but his plans were flawed as there were only 33 tanks to cover a front of 35 miles. He wanted both 4th Indian and 2nd Armoured to counterattack against Msus and Major-General Tuker complied as best he could to make it work. The 7th Indian Brigade moved west and attacked the enemy flank. However, Msus was captured after a further action which split the 1st Armoured Division and gave the Axis options for further advances towards the Djebel hills. On the 28 January Axis columns feinted along the desert route towards Mechili, but the real thrust then headed towards Benghazi which trapped the 7th Indian Brigade south of the port. British formations began to retreat through the hills and held defensive positions which allowed large numbers of supply trucks and units which had disengaged from Benghazi to be shepherded eastwards. Eighth Army had been ejected back from the Antelat sector

---

28   TNA WO 169/4005. XIII Corps G Branch, Jan-Jun 1942. 13 Corps Intelligence
      Summary No.85. 30 Jan 42.pp.4.
29   TNA WO 169/4005. XIII Corps G Branch, Jan-Jun 1942. 13 Corps Intelligence
      Summary No.85. 30 Jan 42.pp.1-2.

and was only able to halt near Gazala after the Axis advance ground to a halt for lack of fuel.

Second Retreat: The impact of terrain and doctrine

The ground near Agedabia included a narrow strip of fairly good going just north of the Wadi Feragh. However this sector developed into terrain which was poor to impossible for wheeled vehicle and impeded Jock column movement so much that the few passable tracks became vital routes across the rough ground. This bad going in this eastern sector of the front was unexpected and forced the columns to abandon damaged vehicles and guns behind. One report indicated that it weakened the unit's ability to defend in that area.[30] There was further soft sand between Agedabia and Antelat which caused vehicles to become bogged down again. Jock Columns were proving to be not as effective in such poor terrain, as they had been during Crusader, on the gravel plateau.[31]

The poor going affected the ability of Jock columns to hold the line and they were forced to retreat. They were trying to hold a long frontline on difficult ground, against bad weather and fast moving Axis columns. By late morning on the first day the Axis had infiltrated the frontline. The difficult ground impeded the artillery gun tractors which become easily bogged down in the soft sand and created traffic jams along the few passable tracks as British units tried to pull out. By mid-afternoon the Jock columns started to lose radio contact with one another causing further retreat. The following day they were dive-bombed by the Luftwaffe but did not see enemy ground troops. The retreat remained orderly as 1st Support Group columns manoeuvred in pairs to cover each other. However they could not stop the Axis from making a rapid advance of nearly 70 miles, leaving some columns behind the front and exposing the supply route to Msus. The 200th Guards Brigade had four Jock columns deployed some 50 miles south of Agedabia, in very difficult terrain.[32] Later reports agreed that these columns had little choice but to retreat once by-passed.

British doctrine was still committing the armour to fight its own battles, when the 2nd Armoured Brigade was dispersed to cover both Antelat and Saunnu 20 miles away.[33] The two Regiments at Antelat attempted to disengage the enemy and re-join its fellow Regiment but were attacked by elements of both Panzer Divisions and suffered heavily. Their supporting artillery fought tenaciously but the Brigade and

---

30   TNA WO 169/4005. XIII Corps G Branch, Jan-Jun 1942. 13 Corps Intelligence Summary No.83. 23 Jan 42.p.8.
31   TNA WO 169/4065. 1st Armoured Support Group, Jan-Mar 1942. Reconstructed Diary, following capture of original.
32   TNA WO 201/530B, 201 Guards Motor Brigade: reports on operations near Agedabia, Jan-April 42.
33   TNA WO169/4065. 1st Armoured Support Group, Jan-Mar 1942. Reconstructed Diary, 22 Jan, p.4.

eight artillery batteries were defeated by stronger and more effective Axis tactics. The Axis consolidated and engaged 2nd Armoured Division again with eighty-five tanks. Hans Schmidt noted how well his anti-tank company worked with Panzers to out-flank and drive British armour out from defended locations in this action.[34]

Ritchie also clashed with his subordinate commanders, which caused a succession of command problems during the retreat. At 13th Corps HQ, Godwen-Austen wanted to evacuate Benghazi, but was over-ruled by Auchinleck who was visiting Ritchie at his Army HQ at Tmimi, so the 7th Indian Brigade was ordered to 'strike vigorously southwards.'[35] Tuker opposed his only forward Brigade being dispersed into more Jock columns, so Ritchie took personal control of the 4th Indian Division to ensure the Brigade then advanced towards Antelat.[36] British units suffered two days of command indecision and this was picked up by Axis signals and enabled Rommel to strike for Benghazi rather than continue to Mechili.[37] The Axis had better intelligence, which noted confusion amongst British commanders and enabled Rommel to out manoeuvre the separated Brigades. The Eighth Army had been decisively defeated; the Armoured Brigade and Jock Columns suffering heavy losses in guns and vehicles, including 70-100 tanks, 40 guns and 1,400 casualties. The Panzerarmee also benefitted from the mass of stores captured in depots and at Benghazi.

Second Retreat: Conclusion

The main problem for British forces remained the size of Cyrenaica and the poor tactical terrain along the chosen British frontline. This was too far south from the nearest supply bases and was too long a front for eight Jock Columns to cover. The appalling terrain slowed down the columns which were more easily by-passed by faster moving enemy units. Other formations were too far in the rear to be an effective support as they were sited to cover the numerous routes across the province. These ran through the Djebel Akhdar hills and across the desert route to the south. Once Axis forces had reached the Libyan plateau, the supply bases here were vulnerable and further divided British forces trying to cover the coast and the inland supply lines. British units were dispersed in their deployment but also in their defensive doctrine, with 2nd Armoured Brigade fighting a separated battle. Therefore both terrain and poor doctrine were heavily influencing the outcome of these actions.

Other factors also contributed to the two Retreats were failures in British Intelligence and Command which were affected by the terrible weather conditions, while in 1942

---

34   Schmidt, *With Rommel in the Desert*, p.129.
35   TNA WO 201/500. General Auchinleck's despatch on Operation `Crusader'. Brief Survey of Operations between 21 Jan and 5 Feb 1942. By Lt Gen AR Godwen-Austen, and Stewart, *Early Battles of Eighth Army*, p.48.
36   Stevens, *Fourth Indian Division*, p.128.
37   Stuart Hamilton, *Armoured Odyssey. 8th Royal Tank Regiment in the Western Desert 1941-1942* (London: Tom Donovan, 1995) pp.30-31.

Ritchie spent vital days disagreeing with his subordinate commanders over how to slow down the Axis advance. The Eighth Army also withdrew three Reconnaissance regiments from the front and the RAF were prevented from providing air reconnaissance due to the bad weather, which disguised the initial Axis advance. British Intelligence was also misled that the Panzerarmee was too weak to do more than make a 'reconnaissance in force,' such as to destroy forward British supply dumps. These were all important issues which hampered British operations but it was the size of Cyrenaica which made any operational defence difficult compounded by the lack of defensible tactical sites

5

Brevity and Battleaxe May-June 1941

This chapter compares the two successive British offensives of May and June 1941, codenamed Brevity and Battleaxe, and will highlight how aspects of terrain impacted on these operations to influence the outcome of each. These offensives were designed to recapture the frontier sector, defeat German armoured formations and make an advance towards Tobruk. Operation Brevity was a chance to take advantage of stationary Axis forces at Tobruk whilst Battleaxe was a more optimistic plan designed to destroy Axis armour, relieve Tobruk and if possible re-take the Cyrenaican airfields in the west to aid Malta bound convoys.

These offensives have both been well documented in various histories, but there has been little real assessment of the impact of the tactical terrain, beyond noting the coastal escarpment features and the Hafid ridge, which so undermined British attacks during Battleaxe. Robin Neillands provides excellent accounts of the armoured assault on the Hafid ridge, but is less clear on the 11th Indian Brigade assault on Halfaya, whilst Barrie Pitt offers more detail on the latter, though neither discusses the impact of terrain.[1] Paddy Griffiths argues that the operation was a failure of, 'reconnaissance, navigation and terrain analysis' by British forces.[2] Memoirs tended to be critical about both operations, Tedder commented in the midst of Battleaxe, 'Afraid I've got no more faith in the army than they have in themselves.'[3] But G.L. Verney, a later commander of 7th Armoured Division believed the offensives were vindicated because Axis forces made no further advance for the next five months.[4] Their discussion tends to focus on the problems of command, the lack of units and good equipment for British Forces who faced well informed and much stronger Axis forces. Colonel Rainer Kreibel gives a detailed study of the Axis defences and doctrine and shows how their main positions were centred on the key heights, but again fails to emphasize the point that it

---

1   Neillands, *The Desert Rats*, pp.72-79, and Pitt, *The Crucible of War, Vol II*, pp.294-309.
2   Griffiths, *Desert Tactics*, p.30.
3   Lord Tedder, *With Prejudice* (London: Cassell & Co, 1966) p.125.
4   G.L. Verney, *The Desert Rats*, p.59.

was the number and complexity of these defences which exacerbated other problems and undermined the British attacks.[5] The Axis defence was more dynamic in their mobility and vigorous counter-attacks which then out-flanked the already weakened British forces, forcing them to retreat. Lewin places this success on better Axis tactics, better intelligence derived from poor British radio security and the markedly better anti-tank weapons.[6] Whilst noting British problems of too many tank variants he also fails to appreciate the tactical terrain. At the operational level, especially during Battleaxe, the lengthy approach march from the railhead impacted on British tank numbers which reached the front, and kept the British HQ 100 miles in the rear.

Operation Brevity, 15-17 May 1941

Wavell was under enormous pressure during May 1941, sustaining a difficult work-load to control five campaigns simultaneously across the Mediterranean and Middle East.[7] Iraq was still in revolt, German intervention into Syria was imminent, the East African campaign had reached a successful conclusion but still diverted his attention and resources, whilst Ultra intelligence clearly indicated an airborne assault on Crete was expected in late May and all of these required his valuable time, and limited troops and resources. Churchill constantly badgered Wavell for a quick offensive because Ultra decrypts also showed the mechanized German 5th Light Division had been defeated at Tobruk and Rommel had been ordered to hold along the frontier, so it was an opportunity to strike before the expected arrival of the new 15th Panzer Division.[8] Wavell, under severe pressure from London to achieve a victory, therefore ordered an offensive on the 1 May to recapture the Libyan frontier positions, 'to secure a good jumping off place for an attack on a larger scale.'[9]

Brevity: Terrain

What has not been emphasized is that the British objectives were too numerous in total and even if achieved they could be easily outflanked by an approach from the desert because the terrain just inland was considered good going for armoured vehicles. The main feature along the frontier sector was the high escarpment which ran near to the coast at Sollum, and forced any major advance by British forces to be divided, (see Fig 5.1). The coast road ascended the cliff at Sollum and again so

5   Bruce Gudmundsson, *Inside the Afrika Korps, The Crusader Battles, 1941-1942* (London: Greenhill, 1999) pp.295-308.
6   Ronald Lewin, *The Life and Death of the Afrika Korps* (Barnsley: Pen & sword, 2003) pp.55-56.
7   TNA WO 201/493.Despatch by General Sir A.P. Wavell, July 1941.Summary of Operations, p.41.
8   Connell, *Wavell, Scholar & Soldier,* p.427.
9   TNA CAB 106/379. Wavell's Despatch: Operations in the Western Desert, p.33.

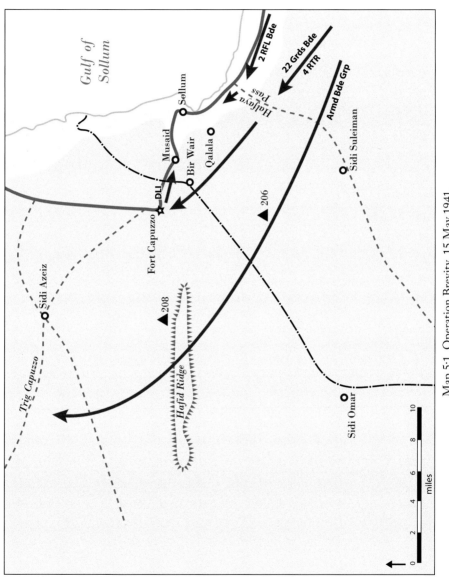

Map 5:1 Operation Brevity, 15 May 1941.

did a track up the Halfaya Pass five miles to the east to the plateau above, before continuing onto Fort Capuzzo. At Halfaya the upper and lower sections of the track were developed into major defensive positions by the Axis, covering the surrounding open ground with heavy anti-tank guns, protected by Infantry, wire and minefields. Any forces attacking the pass needed to capture both positions which meant a more complicated, simultaneous assault.

Beyond Sollum, there was a further 'line' of smaller defensive positions which protected the coast road for eight miles, through Musaid, Bir Wair and Capuzzo. When added to the two positions at Halfaya and those at Sidi-Aziez, these presented a much more formidable area defence of interlocking fire against a British assault, and they were just widely enough dispersed to prevent British forces to prevent an outflanking move on Tobruk. Much of the surrounding desert was largely flat with little cover, offering 'good going' which allowed motorized units to manoeuvre around the defences. Therefore the modest British force available for Brevity was simply unable to cope with the scale of these numerous dispersed positions.

Brevity: Preparations

Lieutenant-General Beresford-Pierce had too few troops and too many objectives. He designated 22nd Guards Brigade to divide its three battalions into four Jock columns.[10] They were to be supported by the 4th Royal Tanks with just 16 Matilda tanks to lead the Infantry assault on Halfaya before moving towards Bir Wair and Capuzzo. The lower Halfaya and Sollum positions were to be assaulted by a Coastal Group of one battalion (2nd Rifle Brigade) supported by artillery. The 'Desert Group' of 2 Cruiser squadrons and three more Jock columns from 7th Support Group was to cover the Halfaya attacks and strike towards Capuzzo and beyond.[11]

Air Marshal Collishaw believed the most effective way to neutralize enemy armour was to deny it petrol and ordered for RAF support to concentrate on ground-strafing sorties against Axis supply columns behind the front.[12] British forces were basically too weak and their doctrine of using a succession separate assaults, along with Jock Columns which had only proven useful in harassing enemy positions, limited the chances of success. In comparison, Axis forces had a line of static units holding their positions, under the command of Colonel von Herff, who also had between 30-50 tanks in direct support. Their supply artery was vulnerable to RAF attack but actually took the shorter inland route to Tobruk along the Trigh Capuzzo, and not the more exposed coast road.

---

10   TNA WO 201/511.Guards Brigade Operations. March – Sept 1941. Operational Order No.11. 14 May 1941, p.3.

11   Pitt, *Crucible of War*, Vol I, p.276, consisting only of 29 reconditioned A9 and A10 tanks, less than a full regiment.

12   TNA AIR 27/1588. 274 Squadron Operations: Diary of events, May 1941.

Brevity: Battle summary

Early on the 15 May, the two positions at Halfaya Pass were assaulted and captured by British Infantry. The momentum continued so that Bir Wair, Musaid and Fort Capuzzo were also overrun. However, 2nd Rifle Brigade struggled to capture lower Halfaya, despite RAF bomber support. The Desert Group advanced beyond Capuzzo onto Sidi-Azeiz, but could not halt the subsequent counter-attack by the 5th Panzer Regiment which retook both, and then inflicted heavy losses on the isolated Jock columns. Brigadier Gott realized that a strong counter-attack was likely and ordered a withdrawal back to Halfaya and the weakened Desert Group wisely delayed a subsequent further counter-attack and also retired.

The Axis counter-attack was made on the following day and used what became a well-tried tactic of attacking in the late afternoon, with the low sun behind their vehicles. This time it avoided closing completely on British positions which enabled the latter to withdraw.[13] Fort Capuzzo was later recaptured because the Jock Columns were overwhelmed by fresh armour and heavier firepower. One report noting, 'there were 40 MkIVs in a fold in the ground near Capuzzo…[they] fired a solid shot which penetrated our tanks…there were also numerous A/T guns of the same type.'[14] By 26 May 15th Panzer Division had its full complement of tanks on the frontier and its supporting 1/104th Rifle Regiment who quickly recaptured both the upper and lower Halfaya positions. The Western Desert Force had been pushed back to its original position and needed fresh armour and troops to make any further progress against the series of increasingly strengthened Axis positions.

Brevity: Conclusion

This operation failed because of the impact of terrain which highlighted the weaknesses in British assault doctrine. There were too many Axis positions and these were too widely separated for weaker British forces to hold once captured. The numerous positions also forced Wavell to use much stronger forces in the subsequent Battleaxe operation to make an effective advance beyond them. The multiple nature and distribution of the positions compounded British weaknesses in numbers, poor equipment and doctrine. Only four armoured squadrons had been used and this was clearly not enough, especially once casualties had been sustained. In doctrinal terms, Cruiser and Infantry units still operated separately and were too dispersed, meaning British forces had not learnt from the errors of the First Retreat in April. The Infantry Matilda tanks had been impervious to Italian guns but now proved vulnerable to the highly effective

---

13   TNA WO 201/493.Despatch by General Sir A.P. Wavell, July 1941.Summary of Operations, p.41.
14   TNA WO 169/1185.7 Armoured Division: Support Group, Jan – Dec 1941; Feb 1942, Intelligence Summary No.26, 18 May 1941.

German anti-tank guns, with 4th RTR noting that better quality shells penetrated their 78mm frontal armour.[15]

Future British combined arms assaults would remain compromised because they revolved around the ability of this tank to survive against these more effective German guns and carry the Infantry onto Axis positions. The Western Desert Force was still using faulty Infantry doctrine by employing Jock columns which dispersed supporting artillery and Infantry in penny-packets on the flanks, rather than supporting the main assaults. The Guards Brigade held Halfaya using Jock columns to harass Axis positions, but made a phased withdrawal when a battlegroup attacked and recaptured the same position two weeks later.[16] These units were unable to cope with subsequent Axis counter-attacks made by more powerful battlegroups. British casualties were not excessive but the battle still left two infantry battalions weakened and numerous tanks were lost.[17]

More importantly, Brevity also signalled likely British intentions for future attempts on the frontier to reach Tobruk. Axis forces gained another month to strengthen their positions and increase their firepower, which would make future assaults on them even more difficult. The arrival of the 15th Panzer Division concentrated German armour at the front and put Western Desert Force further on the immediate defensive, which also contributed to delays in their preparations for Battleaxe.[18]

Battleaxe: 15-17 June 1941

By early June Wavell was under even greater pressure from Churchill who demanded, 'Everything must now be centred upon destroying the German forces in the Western Desert, only by this deed will you gain the security on your western flank…'[19] This second offensive to capture the frontier positions and Tobruk was simply a larger scale version of the Brevity plan with similar objectives but which still ended in failure. At Churchill's insistence, a total of 238 new tanks had been rushed directly through the Mediterranean for the operation.[20] Various studies including Griffiths have concentrated on excellent, detailed narratives of the fighting, but none have emphasized the impact of the terrain despite discussing the Halfaya pass and Hafid ridge battles.[21] This study argues that the importance of the terrain has been underestimated while

15   John Parker, *Desert Rats. From El Alamein to Basra* (London: Bounty Books, 2004) p101. Peter Vaux 4th RTR.
16   TNA WO 201/511. 22nd Guards Brigade: operation instructions, Mar.-Sept. 1941.
17   Playfair, *Mediterranean & Middle East, Vol II*, p.163.
18   TNA WO169/1185.7 Armoured Division: Support Group, Jan – Dec 1941; Feb 1942, Intelligence Summary No.27, 18 May 1941.
19   Connell, *Wavell, Scholar & Soldier*, p.481.
20   Parker, *Desert Rats*, p.101, and Robin Neillands, *The Desert Rats*, p.55. Operation Tiger.
21   Paddy Griffiths, *World War II Desert Tactics* (Oxford: Osprey, 2008) p.29.

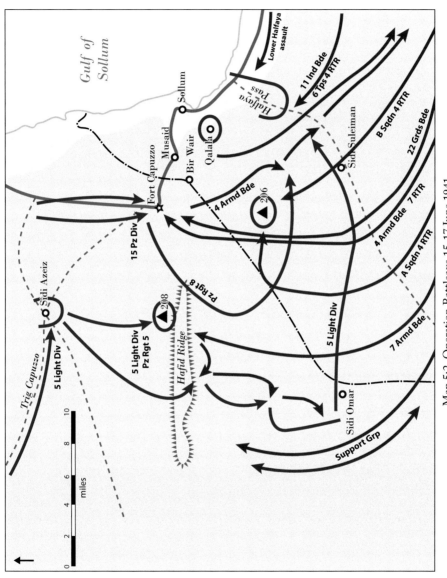

Map 5:2 Operation Battleaxe 15-17 June 1941.

British forces were again attempting to capture too many widely-dispersed objectives, using poor assault doctrines.

Battleaxe: Terrain

The British wanted an 'armoured battle' in the open desert, to defeat the Axis armour and move quickly towards Tobruk.[22] However, their objectives had increased to include capturing both upper and lower Halfaya, followed by Sollum, Fort Capuzzo and its flanking defences at Musaid and Bir Wair. They were expected to complete a follow up advance to Tobruk. However, this was a demanding series of objectives even for two weak Divisions when considering the distances to be covered between the Axis positions.

The approach to lower Halfaya meant crossing two miles of open ground, which was heavily mined. The approach to upper Halfaya, along the top of the escarpment, was broken by numerous ravines which were the only cover available to Infantry along the crest-line. Inland on the plateau, Axis forces under Rommel's direction had developed key areas of high ground and turned them into heavily defended positions. These positions included Pt 206 which dominated the ground on both sides and along with Pt 207 behind it, slowed any direct approach towards Fort Capuzzo, (see Fig. 5.2). Further inland, the Hafid Ridge was a prominent feature about five miles west of Capuzzo, behind which more Axis armour was concentrated.[23] The ridge had three successive crest-lines each with anti-tank guns, armour and artillery in reserve.[24] Near the coast, Fort Capuzzo blocked the road to Bardia but was only lightly held as Axis units held the more valuable higher ground in the rear and to the south-west, which overlooked the whole area.[25]

Battleaxe preparations

British forces were rebuilt as quickly as possible for the operation although weaknesses remained in armour, equipment, and training especially when compared with Axis preparations and deployment across numerous their defensive sites. The Western Desert Force had managed to strengthen two Divisions; the 7th Armoured Division was rebuilt up to two armoured brigades using both new and reconditioned tanks, whilst the 4th Indian Division also rebuilt two Infantry Brigades each of three battalions with supporting artillery. This was clearly still not enough to capture advance beyond their objectives.

22   Stevens, *Fourth Indian Division*, p.60.
23   Joly, *Take these Men*, p.137, though Joly thought it was three miles west.
24   LHCMA GPB Roberts Papers.
25   TNA WO 201/357.Operation `Battleaxe': Lessons of the campaign. An Account of the Frontier Battle.

Churchill had expected great success from the newly arrived 'Tiger cubs,' which despite being re-equipped by mid-June were still experiencing technical problems. Wavell reported that of the new tanks, only sixty-seven were in good order with the rest needing hours of maintenance in workshops.[26] The Armoured Regiments only received their new tanks by the 9 June and so 7th Armoured Division's commander urgently requested five more days for at least some crew training which delayed the start of the operation to the 15 June.[27] The RAF provided air support including 36 Hurricanes, two Blenheim squadrons, one Tomahawk squadron and one reconnaissance squadron, and despite the inexperience of the crews, they provided effective support on the first day.[28]

There were three planned phases to the operation, starting with the defeat of Axis forces at the front and an advance to Bardia-Capuzzo area. This would be followed by an advance to the Tobruk-El Adem sector and the defeat of further enemy forces there, and finally a possible exploitation towards Derna-Mechili and beyond. It was a huge task and Wavell did warn the Prime Minister that despite British strength in tanks and supporting aircraft there still might not be sufficient troops to gain a decisive victory.[29] On the right the 11th Indian Brigade would divide to assault upper and lower Halfaya, with the Cameron Highlanders attacking along the top of the escarpment supported by 20 Matildas. In the centre column, 22nd Guards Brigade was to assault multiple objectives including Pt 206, Pt 207 and Capuzzo.[30] Further inland again, 7th Armoured Brigade was to capture the Hafid ridge and expected to engage an Axis armoured counter-attack in a decisive battle, but Gerald Jackson with 6th RTR, believed it was, 'an ill-fated operation with quite inadequate forces.'[31]

Axis units had been distributed into self-sufficient battlegroups across the strongpoints, from the coast to fifteen miles inland at Sidi Omar. The forward zone was occupied by German and Italian units; the positions at Fort Capuzzo, Musaid and Sollum were strongly held by elements of the Italian Trento Division, along with three batteries of artillery.[32] Rommel had deployed numerous heavy anti-tank guns throughout the front line. All of these positions were supported by lighter weapons and protected by Infantry, wire and minefields. The 15th Panzer Division was deployed as a mobile reserve, whilst the more experienced 5th Light Division remained in reserve near Tobruk. German defensive doctrine emphasised firepower around a key point or

26   Ronald Lewin, *The Life and Death of the Afrika Korps* (Barnsley: Pen & Sword, 2003) pp.55-56.
27   Pitt, *Crucible of War, Vol I*, p.295.
28   Tedder, *With Prejudice*, p.124.
29   Connell, *Wavell*, p.483.
30   TNA WO 201/511. Guards Brigade Operations: March – Sept 1941. Operational Order No.19, p2.
31   Gerald Jackson, *A Long Parting*, Unpublished memoir, undated, p.25.
32   Playfair, *Mediterranaean & Middle East, Vol II*, p.164.

Steutzpunkt, to wear down their attackers before local reserves of armour delivered a powerful counter-attack.[33]

British intelligence provided much less accurate information than the tactical intelligence provided to Rommel by his forward units. On 13 June, it was estimated that the Axis only had 102 tanks and 72 anti-tank guns along the frontier positions whilst the weakened 5th Panzer Regiment was thought to be further back near Tobruk re-fitting and largely unready for combat.[34] Ultra reported Axis shortages of petrol and trucks which mislead analysts into thinking this would limit their ability to make an advance or counter-attack easily. However, RAF attacks on supply shipping in Benghazi during May had limited success as 90% of supplies were still being unloaded.[35] In comparison, Axis intelligence collated by 621 Signals Company, accurately showed British preparations and definite signals activity which indicated an impending offensive to relieve Tobruk. Consequently, Rommel increased numbers of anti-tank guns across the positions which Brevity had previously targeted.[36]

The British were also experiencing command problems when Churchill questioned the appointment of Lieutenant-General Beresford-Pierce to command the Western Desert Force. Beresford-Pierce also struggled to site his HQ nearer the front and was forced to place it sixty miles to the rear at Sidi-Barrani. Any further forward and he would have lost radio contact with the RAF Group HQ at Mataan Baggush 100 miles further to the rear.[37] This left the control of the tactical battle to the two Divisional commanders, Messervy and O'Moore-Creagh. Messervy noted he was issued plans, photos and maps only twelve days before, and realised he had, 'no knowledge of the country, except from…the maps and from one short visit to the area.'[38] The long journey to the front caused the British armoured strength to be reduced again before the operation began, leaving 4th RTR with only 45 Matildas and 6th RTR with just 35 Crusaders.[39] It took two days to move the vehicles up by rail, and a further two days to move the armour 100 miles across the desert while carrying out constant repairs.[40]

33   T.L. Jentz, *Tank Combat in North Africa. The Opening Rounds. Operations Sonnenblume, Brevity, Skorpion and Battleaxe. February 1941-June 1941* (Atglen: Schiffer Publishing, 1998), p.155.
34   TNA WO 201/511. Guards Brigade Operations: March – Sept 1941. Special Intelligence Summary, 13 June.
35   Bennett, *Ultra and Mediterranean Strategy*, pp.45-46
36   Neillands, *Eighth Army*, p.60.
37   Playfair, *Mediterranean & Middle East, Vol II*, pp.165-166.
38   Stevens, *Fourth Indian Division*, p.60.
39   Griffiths, *Desert Tactics*, p.30.
40   Jackson, *A Long Parting*, p.25, including tracks lost and engine problems.

Battleaxe: Battle summary 15-17 June

The first assaults along the top of the escarpment highlighted Axis defensive firepower with the open ground enabling Axis guns to knock out the approaching Matildas at 2,000 yards.[41] The supporting Infantry (11th Indian Brigade) continued onwards before being pushed back by a later Axis counter-attack.[42] The assault at Lower Halfaya was similarly halted by Axis fire and minefields. Here the Infantry were unable to cross the open ground swept by heavy MG fire and this effectively ended the assaults on the two pass positions.[43] British assault doctrine was failing to take account of ground conditions in daylight assaults, without adequate artillery support, which resulted in the loss of valuable armour, and caused each attack to be stalled.

The centre column was more successful and it made combined armoured/ infantry assaults which captured Pt 206, Sollum and Fort Capuzzo, with the Matildas of 7th RTR advancing to occupy the nearby airfield on the following day.[44] However, heavy and accurate Axis gunfire here knocked out many tanks and forced the Regiment to retire with only 14 vehicles on the 17 May. The regiment subsequently engaged an 'overwhelming Axis column', to enable the remnants of 22nd Armoured Brigade on the left to withdraw.[45] The 7th RTR became overextended trying to capture too many enemy objectives and fought a separated battle from its infantry support.

On the left flank, the 7th Armoured Brigade advanced towards the Hafid Ridge. However, visibility was very poor because of the heat and dust which made observation beyond 1,000 yards impossible, and the Brigade was soon under heavy enemy fire. The 2nd RTR made a frontal assault on the second crest-line, with B squadron driving in from the flank and which became heavily engaged amongst the Axis guns.[46] As Joly observed, the armoured assault faltered when support from other squadrons failed to materialize.[47] The remaining British tanks were quickly lost due to the attritional fighting and communication errors which resulted in some tanks driving away in error. This was another example of the armour fighting alone without infantry and artillery support.

The attack on Hafid ridge failed with heavy losses and after a stationery fire-fight 2nd RTR began a long slow retreat pushed back by Axis tanks. The armour

---

41   Parker, *Desert Rats*, p.106, all suffered high casualties, although Peter Vaux believed they were using Italian 6" naval guns at upper Halfaya.
42   Joly, *Take these Men*, p.135.
43   Pitt, *Crucible of War*, pp.297-298.
44   TNA WO 201/511. Guards Brigade Operations: March – Sept 1941. Operations Order 19, p.3.
45   Bovington Archives: 7th RTR War Diary: Diary of events, June 1940-June 1941. It was left with 5 tanks.
46   Patrick Delaforce, *Battles With Panzers, 1RTR & 2RTR at War* (Stroud: Sutton, 2003) p.191.
47   Joly, *Take these Men*, p.140.

lost communication with its artillery fire support which also left 6th RTR isolated and weak. Troop commander Cyril Joly noted, 'the gun OPs were miles behind and hadn't a chance of getting up to us. We've got to get that better organized…have 'em riding in tanks…the present set-up's bloody well useless.'[48] The British attack had been surprised and undermined by the two further crest-lines of the ridge which had enabled the Axis anti-tank guns and armour to deploy in-depth. Major Pip Roberts also believed this was the key reason for the failure of the attack.[49]

Another feature of this mobile warfare was that regiments quickly became scattered across different objectives. Despite this, a weakened 7th Armoured Brigade did worked with the artillery to halt a later attack by 5th Light Division, but was still forced to withdraw 15 miles.[50] The artillery was still an effective force, as noted by Gerald Jackson who watched an Axis column coming under heavy shell fire which compelled them to withdraw.'[51] Even though units were being dispersed, they were still able to engage the enemy effectively. The assault doctrine remained weak, however, as Infantry brigades and cruiser regiments were each fighting an independent battle instead of as a combined force.

Regimental accounts noted the importance of key terrain heights and how these remained the focus of the fighting. As the battle drew to an end the remnants of 7th RTR retreated and,

> The Sqn arrived at Pt 205 which dominates the entire country. Maj Holden therefore decided to hold it…the enemy had overwhelming superiority and attacked from all directions… By 1900hrs the remaining five tanks had run out of ammunition and were short of fuel so Maj[or] Holden decided to withdraw them.[52]

The concluding phase of the battle, on the 17 May showed how better Axis signals intelligence helped Rommel win the final phase of the battle. It confirmed that British commanders had lost faith in the battle and the remaining concentration of British tanks were too far forward near Sollum, so he ordered his fresh battlegroups to swing behind them and thrust north-east towards Halfaya and the coast. The remnants of 7thArmoured Brigade made a fighting retreat from this thrust and Messervy and Beresford-Pierce decided to cancel their planned moves and order a general retreat to save the remaining armour. Wavell had come forward to Beresford-Pierce's HQ on the previous afternoon to gain a better picture of events, but the British Commander had already gone forward to meet his two Divisional commanders, who had controlled

48   Joly, *Take these Men,* p.150.
49   LHCMA Roberts, GPB, Papers. Report on Battleaxe.
50   TNA WO 201/357.Operation `Battleaxe': Lessons of the Campaign, and Delaforce, *Battles With Panzers,* pp.191-192. with 25 tanks remaining.
51   Jackson, *A Long Parting,* p.26.
52   Bovington Archives, 7th RTR History, Events of June 1941.

the tactical battle with little input from him so far.[53] British commanders were now on the spot, like their Axis counter-parts, yet they no longer had the armoured strength or the will to alter the course of the operation.

The battle was influenced by other factors which included poor command and communication issues. The 4th Indian Division blamed poor radio links between air and ground units for the failure of the operation.[54] However, the two Divisional Generals had actually kept good radio security by conversing in Hindustani, but other messages back to 13th Corps HQ were more insecure.[55] The supposedly vital radio message from Creagh back to Beresford-Pierce at 0930hrs on the 17 June, was picked up by 621 Signals Company and confirmed that the British commanders were in doubt about their next move. This intercepted message enabled Rommel to change the direction of his counter-attack to outflank 7th Armoured Division.[56] Yet Rommel failed to acknowledge this in his own account, and stated that ordered his own advance quickly towards Halfaya.[57]

The tactical battle was influenced by terrain due to the quantity and distribution of the Axis defensive positions. These locations gave Axis armour the time to concentrate for an effective counter-attack from a flank position, which in turn undermined the British advance. As in Brevity, the objectives were too widespread for the limited forces and some positions such as the Halfaya Pass needed more tactical finesse to capture. The three crest lines of the Hafid ridge had undermined the British armoured assault as the ill-planned attack was made by armour alone against the deep Axis defence position. It is noted that the British diverted around these positions in November, rather than be delayed by them again, in the approach to Tobruk.

British doctrine had become weakened by the over-use of Jock Columns. The armoured assault on the Hafid Ridge had no infantry support because 7th Support Group operated in Jock columns in a protective screen on the left flank. There had been a lack of combined arms training with Cruiser tanks, and most commanders traditionally used Infantry with 'I' tanks. The Jock columns kept the artillery too widely dispersed and Royal Artillery commanders were critical of the lack of concentration of guns. There was a growing perception the tanks needed mobility more than artillery support fire, and that the, 'over-use of scattered guns in jock columns,' led to armour becoming more self-reliant.[58] The British might have used more concentrated

53   Pitt, *Crucible of War, Vol I,* p.308.
54   TNA WO 201/357. Operation `Battleaxe': Lessons of the campaign. An Account of the Frontier Battle.
55   Pitt, *Crucible of War,* p.308.
56   Hinsley, *British Intelligence, Vol I,* p.399 and Strawson, *Battle for North Africa,* p.83.
57   Liddell-Hart, *The Rommel Papers,* pp141-142, and James Lucas, *Panzer Army Afrika* (London: Macdonald & Jane's, 1977), p.60, and Playfair, *Mediterranean & Middle East, Vol II,* pp.169-170.
58   Martin Farndale, *The Years of Defeat. 1939-1941. History of the Royal Regiment of Artillery* (London: Brasseys, 1996), pp.190-191.

supporting artillery fire which would have been more effective in covering the assault troops onto the positions. Air support from the RAF had concentrated on units behind the frontline and was attritional but did not decisively change the battle.[59]

Battleaxe had been hastily planned and carried out with insufficient forces, when more detailed planning and better intelligence might have led to some tactical gains. British forces had again failed to hold onto any of the numerous objectives and suffered losses which included 1,000 casualties, 91 tanks and 40 aircraft for no gain. British estimates initially thought Axis losses had also been heavy with large numbers of trucks and 700 casualties along with losses of nearly 100 tanks, but after recovery the Axis had lost just 13 tanks with another 50 damaged and recovered.

The command and communication structure was also weakened by the scale of the distances involved, as seen in the site chosen by Beresford-Pierce for his HQ. This was a poor compromise to cope with the fast changing situation in the battle, and was made worse by insecure radio procedures. In comparison, Rommel led from the front and placed his tactical HQ alongside his leading armoured units, meaning he was able to respond more quickly to British attacks.

British forces needed fresh reinforcements before any further advance could be considered and Churchill finally sacked Wavell who was exchanged with Auchinleck, as CinC India.[60] The new CinC also insisted on a proper reorganisation of British forces before any further offensive would take place. This created the Eighth Army with new equipment and a training period of five months before the next offensive, Operation Crusader, took place. British planners also had to contend with how to overcome the operational terrain problem; of moving a large force across eighty miles of desert, by-passing heavy defences to engage and defeat the enemy.

59   TNA AIR 27/1588. 274 Squadron Operations: summary of events 1 June-31 July 1941.
60   Connell, *Wavell*, p.484.

6

Operation 'Crusader' October-December 1941

This chapter considers the major British offensive of late 1941 which was designated Operation Crusader. It looks at the impact of terrain upon the operational level planning and command decisions, as well as how the tactical ground affected various key battles during the operation. The effect on the operational level planning was again influenced by the scale of the distances traversed by Eighth Army before Tobruk could be relieved, as well as fighting across two different sectors of Libya. The impact of the tactical terrain will be examined as the key battles unfolded in three different sectors. These features became the focus of the fighting and influenced the outcome as much as the issues of command, training, and equipment, which have been the focus of most of the previous historiography about the battle. British doctrine will also be considered to show how it evolved from previous operations.

Other studies about Crusader have concentrated on the narrative of this complex twenty day battle and argue that the outcome was largely influenced by other military factors. De Guingand's early memoir noted that Crusader received little attention and was one of the hardest fought battles for the Eighth Army, which deserved credit for defeating a more experienced Axis force. Geoffrey Cox's memoir is one of the very few to note the vital terrain feature which influenced the battle considered the relief of Tobruk was important but the battle had become eclipsed by Second Alamein.[1] Tim Moreman notes that British doctrine needed to improve, and change its dispersion of formations,[2] while Michael Carver discusses the failures of poor equipment and doctrine, but which again misses the importance of the impact of terrain on the tactical battle.[3] John Strawson argues that the British command was weaker, and the Axis had better gun-armour equipment which affected doctrine but again terrain is

---

1 De Guingand, *Operation Victory,* p.99, and Cox, *A Tale of Two Battles,* p.196.
2 Tim Moreman, *Desert Rats. British 8th Army in North Africa 1941-43* (Oxford: Osprey, 2007) pp.32-35.
3 Michael Carver, *Dilemmas of the Desert War. The Libyan Campaign 1940-1942* (Staplehurst: Spellmount, 2002) pp.29 and 51.

not mentioned as a factor.[4] Barrie Pitt offers a powerful narrative which again shows the separated armoured and infantry actions but he made little of the terrain impact.[5] Adrian Stewart and Richard Humble both provide detailed narratives and focus on command problems but neither comment on the impact of terrain.[6] Therefore this study argues that terrain again played an important part in how British units fought, where they fought and the outcome of key battles. This operation was an important step for British forces gaining more combat experience in learning how to defeat Axis forces, but there were crucial lessons still not being learnt which were to influence future doctrine in the months ahead.

Crusader terrain: The Frontier sector

At the operational level, the scale of Cyrenaica and its terrain influenced British planning, due to the distances between the Axis frontier defences and the primary objective, Tobruk. The strength of the frontier defences forced the Eighth Army to divert around them, increasing the distance of the approach march towards the Tobruk sector. This then created two areas of British operations and drew away large numbers of British units just to contain the frontier sector. The frontier defences also diverted Rommel's attention away from the more vital Sidi Rezegh battle, which gave Eighth Army forces there a chance to regroup for the final phase of operations to relieve Tobruk.

Tactically the Axis frontier positions had been strengthened over the previous four months, from Sollum to the Omars and were sited on the dominating heights for twenty miles along the frontier wire. New Zealand Intelligence Officer Geoffrey Cox thought that they provided, 'the Germans there with a very defensible line.'[7] The problem for British forces was that each position had to be contained, assaulted and captured, during which time the Axis garrisons were extending local minefields throughout the blockade.[8] At the southern end of the line, the Omars were considered the most formidable of positions, which consisted of three adjacent strong points, all sited to cover each other. These positions were blockaded for several weeks and were only assaulted at the end of Operation Crusader.

4   John Strawson, *The Battle for North Africa* (New York: Charles Scribner's Sons, 1969) pp.103-107
5   Pitt, *Crucible of War, Vol II*, pp.43-153.
6   Adrian Stewart, *The Early Battles of the Eighth Army. 'Crusader' to the Alamein Line 1941-1942* (Barnsley: Leo Cooper, 2002) p.39 and Richard Humble, *Crusader Eighth Army's forgotten victory. November 1941-January 1942* (Barnsley: Leo Cooper, 1987) p.200. A Pyrrhic victory was a battle won, but at great cost to the winning side.
7   Cox, *A Tale of Two Battles*, p.163.
8   Stevens, *Fourth Indian Division*, p.99.

Crusader terrain: The Sidi Rezegh sector

The ridges south-east of Tobruk became the main focus of the fighting during Crusader and largely defined the outcome of the battle. The terrain here was dominated by three parallel escarpments and the high ground along each provided good artillery observation over lower ground on either side, which enabled units to target concentrations of vehicles and men. The control of this area and of the Sidi Rezegh airfield played a major role in defining success and failure for both sides. The airfield became a focus for British commanders because it was an important Axis supply route and its capture would force the Luftwaffe further away from the frontier.[9]

The tactical terrain in this sector included a 'quadrilateral' of heights near the Sidi Rezegh airfield all of which became objectives and which dispersed British forces trying to capture them. The three escarpments ran broadly east-west and were the most prominent terrain features in this sector. The first or northerly one was the Ed-Duda ridge, which overlooked the Axis bypass road around the Tobruk perimeter. It contained the Panzergruppe HQ and was the objective for the break-out by 70th Division from Tobruk south-east towards Eighth Army. The second or middle escarpment was situated south of the Trigh Capuzzo, and was the highest feature reaching 192 metres in places. Other key heights along this ridge were Pt 163, overlooking the airfield on its southern side and five miles east at Pt 175, another prominent circular hill was made naturally defensive by defiles on either side.[10]

The ridge was passable for vehicles onto the southern slopes but was too steep on the northern slopes to descend except in a few places.[11] The third escarpment was three miles south of Sidi Rezegh airfield and became more prominent further westwards to overlook the El-Adem airfield. The south side of this ridge provided a staging area for both sides as they made approaches north towards the airfield.

The final area of ground which saw major fighting was just south-east of the Tobruk perimeter, where numerous large Axis defensive positions were sited across low ground on the routes towards the northern escarpment at the Ed Duda ridge. These three operational sectors of eastern Cyrenaica influenced Eighth Army command decisions during planning and heavily contributed to the outcome of the fighting at the tactical level as much as other military factors.

Crusader: Preparations

Auchinleck delayed another summer offensive, despite heavy pressure from Churchill, because he argued that Army needed time to reorganize, train and re-equip, 'as an

---

9   TNA WO 201/361. 7th Armoured Division: Account of Operations in Libya, 1941, Nov-Dec, pp.31.
10   Cox, *A Tale of Two Battles,* p.160.
11   Jackson, *A Long Parting,* p.31.

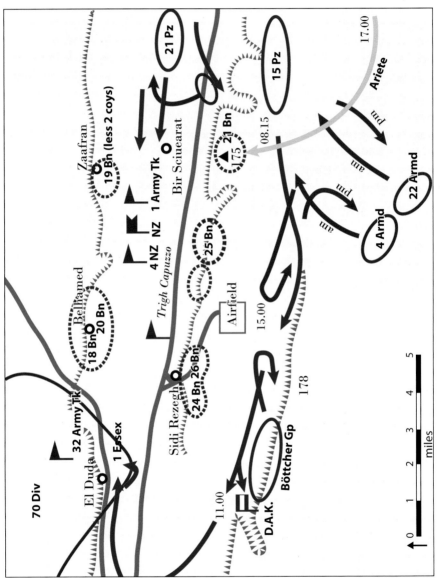

Map 6:1 Crusader, Sidi Rezegh, November–December 1941.

essential part of the preparations for driving the enemy out of Libya.'[12] Even though fresh reinforcements, including American Stuart tanks and British Cruisers arrived in August and September, he realized the armoured regiments would not be trained or prepared enough until at least mid-November.[13] The subsequent preparations for Crusader took place on a vast scale and ensured that the Army was well equipped, though training levels varied between units. Reinforcements came in from Britain and the Empire, including 27,300 men in new formations and 17,000 for existing units along with 2,100 new tanks, which gave Auchinleck the three to two ratio of armour he wanted to begin the offensive. Other new equipment arrived up to October including over 34,000 trucks, 600 field guns and 200 anti-tank guns along with thousands of tons of weapons and ammunition.[14]

The Eighth Army used the four months build up to reorganize and improve training. The Infantry were grouped mainly in 13th Corps, under Lieutenant-General Godwen-Austen, with 2nd New Zealand Division and 4th Indian Division both increased to three Brigades each, supported by the 1st Army Tank Brigade. The main armoured formation was 30th Corps, under Lieutenant-General Norrie, the 7th Armoured Division had three full Armoured Brigades plus its Support Group, while the 1st South African Division had two Infantry Brigades and the experienced 22nd Guards Brigade attached. Some units such as the South Africans requested further training so the mid-November start date was delayed a little more, despite immense pressure from Churchill.[15] Despite the lengthy build-up, not all units had the time for doctrinal training and consequently there was little real change in battle tactics.

The RAF made thorough preparations to achieve air superiority and support for the Army and had built up 500 aircraft in nine bomber and nineteen fighter squadrons. Liaison with the Army improved as Air Vice-Marshal Coningham sited his HQ alongside Eighth Army HQ for closer cooperation.[16] The bombers began a month long, phased campaign which targeted the major Axis airbases at Derna, Tmimi and Gazala, increasing the intensity of raids in the final week before the ground offensive.[17] The RAF provided a combination of regular fighter sweeps over the battlefield and medium-bombing raids on enemy concentrations of MET,[18] along with deeper raids on enemy airfields and supply routes.[19] A new fighter-bomber squadron was created to specifically target Axis supply trucks and air cover improved as the fighter squadrons

---

12   TNA PREM 3/285. Gen. Auchinleck's Despatch 1941 Jul.-Oct. etc. p.2.
13   TNA WO 201/2357. Libya, Cyrenaica and Tripolitania planning. 1941 July – 1942 Feb. Cipher 84786. Mid-East to Troopers (CIGS). 23 July 1941.
14   TNA PREM 3/285. Gen. Auchinleck's Despatch 1941 Jul.-Oct. etc. p.23.
15   Carel Birkby, *Uncle George. The Boer Boyhood, Letters and Battles of Lieutenant-General George Edwin Brink,* (Johannesburg: Jonathan Ball, 1987) p.170 and pp.191-192.
16   TNA PREM 3/285. Gen. Auchinleck's Despatch 1941 Jul.-Oct. etc. p28.
17   TNA WO 201/363. Operation Crusader. Air Operations.
18   Playfair, *Mediterranean & Middle East, Vol III,* p.41.
19   TNA WO 201/363. Operation `Crusader': air situation: diary of events. 1941 Nov-Dec.

were made ready to take over landing grounds just behind the front.[20] Problems still remained over operational control and there were delays in signalling targets back to squadrons for them to react in time but overall the RAF provided solid support for the Army, which was an improvement on previous operations.

Auchinleck was criticized about his choice of commander for the Eighth Army prior to this vital offensive. He appointed General Sir Alan Cunningham, who had defeated the Italians in East Africa, but who had not yet faced German forces and had no experience in armoured warfare. The CinC defended his decision to London despite their wishes for the more experienced Maitland-Wilson to have been appointed. British forces were to suffer from command problems during the operation when Cunningham suffered a breakdown at a critical moment and Auchinleck had to take direct command for a period. Cunningham's style of command was seen by contemporaries as weak. Brigadier John Harding, then BGS at 13th Corps HQ noted that, 'Orders formed a basis for discussion rather than something that had to be done.'[21] There were also errors in the selection of plans made by GHQ and approved by Auchinleck, which were forced on Cunningham. The final choice was a compromise of options designed to protect the vulnerable Infantry formations against armoured assault and bring the Panzer Divisions to battle.

The main task of 30th Armoured Corps was to advance south of Tobruk and await the Axis response to bring about an armoured battle, whilst the Infantry of 13th Corps would screen the frontier defences and then advance west once the Axis armour had been defeated.[22] The plan was altered and weakened after objections from the New Zealand General Freyberg and Godwen-Austen at 13th Corps, who both wanted to protect their Infantry if attacked by armour, consequently the 4th Armoured Brigade was re-assigned to cover the Infantry flank. General Freyberg was seriously worried because his battalions only had four anti-tank guns each, and he feared they would be easily overrun by Panzers, as had happened in Greece.[23] The New Zealand Division would be divided to screen the frontier defences and advance west towards Tobruk, while the 4th Indian Division was to assault the Libyan Omars to clear the forward supply routes.

In Tobruk, the breakout by 70th Division was well planned in every detail by Brigadier Willison of the 32nd Army Tank Brigade, who trained his troops in combined arms assaults. They had the difficult task of advancing ten miles to the Ed-Duda ridge through some extensive Axis defences. This part of Crusader was more successful because Willison ensured all ranks understood their tasks and became

20   TNA WO 201/355. Action at Sidi Rezegh: 1st Kings Royal Rifle Corps.
21   Stewart, *Early Battles*, p.16 and Humble, *Crusader*, pp.74–75.
22   TNA WO 201/2357. Libya, Cyrenaica and Tripolitania planning. 1941 July – 1942 Feb, p.4
23   http://www.nzetc.org/tm/scholarly/tei-WH2-21Ba-c5.html. 21 Battalion History, p.119, accessed 29.3.12.

used to working together.[24] Other diversionary attacks included Commando and SAS raids as well as an 'Oasis Force', a unit designed to create havoc in the Axis rear supply routes and cut the road near Benghazi. Although some of these diversionary attacks failed, Oasis Force did cause some anxiety to the Panzergruppe HQ who brought in additional air units from Sicily in reply.[25] Overall, the task of planning for Crusader involved bringing all these elements together to defeat the Axis forces. They were a complex set of objectives which was asking a lot from a newly formed army.

Axis forces had been building up to assault Tobruk in November since Rommel's victory in mid-June. However, both German and Italian Divisions were struggling to increase men and resources due to the stranglehold on Axis supplies by the Royal Navy and RAF on Malta. Their Air Forces were now weaker than the RAF, as there were only 300 Axis aircraft operational in Libya although they could call on reserves of planes from elsewhere. The Axis supply shortage led to petrol shortages by November and this had principally delayed Rommel's planned assault on Tobruk which was just nearing completion, when Crusader began.

Sidi Rezegh: Battle summary

Only a few examples of the fighting can be given here as the twenty days of combat involved a mass of combats many of which were interconnected by terrain, command and issues of action-reaction. One of the early successes for the Eighth Army was the discipline and precision by which it advanced into Cyrenaica with numerous large Brigade Groups. The left flank was protected by the Reconnaissance Regiments from 1st South African Division because of their strength and expertise.[26] The advance placed the bulk of 30th Corps south-east of Tobruk awaiting a reaction from the Panzer Divisions. The reaction was slow because Rommel disbelieved early reports about the British advance and there was no air reconnaissance due to the stormy weather which flooded all Axis airfields. Eighth Army had achieved a major operational success by this manoeuvre behind enemy lines. The subsequent battle for Sidi Rezegh Airfield developed through a series of armoured engagements and an Infantry defence against attacking Axis battlegroups, when 13th Corps Brigades made an advance towards Sidi Rezegh, either side of the second escarpment.

The impact of terrain and doctrine on the battle

In the early armoured engagements, units became more dispersed in order to capture widespread objectives and/or engage the Axis armour. The later Infantry assaults also

24   Bovington Archives. Breakout From Tobruk November 21 1941, by Willison.
25   TNA HW 1/237, North Africa: GAF measures to counter possible British break through Nov 20-21; Italy and Africa Air Operations, 21.11.41.
26   John Rylands Archive Auchinleck Papers, AUC/427, 8.11.41.

dispersed as they attempted to overcome key landscape features on the escarpments in order to gain the higher ground. British doctrine still focussed on separate actions by Armour and Infantry rather than by combined assault. In one early encounter 4th Armoured Brigade engaged a battlegroup from 21st Panzer Division at Gabr-Saleh, at only two-thirds strength, because it had been dispersed. The terrain also influenced the fighting at Sidi Rezegh when the 6th RTR captured the airfield but was drawn into attacking Axis positions on the ridge above.[27]

British commanders continued to direct separate Armoured Brigades to engage enemy formations; 4th Armoured Brigade spent most of the first five days chasing Axis formations but with little success. Armoured Regiments were also directed across the Sidi Rezegh ridge and north-west towards the Ed-Duda ridge, Lieutenant-General Norrie directed the 7th Armoured Brigade to make this link-up with the 70th Division, because Axis forces were thought to be weaker there. The attack failed because of the terrain and due to command errors and poor doctrine. The attack initially combined two Armoured Regiments with the 2nd Rifle Brigade to assault the Ed-Duda ridge but again, the 7th Hussars were pulled back to defend the airfield. The attack was initially successful with Pt 167 secured, after which just two squadrons from 6th RTR continued the advance towards Ed-Duda, but these were halted by strong enemy gun positions on low ground, which left the unit decimated.[28] A combined assault had been reduced to a weak armoured thrust which had been easily halted by well sited guns.

Another issue for British tactics was that newly arrived units showed their inexperience in combat and doctrine, despite long months of training in the UK. The 22nd Armoured Brigade engaged the Ariete Division at Bir el Gubi because it was considered an easier objective. They began with a frontal assault by one regiment supported by a single artillery battery, 'the position was overrun in a dashing cavalry charge… (but we lost 35 of our 53 [Crusaders])…[and] we were not able to hold the ground and were ordered to retreat.'[29] The two remaining Regiments attacked later and halted by minefields and anti-tank fire, so that the Brigade was outflanked and forced to withdraw by a later Axis counter-attack. British Armoured Brigades were not combining with Infantry and were delivering poorly coordinated frontal assaults on strong Axis positions for no gain.

Another feature of the separated armoured battle was the high attrition rates suffered by Regiments against these defended positions. Having been weakened in the early actions, the 7th Armoured Brigade and its Support Group defended the Sidi Rezegh ridge and airfield over two days which left both formations very weak by the

27   Jackson, *A Long Parting,* p.31.
28   Bovington Archives 6th RTR War Diary. November 1941, including the CO, Lieut-Colonel Lister and two Squadron commanders.
29   IWM Box No. 6911. 97/36/1, Papers of Sgt W.R. Hill. 2nd Gloucester Hussars Yeomanry and LRDG, p.14.

23 November.[30] Units were reformed and re-equipped around surviving personnel, but were largely incapable of further offensive action. The weakened units forced the 4th Armoured Brigade to return the airfield but its two remaining Regiments, the 3rd and 5th RTR, but these also suffered further heavy losses and were reduced to just 12 tanks. British armour suffering attrition faster than tanks and crews could be replaced. The weakened units also had to attack Axis defensive positions on the Sidi Rezegh ridge which held low profile anti-tank guns in rough ground and caused further losses.

Other factors which influenced the outcome were failures of doctrine and Command. British doctrine proved weak when Armoured Regiments disengaged because of their practice for replenishing of fuel and ammunition, the 3rd RTR initially assisted 1st South African Division's defence on low ground but was ordered away to replenish its own munitions and fuel leaving the isolated Infantry Brigade which was overrun later in the day.[31]

Another failure was for British HQs to direct Regiments towards different objectives. Informed by Ultra intelligence, General Cunningham changed his plans on the 21 November to meet an expected Panzer thrust. The 4th and 22nd Armoured Brigades were combined to receive it, but Cunningham also then separated the 1st South African Division to screen both Bir el Gubi and Sidi Rezegh airfield. HQs were also quickly put out of action by the mobile nature of operations when they were overrun by enemy columns, the 4th Armoured HQ was overrun and was temporarily out of action, whilst the 8th Hussars lost 35 tanks captured in night-close leaguer which meant it was unable to support the vulnerable 5th South African Brigade, which was overrun on open ground the following day.[32] Eighth Army directed forces to hold the both Sidi Rezegh airfield and the Third Escarpment to the south, so that a weakened 22nd Armoured Brigade reached the escarpment and assisted the weak 2nd RTR against strong Panzer attacks. The Brigade was held up by anti-tank fire and dust which created total confusion because of the lack of visibility. They moved to outflank these guns but the Brigade remained caught on the ridge for the rest of the day.[33] Armoured battles were confused affairs, hampered by numerous problems, though they were often committed to capture or hold key terrain features.

The Infantry Brigades also fought separate battles as they approached Sidi Rezegh, the 2nd NZ Division and the 5th SA Brigades both fought separate actions as they made their approach marches towards the airfield. The South Africans were too slow approaching from the south and were caught in the open and overrun by a powerful attack by DAK.[34] In comparison on the frontier sector, the 4th Indian Division and

30   Bovington Archives 6th RTR War Diary. November 1941.
31   Joly, *Take these men*, p.206.
32   Birkby, *Uncle George*, p.218.
33   Bovington Archives 2nd RTR War Diary. Account of Operations of Composite
     Squadron, 22 November 1941. Two Regiments only; the 4th CLY and 2nd RTR.
34   Birkby, *Uncle George*, pp.183-240, is based on Brink's unpublished report of Jan 1942.

1st Army Tank Brigade, made set-piece combined assaults supported by 'I' Tanks, as they had done during Compass.

The 2nd NZ Division was assigned multiple objectives after an approach march towards Sidi Rezegh which was 100 miles away and took four nights to complete. Each Brigade had a different objective, the 4th Brigade moved north-west to cut the Tobruk road, while the 6th Brigade moved directly west to support Sidi Rezegh, each of them was supported by a Regiment of 'I' tanks. The Brigades took four days to reach Pt 175, because they also had to clear Axis battlegroups from their rear to maintain their supply routes. The 6th NZ Brigade moved along the central escarpment and 4th Brigade was north of it, towards Belhamed ridge and both were in continuous contact with the enemy which caused heavy casualties and forced two battalions to be amalgamated. The key Pt 175 was taken after hard fighting along the ridge by 6th NZ Brigade.[35]

The Infantry assaults had been weakened because they were made without any powerful armoured support, the attack by the 4th Brigade on Belhamed was made by two battalions with no artillery support after an approach march of 6,000 yards. Belhamed was captured but was then subjected to heavy shelling, which caused further high casualties amongst the units which were surrounded by Axis positions on lower ground still between them and Sidi Rezegh ridge. [36] The separation of Brigades was leaving them weakened and isolated by pockets of Axis positions who used firepower to cripple any moves made by Eighth Army.

The heavy attrition forced on the Infantry forced the New Zealanders to make a weak daylight assault on the low ground with just two companies of 20th Infantry Battalion and three tanks to clear the machine gun positions which was a complete failure. The supporting artillery quickly ran out of ammunition and smoke.[37] Casualties continued to be suffered until the battalion was overrun by a large Axis Battlegroup. In comparison the 19th Battalion had by-passed the Belhamed ridge to the north and made contact with the Tobruk garrison on the Ed-Duda ridge, though this link was briefly closed again by Axis attacks.[38] The need to capture Belhamed and Pt 175 had exhausted the 4th NZ Brigade in a succession of assaults which highlighted the influence of terrain and the weakness of the assault doctrine.

The combination of factors of terrain, numerous objectives and weak formations highlighted the weaknesses in doctrine. British forces further east targeted the Axis positions dug-in near Bir el Gubi and along the Trigh Capuzzo. Those on the Trigh were considered too well dug in, so 7th Armoured Division moved against the Italian units near El-Gubi again. Unfortunately the 11th Indian Brigade with just one

35   Kippenburger, *Infantry Brigadier*, p.93.
36   Kippenburger, *Infantry Brigadier*, p.94, (or 3.4 miles).
37   http://www.nzetc.org/tm/scholarly/tei-WH2-20Ba-c7.html Chapter 7, 20th Battalion and the Armour, p188. Accessed 31 March 2012.
38   Humble, *Crusader*, p.145.

squadron of Tanks and the 4th Armoured Brigade with 98 tanks and its Support Group, all fought separate actions rather than making a combined assault. The higher ground were again the main objectives of for each assault, the 11th Indian's attack was only partially successful in securing Pt 182 which overlooked the position and they failed to secure Pt 174 nearby.[39]

The improvised doctrine developed in desert fighting defined that a Support Group and Reconnaissance Regiment would hold off an enemy force using Jock Columns and harassment tactics when the Armoured Division had suffered major losses, until it had recovered sufficiently enough to return to the offensive again.[40] This is what happened during Crusader and successes for the Jock columns ensured their continued use well into 1942. The 7th Armoured Division had followed this defensive doctrine and appeared to be fighting with all units, but in reality the Brigades still fought separate actions. The Jock Columns appeared to have inflicted enough damage to contribute to Rommel's decision to pull back from the frontier and bring about the end of the battle. They provoked optimistic reports and comments such as the tactic being a,'buccaneering...piratical sort of game to which Englishmen took likes ducks to water.'[41]

Operation Crusader was an important British offensive which lasted for 20 days and resulted in a costly victory. They had succeeded in relieving Tobruk and pushed back Axis forces out of most of Cyrenaica. They retreated to a defensible position near Mersa Brega so that Eighth Army was able to re-occupy Benghazi and the western airfields. Historians have failed to properly emphasize the importance of the terrain which influenced the fighting throughout. The terrain features at Sidi Rezegh and Pt 175 had dominated the key battles in the central sector of the battlefield and they had become the main objectives of British operations. Equally, further north, the Ed Duda feature had divided the forces breaking out of Tobruk with Eighth Army near Sidi Rezegh. The tactical terrain in this sector included a 'quadrilateral' of heights near the Sidi Rezegh airfield all of which became objectives and which dispersed British forces trying to capture them. The operational distances in this part of Cyrenaica had also influenced British planning and on-going decisions by Eighth Army HQ, who divided its Brigades to either blockade the frontier with Infantry or sent its Armoured Brigades to Tobruk to engage the Axis.

The victory drew British forces far forward again into Cyrenaica, which left them over-extended, and short of supplies but with another long front line held by the improvised Jock Columns. British forces would again be vulnerable to future Axis counter-attacks. They had not developed their doctrine to be fully concentrated or

39   TNA WO 201/361. 7th Armoured Division: Account of Operations in Libya, 1941, Nov-Dec, p35.
40   TNA WO 201/361. 7th Armoured Division: Account of Operations in Libya, 1941, Nov-Dec, pp.35-36.
41   Alexander Clifford, *Crusader* (London: George G. Harrap & Co,1942) p.108.

using combined arms again. Units were still directed towards too many objectives which were too widespread. British doctrine continued using dispersal tactics as there was an increased use of Jock columns within major operations. This improvised tactical doctrine undermined the subsequent defence of western Cyrenaica in January 1942, as previously discussed. Following this Second Retreat, Eighth Army settled on a line south of Gazala, which would become the next major battle in the late spring/summer of 1942.

7

Gazala and Tobruk, May-June 1942

The battles for the Gazala line during May and June 1942 were the Eighth Army's second attempt at a defensive battle that year and ended in a major defeat. Strategically it was the last defensive position in eastern Cyrenaica, but operationally it was a battle for the defence of Tobruk and its adjacent supply bases. However, it failed to develop into the armoured counter-stroke envisaged by Ritchie and Auchinleck. At the tactical level, the Eighth Army was outmanoeuvred from a series of ridgeline positions. Again key terrain features had a repeated impact throughout the tactical battle and also on British doctrine. Gazala was a defensive battle over an artificial defensive 'line' in the desert made up of adjacent or distant Brigade 'boxes' or positions. Once each of these positions had been lost Eighth Army had little choice but to retreat beyond the frontier. The Army had also failed to improve its doctrine of combined arms in either attack or defence, due to weaknesses in command and the on-going problems of poor quality armour and training, which until now, have always been cited as the main reasons for British failure.

Until recently the battle has remained much less obvious in the historiography, often being part of the story of the general retreat from El Agheila to Alamein and of course overshadowed by the later victory at Second Alamein. Alan Moorehead believed that it was the loss of the southern Bir Hacheim box which undermined the Gazala line, combined with the loss of armour on the 12 June, whilst Niall Barr concentrates on the problems of command and lack of an effective tactical doctrine in the Eighth Army, which led to the British defeat.[1] The official history blames the defeat of British armour on the 12-13 June which enabled Axis forces to capture Tobruk. Michael Carver offers the most detailed study of the battle but essentially defends Lieutenant-General Ritchie's record as Eighth Army CinC and blames poor command by Auchinleck down to Divisional level commanders and poor doctrine.[2]

---

1   Moorehead, *African Trilogy*, pp.333-336, and Barr, *Pendulum of War*, pp.15-17.
2   Playfair, *Mediterranean and Middle East. Vol III*, p.252, and Carver, *Dilemmas of the Desert War*.

Adrian Stewart also blames poor command as does Barrie Pitt's narrative which high-lights the loss of armour and the command confusion in another fast moving mobile battle.[3] John Strawson thought the major loss of armour from the 12-13 June was the turning point along with an over-rigid plan and the lack of combined arms doctrine.[4] Lieutenant-General Francis Tuker blamed the lack of direction from both Eighth Army HQ and Auchinleck at GHQ, following the defeat in the Cauldron on the 5-6 June. [5] Ken Ford's recent account offers a fresh narrative but argues there were no discernible terrain features and that Rommel largely dictated the battle.[6] However the primary sources show that the tactical terrain of the battlefield also influenced the phases of the battle and materially contributed to the outcome of the fighting.

Gazala: terrain

The British sited their defences at Gazala on the best available terrain features in that sector of eastern Cyrenaica, where Tobruk could be protected, but forward of its 1941 defensive perimeter. The line was created to be a strong defensive position to protect Tobruk and the new Belhamed railhead. It was based on a forty-five mile long minefield running south/south-east from Gazala on the coast road and which covered the main Trigh routes going east.[7] Ritchie planned to hold it using defensive 'Boxes' which overlooked the extensive mine-belt. Some of the boxes were Interlocking and covered the coast road in the north whilst the desert flank was protected by the more distant Bir Hacheim box.

In the centre of the line the main feature was the Sidi-Muftah depression, through which the Trigh Capuzzo passed east-west. Along its northern edge was the Sidra ridge which also dominated the open plain to the north behind the minefield which also led towards the coast road and Tobruk. The eastern edge of the Sidi-Muftah depression was the Aslagh ridge which also overlooked the Bir-Hacheim track running north-east to Tobruk. The plain north of the Sidra ridge had some key heights which were later used as 'defended localities' but their weakness, besides being too small as defensive postions, was that they were easily outflanked and too isolated. The plain continued north to the next heights which included a steep escarpment overlooking the coast road into Tobruk. This ridge included a series of boxes or 'keeps' along the ridgeline at Mrassas, Acroma and El-Adem, designed to protect the port. The concept of dispersion of forces continued in British command thinking as further 'keeps' and lines of minefields were under construction during the battle.[8]

3   Pitt, *Crucible of War, Vol II*, p.261. Using the official South African history.
4   Strawson, *Battle for North Africa*, pp.127-128.
5   Stewart, *Early Battles*, p.67 and Pitt, *Crucible of War, Vol II*, pp.222-231, and Tuker, *Approach to Battle*, pp.126-129.
6   Ken Ford, *Gazala 1942. Rommel's Greatest Victory* (Oxford: Osprey, 2008) p.14 and p.93.
7   The minefield was made up of mines taken mostly from the old Tobruk perimeter line.
8   TNA WO 201/2692.Operational Reports: Western Desert. May-July 1942, p.5.

The centre position of the British line was an open plateau east of the Sidra ridge, quickly named the 'Knightsbridge box'. It was constructed by the 201st Guards Brigade and was sited to dominate the junction and ridgeline at Pt 167 near the crossroads of the Trigh Capuzzo and Bir Hacheim tracks. These ran east towards the El-Adem group of airfields and this box became crucial to holding the centre of the line. Knightsbridge was at the centre of a series of ridges which included the Maabus and Rigel ridges to the north, the Hagieg-Batruna ridge north-east and Bir Bir-Belleiffa ridge running east, which all formed terrain which could hold an Axis approach from the south. At the southern end of the line, the Bir Hacheim box was based on a low ridge which overlooked ground to the south and west; the defensive area itself was dominated by a pivotal observation point at Pt 186, which if captured made the site untenable.[9] The southern end of the line had a second belt of minefields running back north-east, like the bottom of a reverse J, to the Aslagh ridge near the centre of the line. Most of the mines came from the old perimeter defences around Tobruk, which of course further weakened any last line of defence around the port.

The weakness of the Gazala line due the open flank has been well documented and is not disputed. Ritchie spent months planning for an armoured battle in this sector. However, the line could be fully outflanked if Axis forces broke northwards, through and past the Knightsbridge Box into the plain north of the Rigel ridge or east along the Trigh Capuzzo.[10] The line had been designed to hold an enemy from the west but it was also equally important for the Eighth Army to hold against an advance from the south and the Knightsbridge sector was the only place to do this. The terrain was at the forefront of Ritchie's defensive planning. He was, 'concerned to keep control of the pivotal positions...to keep his armour within close distance ready.'[11] This example shows how Ritchie's thinking was influenced by the prominent ridges in the centre of the line and the doctrine of defensive boxes, around which the armour would fight.

Gazala: Plans and preparations

The Infantry Brigades were deployed in boxes behind the minefield line. These were defensive positions for Infantry and artillery batteries, each designed to hold independently for three weeks and were also surrounded by wire and minefields. Ritchie wanted the nearby armoured brigades to manoeuvre and counter-attack the enemy after they had been weakened by attacking the box defences. As late as the 26 May, GHQ confirmed the importance of a defensive line backed by armour Brigades. It called for 'defended localities' (smaller box defences) to be reduced in number and for

9   Richard Holmes, *Bir Hacheim. Desert Citadel* (London: Pan Ballantine, 1971) p.92.
10   NAM 2009-12-19-4-1, Report by Maj Gen E.Dorman Smith. 'Operations in the Western Desert 27 may 1942 – 2 July 1942'. August 1942.
11   TNA WO 201/2692.Operational Reports: Western Desert. May-July 1942, p.8.

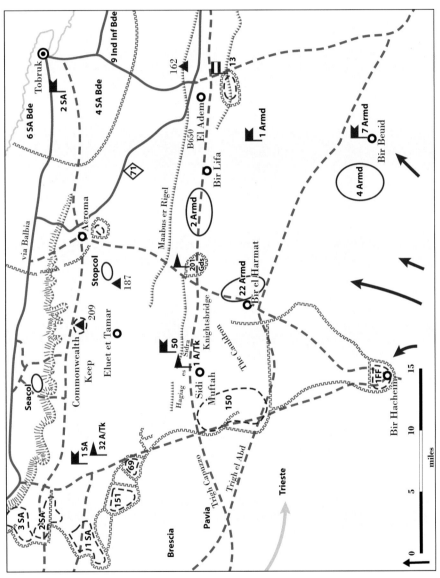

Map 7:1 The Gazala line, May-June 1942.

units to counter-attack from within the battle area.[12] The Eighth Army was allowing Panzerarmee to make the first strike which was a sensible option, given the lack of training for many units within Eighth Army in combined arms doctrine but was a dangerous one if the Axis succeeded in breaking through the line to Tobruk. Ritchie's follow up plan was then for an armoured counter-attack which would decisively defeat Panzerarmee.[13]

Despite increases in the Eighth Army's strength there were too few Brigade Groups to hold the whole line because there was still not enough manpower. Therefore an Axis approach around the open desert flank could not be prevented. In mid-February, Joint Planners at GHQ reported that the Eighth Army would have the forces necessary for an offensive to begin by early May, despite an equivalent Axis build up and dealing with the problems of operations in summer heat. It wanted a limited advance to capture the Derna-Martuba area and ideally to capture Benghazi.[14] Yet by mid-March, 'Q' Branch planners noted there was still a lack of direction and offered only cautious plans to supply a limited number of brigades at either 130 miles or 200 miles distant from Tobruk. To achieve even this modest advance across Cyrenaica, the two supply bases at Tobruk would operate at the maximum rate.[15] These administrative problems contributed to a more cautious approach by Ritchie, despite heavy pressure from the Prime Minister and the COS for a renewed offensive to relieve the air assault currently battering Malta.

The coastal sector was more strongly held by three South African Brigade boxes and two Brigades from 50th Division. It's third Brigade, was belatedly moved south to cover a gap in the centre at the Sidi-Muftah depression. This new defensive box was quite isolated – being six miles from its neighbouring Brigade in the north and ten miles from the Free French Brigade at Bir Hacheim. It had a twenty mile perimeter and no protective minefield across the rear.[16] At Bir Hacheim, the southern edge of the Eighth Army's defence was held by the 1st Free French Brigade who had deployed large numbers of additional anti-tank and artillery guns which were well disguised and dug-in.[17]

The Armoured brigades were positioned behind the line to counter-attack enemy thrusts. Ritchie was concerned to, 'retain his armour, for a concentrated effort' and he

12 TNA WO 201/538.Eighth Army: lessons from Operations, Sept 1941-Aug 1942.'Fixed Defences and the Defences Battle. 26 May 42, p.2.

13 TNA WO 201/2692.Operational Reports: Western Desert. May-July 1942, p.4.

14 TNA WO 201/371.Major operations `G' Planning: campaign. Feb-Apr 1942. JPS Paper No.86.Western Desert Policy II.

15 TNA WO 201/419.Cyrenaica campaign: planning. March 1942.BM/Q (P)/42/3. 12 March 42.

16 E.W. Clay, *The Path of the 50th. The Story of the 50th (Northumbrian) Division in the Second World War 1939-1945* (Aldershot: Gale & Polden, 1950) p.54.

17 The 75mm gun on display at the Musée de l'Armée in Paris, shows the upper gunshield cut off to give the weapon a very low profile, visited April 2011.

held lengthy discussions on where these would be best deployed to engage the Axis armour.[18] Auchinleck believed the Axis would attack in the centre and north whilst Ritchie thought they would swing around the southern flank at Bir Hacheim. At 30th Corps, Lieutenant-General Norrie predicted that the main offensive would be in the north, and directed the armoured brigades to fight a separate battle.[19] The 4th Armoured Brigade was deployed in the south to fight using ridges three miles east of Bir Hacheim. Lieutenant-Colonel Roberts, of 3rd RTR noted how they spent weeks selecting a near perfect hull down 'battle position' from which to defend against the Axis advance, but were unable to reach it in time for the actual battle.[20]

By now the Eighth Army had become a major force with numerous Brigade Groups in Cyrenaica. The armour was mostly in 30th Corps and consisted of 1st and 7th Armoured Divisions and three Motor Infantry Brigade Groups. The 13th Corps now had three Infantry Divisions, supported by one Army Tank Brigade and an additional Infantry Brigade. The lack of training remained an issue within many of these formations; some troops had only recently arrived at the front and were inexperienced in desert conditions. The Armoured Brigades were equipped with new weapons to fight the German armour, including American Grant tanks and a limited number of better 6pdr anti-tank guns, both of which gave improved firepower. Artillery and anti-tank regiments were reorganized but there were only enough Grants to partially equip each regiment and only a few batteries had received the new guns.[21] Brigadier Briggs, commanding 2nd Armoured Brigade, noted that one of his regiments had received their new Grant tanks just a few days before the offensive began.[22] This limited the vital training time that tank crews had with the new equipment.

The Axis forces had spent months being re-equipped and were well prepared for this offensive. The Panzerarmee also reorganized its structure with the emphasis more firepower and fewer men. Rommel also created his own mixed Kampstaffel battalion and had the best mobile Italian divisions, Ariete and Trieste, which gave him five well-balanced Divisions for the offensive. Other Italian Infantry Divisions held the line opposite the mine-belt and provided diversionary attacks in the north, to pin down the British frontline boxes. The Axis plan included a night-time approach march south around the British line, then swinging north-east, to overrun Bir Hacheim and defeat the British armour, followed by a rapid advance north to capture Tobruk.

18   NAM 2009-12-19-4-1, Report by Maj Gen E. Dorman Smith. 'Operations in the Western Desert 27 may 1942 – 2 July 1942'. August 1942.
19   Carver, *Dilemmas of the Desert War*, pp.67-73.
20   Bovington Archives 3RTR Diary and papers. 'Some experiences of an Armoured Commander in the Middle East'. 'Pip' Roberts.
21   TNA WO 201/532.Eighth Army: Commanders conferences.1941 Dec.-1942 May. State of 2pdr, 25pdr and 5.5" Equipments, 11 May 1942, p.2.
22   IWM 8109. 99/1/2.Papers of Maj. Gen. R. Briggs.2ndArmdBde. 2/5. Western Desert Dec 41-Oct 42.

Despite the reverses in February, the Eighth Army believed it was ready to fight the Panzerarmee again. Morale remained high and the men still had, 'absolute confidence' in the Allied cause but there was impatience at getting on with winning the war. By mid-May one report noted, 'current morale is exceedingly high. Men are convinced an offensive will soon begin and a considerable number express the opinion that this time they will finish the enemy once and for all.'[23] However, other censorship summaries noted praise for Rommel and a lack of confidence in their own commanders who were blamed for recent failures. Jonathan Fennell argues that British morale was more brittle in this period. Overall British forces were becoming more experienced and were well supplied if somewhat disparate in quality of experience, training and equipment but faced a well-organized and experienced enemy with a dynamic commander and better tactical doctrine. These factors certainly influenced the coming battle but British tactical thinking and planning also hinged on holding key terrain features and so terrain was became an additional vital factor in determining the outcome of battle.

Gazala: Battle summary

Gazala developed into a lengthy and complex battle for the Eighth Army. The first tactical engagements took place across a series of ridges in the southern sector when two Motorised Brigades were contacted and overrun within hours. Following this the British armoured Brigades were also engaged and many Regiments were quickly reduced to weak numbers in strength. Rommel also overstretched Panzerarmee and had to regroup in the position which became known as the Cauldron. From here he was able to replenish his units who then made two major assaults; one on the Free French at Bir Hacheim and the 150th Brigade in the Sidi-Muftah boxes, the former held out until the 12 June but the latter succumbed more quickly when the key heights around it were captured by the Axis. Both positions were also isolated from reinforcements and weak attempts by Eighth Army to relieve them.

Part of the relief operations included continuous but separated attempts by British armour to engage along the flanks of these assaults and in the ill-fated Operation Aberdeen, where armour combined with 5th Indian Division, when the Panzerarmee went over to the defensive for a brief period on the 5-6 June. By isolating and eliminating the two southern most boxes, Rommel had placed Panzerarmee in a central position from which he could then 'unlock' the central sector of the battlefield. These became the series of actions which included a second phase of armoured engagements in defence of the Knightsbridge box and the Maabus-Rigel ridge, followed by a larger battle during 12-13 June. The armoured losses on these two days have been considered by many to be the turning point of the battle, yet the 6th RTR regimental diary noted

---

23   TNA WO 201/532.Eighth Army: Commanders conferences.1941 Dec.-1942 May. Morale in the M.E.F. May 1942.

it was the losses prior to these two days – which weakened the Brigade irreparably and left it unable to cope with the heavy fighting which followed on the 12-13 June.

The final stages of the battle occurred as both Bir Hacheim and Knightsbridge boxes and the central ridgeline were abandoned, with Eighth Army units retreating rapidly north to the Acroma/El-Adem ridge-line around Tobruk. This also forced the static 1st South African Division and 50th Divisions to retreat from their boxes and escape to the frontier. The final phase included the capture of the Acroma/El Adem ridge and the rapid assault which led to the fall of Tobruk. Eighth Army was forced to fall back to the frontier and beyond.

Gazala: the impact of terrain and doctrine on the battle

The effectiveness of British doctrine is perhaps reflected by the rapid losses suffered by the Armoured Brigades as they engaged the approaching Axis columns separately from the Infantry. During these early engagements their battle quickly became attritional with two regiments of the 4th Armoured Brigade losing most of their tanks on the first day.[24] The 8th Hussars concluded that, 'Owing to the rapidity of [the Axis] advance…no adequate warning was received by the regiment… [so] the enemy was able to affect a surprise attack.'[25] Their early losses compounded the problem of British armour having too few heavy tanks; 3rd RTR had just 24 Grants and lost 19 of these on the first day.[26] The 4th Brigade had 100 Grants, however the other Brigades had only 50 Grants.[27] The adjacent 2nd Armoured Brigade was 'sadly depleted' and by the 31 May only one regiment, the Queen's Bays, remained as a viable unit.[28] The 1st Army Tank Brigade also fought separately from the Infantry, the 44th RTR engaged Axis armour from the Aslagh ridge, using it as cover for hull down positions, but lost heavily in a close quarter tank melee. The terrain impacted on the battle because the Regiment's advance was halted by the steepness of the Hagiaget-Rigel ridge, so that only one squadron actually closed with the larger enemy formation and the regiment lost another third of the unit.[29] The constant daily battles were rapidly wearing out

24   TNA WO 169/4486. 8 King's Royal Irish Hussars, Diary.1941 Nov.- 1942 Dec. 27 May 42.
25   TNA WO 169/4486. 8 King's Royal Irish Hussars, Diary.1941 Nov.- 1942 Dec. Temporary Diary 27 May.
26   Bovington Archives 3rd RTR Files. Some notes on the Knightsbridge battles after conversations with General Roberts (who commanded 3rd RTR there).
27   LHCMA Roberts GPB, Papers. Comparison of British and German Tanks, May 1942, report by Major Carver.
28   IWM.8109. 99/1/2.Papers of Maj. Gen. R. Briggs. 2ndArmd Bde. 2/5. Western Desert Dec 41-Oct 42.
29   TNA WO 201/539.Eighth Army: intelligence matters. Nov 41-Aug 42.Report By Brigade Major, 1st Army Tank Brigade, on the action Fought By 50 Div. Mobile Reserve, p.1, (18 out of 51 tanks).

British Armoured Regiments through losses to crews and vehicles which left them too weak in subsequent actions.

With the Infantry deployed inside the boxes, this continued the doctrine of fighting separate battles with occasional support by artillery. The first major defence of a box was made by the recently arrived 150th Brigade, a territorial unit with little experience of the desert. Some units were inexperienced in combat, yet the Brigade Major believed it was more due to the loss of higher ground which decided Brigadier Haydon to retreat to new positions nearby.[30] The 5th Green Howards noted, 'the enemy continues massing in the east, overlooking the box and shelling heavily all the time.'[31] The capture of the height B.175 late on the 30 May gave Panzerarmee a good view of the Brigade defences which were then heavily and accurately shelled the following day.[32]

The 150th Brigade had been rushed to occupy this area just prior to the battle, and had little time to construct effective defensive positions in low ground. This hurried deployment was a serious problem and Axis forces took full advantage of gaining the high ground and preventing British support from reaching the Brigade. One young officer, Dan Billany, an Infantry platoon officer with the Brigade noted how the constant moves within the new box left the Infantry physically exhausted and fighting from inadequately prepared positions, often just shell scrapes, in comparison to the first defences they had dug.[33] After spending three days assaulting the position, the Panzerarmee reached a turning point when 232 Field Engineer Company was overrun and this gave the Axis, 'a vantage point from which a greater part of the Brigade position could be overlooked.'[34] Each defensive position was then ruthlessly knocked out and the final sectors were overrun on the 1 June. Attempts were made to relieve the Infantry by the weakened 4th Armoured Brigade who attacked the eastern side of the Cauldron, but were repulsed with heavy losses, on the 2 June 5th RTR lost most of their Grant tanks and 51 men, including its experienced CO, Colonel Uniacke. Army policy had new crew men joining these units, but it took time for both veteran and new men to used to each other, ideally not in the midst of battle.[35] The Eighth Army had lost a key central position which threatened the Knightsbridge ridgeline and outflanked the boxes to the north. It also left Bir Hacheim more isolated from

30 TNA WO 201/539. Eighth Army Intelligence Matters: Nov 1941-Aug 1942.Report by Major E.D. Rash, Bde Major 1st Army Tank Bde, on the action fought by 50 Div. Mobile Reserve. Dated 6 June 1942, after Major Rash had escaped from Axis capture.
31 TNA WO 169/5021, 5th Green Howards Diary. January-Nov 1942. Battle of 150 Brigade, 26 May-1 June 1942, p.2.
32 Bovington Archives 44th RTR, Diary. Action fought by the 44thBn RTR 27 May – 1 June 1942 as witnessed by 2/Lt K Dodwell, 44thBn RTR.
33 Dan Billany, *The Trap* (London; Panther, 1964) pp.263-265. A novel but clearly based on the author's own experiences before his capture in June 1942.
34 Clay, *The Path of the 50th*, p.59.
35 Mark Urban, *The Tank War. The British band of Brothers – one tank regiment's World War II* (London: Abacus, 2013) pp.114-117.

ground support. Ritchie's defensive doctrine had been undermined and the armoured counter-attacks were constantly suffering attrition which was unsustainable, despite fresh crews and tanks being brought into the battle.

Operation Aberdeen and the Cauldron

Following the initial armoured battles, Panzerarmee had overstretched itself and regrouped in the Sidi-Muftah depression (or 'Cauldron' as it became known). This was to re-group and open up new supply routes directly east through the mine-belt, to the Axis rear. Operation Aberdeen developed from an earlier plan to relieve the 150th Brigade, into an assault on the weakened Panzerarmee. On the northern side of the depression was the Sidra ridge, with multiple 'peaks' along its eastern sector.[36] The depression was a vital area of operational ground which needed to be re-gained from Axis control, due to the proximity to both the Bir Hacheim and Knightsbridge boxes. The operation highlighted the failings of poor planning and a continuing disjointed doctrine by British forces.

The Eighth Army had reacted too slowly to save the 150th Brigade and now planned to assault three Axis Divisions with just two Infantry Brigades, one Armoured Brigade supported by four Artillery Regiments. All the units which advanced into the depression faced tremendously heavy fire from Axis artillery and anti-tank guns which forced them to turn away or dig-in. The 22nd Armoured Brigade was assailed by masses of anti-tank and artillery fire on their approach. One Regiment, the 3rd County of London Yeomanry, encountered a German 88mm Battery and simply, 'went straight at them,' with their Colonel shouting, 'Yoiks Tally Ho!'[37] Not really an effective way for an Armoured Regiment to be directed. The Artillery Observer accompanying attempted to call in supporting fire, but the enemy position was obscured by dust and smoke and he was forced to withdraw out of the action. The 2nd Gloucester Hussars went in with one squadron of 12 Grants and two squadrons of Light Honey tanks. Their Diary notes the different tasks squadrons were given in support of other units, and the Regiment defended against some powerful German counter-attacks whilst holding low ridgelines. Within two days, there were just 2 Grants and fourteen Light tanks remaining in two weak squadrons.[38]

The 10th Indian Brigade was pinned down and then were, 'eliminated…with ease, as they had no mines or anti-tank guns.'[39] However the Infantry had again been given multiple objectives and battalions were quickly separated from each other and became trapped in the low ground or dispersed along the Sidra Ridge trying to dominate the

36   Billany, *The Trap*, p.205. A peak of just 20 feet high often had a viewpoint of up to 5 miles.
37   Peter Hart, *Voices From the Front: The South Notts Hussars, The Western Desert 1940-1942* (Barnsley; Pen & Sword Military) p.204.
38   http://www.warlinks.com/armour/2nd_rgh/2nd_rgh_42.php, Diary entries for 5-7 June 1942.
39   LHCMA. Daniels papers.

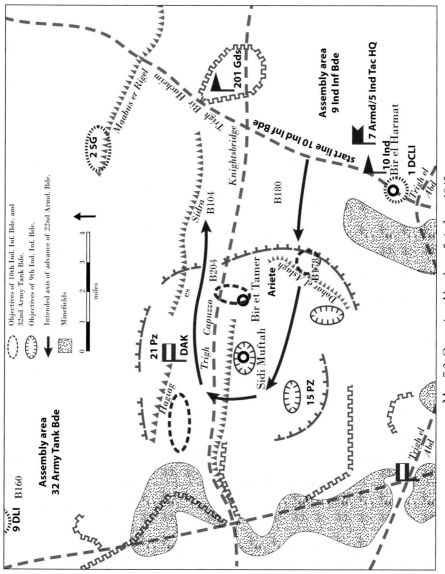

Map 7.2 Operation Aberdeen, 5–6 June 1942.

various peaks. The operation was a rare attempt at a British combined arms assault which failed under the weight of enemy fire and poor coordination.

Axis armour then counter-attacked to outflank the British artillery on the Aslagh ridge before moving through a gap in the rear minefield to overrun the Headquarters of both 5th Indian Division and 7thArmoured Division, which had been controlling the operation, along with an isolated Infantry battalion only just arrived at the front. This left the stranded Infantry without any command.[40] Major Daniel described the attack which overran his unit on the ridge. He also notes that his Regiment, the 107th RHA (South Notts Hussars), could not dig-in effectively,

> Topping a rise we were met with a hail of shells. We dropped into action…on a horrible stony ridge, which proved our undoing…in front [there] was a nice large bowl [the Cauldron]. More and more German tanks appeared until they had totally surrounded us, standing off at a safe distance, whilst their guns proceeded to pound every vehicle to pieces. Our casualties became very heavy…my orders were precise, "to stand and fight where we were to the last man and the last round.[41]

The stony ridge prevented the Gunners' from digging-in to provide cover, whilst their separation from the Infantry Brigades across the Cauldron, enabled the German armour to pick off each gun from a distance before closing in to eliminate the remaining crews. Richard Doherty's study offers some detail of the artillery role during the operation, in which the four Field Regiments were deployed across the edges of the Cauldron firing in support of either the Infantry or the Artillery. Unfortunately this separated deployment contributed to their individual demise as Axis counter-attacks closed around each formation. It was a heroic resistance but still ended with ninety six field guns and one Regiment of valuable 6pdr anti-tank guns and all their crews were lost overall.[42]

A simultaneous second phase of Aberdeen was the attack from the north against the 21st Panzer Division, defending the Sidra ridge. Advancing up a gentle slope the slow moving 'I' tanks of the 32ndArmy Tank Brigade were committed, supported by a single Infantry battalion in trucks with fire support from a single battery.[43] Smoke briefly obscured their advance but soon this attack also received a storm of artillery and anti-tank fire which forced 7th RTR tanks to swerve right in front of the neighbouring

40   Holland, *Together We Stand*, p.116.
41   LHCMA. Daniels papers.
42   Richard Doherty, *Ubique, The Royal Artillery in the Second World War* (Stroud: History Press, 2008) pp.120-121.
43   Bovington Archives. Major Tatum puts 42nd RTR at 32 tanks, 7thRTR at near full strength i.e. 50 tanks and 8th RTR as 1 squadron.

42nd RTR.[44] More than fifty tanks were rapidly lost and the surviving vehicles fought off a local counter-attack and retreated. Terrain played an important part here too because, 'the slope to the ridge was hardly discernible and some tanks reached the high ground without actually being aware of it', the armour was easily silhouetted to anti-tank guns deployed on the rear slopes of the ridge.[45] Overall the failure of the two armoured assaults left the artillery and Infantry isolated and overrun. The British lost nearly one hundred 25pdr guns and most of six battalions, along with more than eighty tanks. Operation Aberdeen was a failed attempt to make a fully coordinated and combined arms assault against the enemy. The Divisional Commanders had been given no opportunity for thorough planning and the coordination and doctrine of the assault units was a joint attack in theory, which in reality none of the arms fought together once the action began. This was compounded by the fact that Axis defensive doctrine had proved much more effective in defence and also in counterattacking British positions.

Gazala: The final phase

Following Operation Aberdeen, British efforts concentrated on maintaining a hold on the ridges near the Knightsbridge box and Bir Hacheim. The armoured brigades made further piecemeal attacks on Axis columns and adjacent ridge-top positions, but with limited success. On the 8 June, the 6th RTR had been ordered to, 'smarten up the Germans but on no account to lose any tanks.'[46] They advanced to attack a ridge south of Knightsbridge with just two squadrons of Grants and with no artillery support and suffered the inevitable casualties. At Army HQ, Ritchie maintained an fatally optimistic view of events which blinded him to the reality of a rapidly declining situation. Even after Aberdeen had failed, he considered the defensive line to be quite strong.

Operationally the Panzerarmee was now well positioned in the Cauldron to cut off Bir Hacheim, envelop Knightsbridge and threaten eastwards towards El-Adem further along the central ridge. Equally, the Eighth Army became overstretched along the Knightsbridge ridges as they sought to prevent Axis columns from breaking through them. In the south the Hacheim box had been stoutly defended by the Free French Brigade for fifteen days and had been sustained by nightly re-supply columns. Their defence was aided by their low profile guns dug into near invisible positions around the slope at Pt 186, and was supported by extensive RAF operations. The Luftwaffe made over 1,300 sorties on the tough Foreign Legion Brigade, leaving them isolated from supply and fatigued by ten days of battle. General Ritchie finally

---

44   This assault has often been noted as running onto a minefield, however the accounts show it was the weight of German firepower which repulsed the slow moving British tanks, combined with the effect of the sloping ridgeline.

45   Bovington Archives Report by Major J.W.G. Tatum, 42nd RTR. On the attack on the Sidra Ridge, 5 June 42.

46   Jackson, A Long Parting, p.41.

withdrew this exhausted garrison when he felt that it could no-longer be re-supplied. British tactics were becoming improvised again with the operation of Jock Columns against the flanks and rear of the Axis forces in the southern sector, but these had little effect. The Panzerarmee now controlled the Cauldron sector and Bir Hacheim was isolated from effective British support.

After the Axis forces had gained control of specific sectors of the battlefield, they were able to 'unlock' other, nearby British positions. The withdrawal of the Free French Brigade from Bir Hacheim allowed the Axis to concentrate their efforts against the Knightsbridge box and the adjacent ridgelines. The subsequent armoured battles either side of Knightsbridge proved costly because British commanders remained offensively minded despite their armour being weak. On the 12 June, 6th RTR was ordered forward to capture Pt 171, despite being weak in numbers, and low on fuel and ammunition. Axis forces then countered with a powerful and sustained bombardment on the height before making an attack with Panzers and 88mm guns. The battle climaxed on the 13 June as 6th RTR planned to make a final stand back on the main ridge, but was instead ordered north to Tobruk along with the remaining armour. The adjacent 22nd Armoured Brigade (already just the strength of one Regiment of light tanks) diary noted, 'If the enemy had got onto the escarpment over-looking the Bir-Bellafun valley that night, the withdrawal of the [Knightsbridge] box…would have been impossible.'[47] British armour was still being worn down trying to hold ridgeline positions and the continuous combat resulted in the armoured regiments being mauled, leaving their crews exhausted.

The continuous battles for the ridges were linked to the British use of armour in separated assaults in the southern battlefield. The armoured brigades suffered further heavy losses from the 7-13 June as they fought to hold the ridges around Knightsbridge. Ritchie reported, 'Yesterday we were unable to prevent enemy from establishing himself on [the]escarpment running westwards to HAGIAG[and]… occupying RIGEL RIDGE, driving our armour North towards ACROMA, thus so much endangering the KNIGHTSBRIDGE BOX, that its evacuation was ordered.'[48] Brigadier Briggs, commanding 2nd Armoured Brigade, was surprised when the Knightsbridge box, 'a feature, well dug in, well wired in and mined and occupied by 201st Guards Brigade and 2nd RHA,' was given up without a fight similar to that made by the Free French at Bir Hacheim.[49] It was a telling moment for British defensive doctrine.

There was further command confusion as the battle became more fluid. By the 14 June Auchinleck signalled Ritchie, that even if the Gazala line needed to be evacuated,

47   Bovington Archive 4CLY Diary.
48   TNA WO 201/404.Operations: telegrams and reports, June 1942.Telegram: To Mideast from Main Army, U1388, 14/6.
49   IWM 8109. 99/1/2.Papers of Maj. Gen. R. Briggs. 2nd Armd Bde. 2/5. Western Desert Dec 41-Oct 42.His address to the Queens Bays, 14 June 1943.

Acroma and El Adem should be held, while he built up reinforcements. Two days later Auchinleck signalled that El Adem was now the 'decisive point' of the battle, despite the problem that the 29th Indian Brigade defending it, had already been split up.[50] He believed Axis forces could still be held as they advanced from Knightsbridge, even though there were 15 miles between the two locations. Ritchie was dispersing Infantry battalions to adjacent 'defended localities' whilst Auchinleck wanted the Infantry to concentrate on a specific position. Confusion continued when El-Adem was later evacuated as part of the overall retreat from the Gazala line. The remaining elements of the 29th Brigade formed five Jock columns and were given a harassing role against the 90th Light Division. After the loss of so much armour during this battle, British defensive tactics had again resorted to forming Jock columns which proved much less effective against the Axis Battle groups. During Crusader, the attacks had contributed to a Panzerarmee already in retreat, now they faced an enemy who was equally exhausted, but whose morale was jubilant because Eighth Army units were in retreat from Gazala, either towards Tobruk or the frontier.

Terrain had again played a crucial part influencing the final stage of the battle. Eighth Army had been defeated trying to hold a series of defensive positions along the ridges near Acroma-El Adem and was forced to retreat to the frontier which left Tobruk exposed and unready for a renewed siege. The port was lost because of further command confusion about the situation and a rapid, well directed Axis assault at the weakest point of the defences. The subsequent losses in supply tonnage were enormous, as was the capture of approximately 33,000 men which had to be added to the losses in armour, crews, infantry and artillery suffered since the 27 May.

Gazala: Conclusion

The Eighth Army had been decisively defeated at Gazala, and the influence of the terrain played a key role in each of the engagements. Operationally the Brigades Boxes in the southern part of the line at Sidi-Muftah, Knightsbridge and Bir Hacheim had been sited too far apart and were unable to support each other. Tactically, the British obsession with trying to hold the Sidi-Muftah depression cost the Army dearly in terms of men and equipment, because of the attritional fighting which continued around those ridgelines. Later, the higher ground around the Knightsbridge Box became the defining point on the battlefield, once the brigades retreated from it, there was little to stop further Axis advances towards Tobruk. Other factors such as poor battle tactics, poor command and equipment failures also contributed heavily to the British defeat. The Panzerarmee and its commander General Rommel had also dominated operations at crucial moments throughout. It used a more effective doctrine to

---

50   TNA WO 201/405. Telegrams 12-16 June 1942. No.CS/1266. 16 June. The 1st Worcesters battalion and attached artillery were sent to hold Pt 187 in the west, and the 3/12th Frontier Regiment to Pt.B. 650, nearby.

carry out a series of assaults, which, along with a determined defence of the Cauldron position, unlocked the southern and central sectors of the battlefield, which led to whole position being undermined.

There had been other problems including poor British command decisions which had contributed to the in-effective use of the Armoured Brigades throughout the battle. British troops had been let down by bad decision making by Corps and Divisional commanders who were sluggish and un-cooperative. Messervy was a highly experienced Infantry leader but was thought to have little experience of commanding armour. Veteran tankman Jake Wardrop however, thought him a, 'slow, silly old man…'[51] Before Operation Aberdeen, the Corps commanders Norrie and Gott queried the plans for the attack and left the operational control to the two harassed Divisional commanders. When Brigadiers managed to combine their weakened units, their tactics still appeared to be direct frontal assaults with limited artillery support. This fire support was affected by a lack of suitable vehicles for the Forward Observation Officers and communications had been easily lost when the rear link tanks were also quickly knocked out. Therefore the armoured assaults had lacked the proper fire support needed. Overall British doctrine had failed to develop and this had left the Eighth Army defeated and with a weakened morale. Yet it had been the impact of the operational and tactical terrain in the southern sector of the line which had contributed to the defeat and had left British forces with no option but to retreat to the next available defensive position at Mersa Matruh in Egypt.

---

51   George Forty (ed.), *Tanks Across the Desert. The War Diary of Jake Wardrop* (London: William Kimber and Co, 1981) p.77.

8

Mersa Matruh and First Alamein, June-July 1942

The British retreat into Egypt and the defeat at Mersa Matruh on the 25-26 June 1942 are covered here along with the longer battle of First Alamein from the 30 June to late July 1942. At Mersa Matruh Eighth Army was still trying to hold too wide an area of ground which stretched for at least 20 miles inland with exhausted and too few organised formations. In contrast, at El Alamein there were many more units by August and more numerous terrain features, which gave them a 'hook' on which to anchor their defences. However, at Mersa Matruh British doctrine was also still chaotic with changes in command, organisation and defensive tactics. Later on, by First Alamein, there was an improvement in defensive doctrine but the problems of poor cooperation between armour and Infantry during attacks continued. The two battles have been linked because they represent the last two actions in which General Auchinleck commanded both the Eighth Army directly and Middle East Command. They also represent the nadir of British defensive doctrine, which was followed by improvements, but where there were still problems in assault tactics.

Mersa Matruh background

The battle for Mersa Matruh was a relatively minor action when compared to Gazala or First Alamein and was another example of how the terrain was exploited by Axis forces to outflank Eighth Army and force it to retreat. One positive change was that there was increased RAF support which became a new weapon for British commanders. This use of tactical air support for ground operations was to be developed and extended for the remainder of the campaign.

After the loss of Tobruk, Ritchie believed an Axis advance into Egypt was inevitable and so despite the Eighth Army withdrawing in some confusion from Cyrenaica, a holding action at Mersa Matruh was planned.[1] The Army attempted to hold an area of ground consisting of two plateaus running parallel with the coast road, where

---

1   TNA WO 201/379.Operations in North Africa: General Ritchie's report, May-June 1942.

unfortunately there were no defensive features. This decision contributed to the subsequent defeat and further retreat to Alamein.

As with the Second Retreat, most narratives such as Clayton and Craig, have glossed over the action at Mersa Matruh to concentrate on First Alamein or later battles.[2] Whilst the terrain may have been noted in terms of the narrative, the impact of it has been largely ignored. Other commentators, including Adrian Stewart and Barrie Pitt, both provide detailed narratives which focus on the poor British command and confusion, particularly that from an over-tired Lieutenant-General Gott, as being the main issue leading to British defeat,[3] although Ritchie and Auchinleck should also have accepted some of the blame for trying to stem the tide of the Axis advance in such a weak sector of the coast.

Mersa Matruh: Terrain

The fighting near Matruh took place along the ridges and high ground south of the supply base. The port was classified as a fortress, but with nowhere near the defences of those which surrounded Bardia or Tobruk and which consisted of old or incomplete minefields along its southern and western sides. Near the coast there was a low, cliff-like escarpment which was the continuation from the ridge near the frontier at Sollum, except at Mersa it was lower and with just a few tracks and the railway traversing it onto the middle plateau. This central area was protected by a much thinner minefield stretching ten miles across it to upper escarpment inland. This higher ridge was a narrow area of higher ground consisting of hard limestone rock which prevented any defensive positions being made. There were very few routes which traversed this higher ridge onto the central plateau and units were deployed to block these few track descents using the ill-fated 'defended localities' once more. The going for vehicles along the higher escarpment was good east-west and this route outflanked both the defended localities along the upper ridge and the central plateau. East of Matruh the terrain was described as, 'undulating coastal desert of mixed going,' for the next one hundred miles to Alamein but there were also rough areas of ground or slow going terrain which damaged vehicles and used up valuable supplies of petrol.[4]

Mersa Matruh: Preparations

The Eighth Army had retreated past the frontier positions while the Panzerarmee diverted around them via Maddalena to the south and then headed east towards Mersa Matruh. Auchinleck and his advisor Major-General Eric Dorman-Smith took

2   Clayton & Craig, *End of the Beginning*, pp.161-176.
3   Stewart, *Early Battles*, pp.96-101, and Pitt, *Crucible, Vol II*, pp.272-282.
4   Charles D. Belgrave, *Siwa. The Oasis of Jupiter Ammon*, (London: John Lane.1923.) p.5. And Mellenthin, *Panzer Battles*, p.124.

Map 8:1 Matruh defences and minefields, 26 June 1942.

over direct command of the Eighth Army from Ritchie on the 25 June and developed plans to halt the Axis advance here, leaving staff officers to reorganize formations as they crossed the frontier.[5] The Army was still overall much stronger than the advancing three German Divisions at this point. The coast road route was defended by a newly formed 10th Corps with three Brigades from the 10th Indian Division in Matruh itself and two Brigades from the 50th Division at Gerawala further east along the coast. Both Divisions essentially defended the coastal sector for ten miles inland to the first escarpment.

Inland the 5th Indian Division had only one brigade remaining and two artillery regiments from which two Jock columns were deployed to hold the central plateau and the remaining units were scattered over three sites along the higher escarpment. Further east the 2nd New Zealand Division protected the Minqar Qaim track on the higher escarpment but they lacked transport, whilst the remnants of 1st Armoured Division deployed two Armoured Brigades.[6] Axis forces were even weaker because the Panzerarmee's strength had been greatly exhausted by the continuous fighting. The DAK now had just sixty tanks, while the Ariete Division had just seventy M13s.[7] The 21st Panzer Division had been reduced to just 600 men and 23 tanks by the 27 June, whilst 90th Light Division was using British trucks for half of its transport.[8] Rather than reform and replenish, Rommel drove his dog-tired units eastwards, and was correct to gamble that speed would undermine any defence British forces might put together. At Matruh he was fortunate to advance across the weakly held central plateau although this decision was based on chance rather than good intelligence.

Mersa Matruh: Battle summary and the impact of terrain and doctrine

On the evening of the 26 June, Engineers from two Axis battlegroups broke through the narrow minefield and the battlegroups quickly drove through the two Jock columns holding the central plateau.[9] Eighth Army HQ was confused by reports about the loss of the 29th Indian Brigade and a possible breakthrough by 150 tanks, although this was clearly an over estimation of Axis strength.[10] The two battlegroups then made further advances on the 27 June. The 15th Panzer Division now advanced along the higher ground above both escarpments to outflank both 1st Armoured Division and 2nd NZ Division which forced them to retreat.[11] The Axis advance was briefly halted on the 27 June, as the battlegroups were still weak, separated from each other and

5   TNA WO 201/2692. Operations May-July 42. Withdrawal to Alamein, p.22.
6   Playfair, *Mediterranean and Middle East. Vol III*, pp.333 and 284-285.
7   TNA WO 201/390. The Battle for Egypt: Operational Reports.1942 May-Sept 1942, p.5.
8   Mellenthin, *Panzer Battles*, pp.121-122.
9   IWM Papers of Maj. J.M. McSwiney.2 LAA Bty, pp.15-16.
10   TNA WO 201/390. The Battle for Egypt: Operational Reports.1942 May-Sept 1942, p.5.
11   TNA WO 201/2692. Operations May-July 42. Withdrawal to Alamein, pp.23-24.

short of supplies.[12] They advanced again next day and blocked the coast road. They then by-passed the more powerfully held flanks with a central thrust by 21st Panzer which turned south and outflanked the New Zealand Brigades on the escarpment at Minqar Qiam.[13] On the coast, 10th Corps was also forced to retreat overnight on the 28-29 June, losing 6,000 men and left large amounts of ammunition and equipment behind.

The defensive deployment near Matruh had been determined by the landscape features of the area. There were few features on which the British could develop a stronger line, and HQ made some questionable deployment decisions. Eighth Army had been left with few intact formations following Gazala, so it had logically strengthened the coastal route east with five Brigades. Auchinleck and Dorman-Smith had left the central plateau and higher ground too weakly defended, which was possibly due to inexperience in dealing with fast-moving Axis operations. Equally the battle had been won by a more mobile Panzerarmee which took advantage of the good going along these two upper routes and advanced 21st Panzer Division through the centre and 15th Panzer Division along the higher plateau.

The Axis advance was also affected by better RAF support for the Eighth Army. The Air Force was now fully committed to attacking Axis ground units and supply routes which gave some protection to the retreating units, with some commentators believing that this saved the retreat from becoming a worse rout.[14] The Army continued to be protected largely by RAF sorties which targeted Axis vehicle concentrations as they advanced towards Matruh. These harassing attacks slowed down the speed of the Axis advance considerably by bombing and ground strafing.[15] Both sides were also affected by the daily heat-haze and sandstorms which confused troops as they moved towards Alamein.[16]

Mersa Matruh: Conclusion

The Eighth army had been defeated once again by trying to hold a line of passable terrain with too few units and a reliance on poor defensive doctrine. The central and higher plateaux proved to be good going for motorised units and enabled the Axis to outflank British forces. The Jock columns were again too weak to halt the Battlegroups advance and there was too much reliance placed on them by commanders who failed to realise their ineffectiveness. The remaining Brigade units were too widely dispersed across the coastal sector and unable to provide mutual support. The defended localities

---

12   Mellenthin, *Panzer Battles*, p.121.
13   The New Zealanders broke through the enemy line in a dramatic night-time drive through the Axis leaguers to re-join the Eighth Army near Alamein.
14   Gladman, *Intelligence and Anglo-American Air Support*, p97.
15   TNA WO 201/390.The Battle for Egypt: Operational Reports.1942 May-Sept 1942, p.5.
16   TNA WO 169/4486.8 King's Royal Irish Hussars, Diary.1941 Nov. – 1942 Dec. 27 June 1942.

on the higher plateau were also by-passed by Axis units who made good use of the improved ground conditions in this area. There had been no improvement in British defensive doctrine, with the exception of improved RAF support. During the battle there was a high level of confusion during fighting with little coherence between armour and infantry. The Eighth Army had no option but to retreat again to the only remaining defensible line near Alamein which provided two secure flanks, had nearby supply bases and a more powerful RAF able to provide close support.

First Alamein: Introduction

British operations at the First Battle of Alamein focussed on the capture of key heights including the Ruweisat ridge and the depressions which flanked it; along with the Tel el Eissa ridge near the coast. This cluster of more numerous features had a greater impact on the British operations here than previously at Mersa Matruh. During the battle, Infantry assaults again proved initially successful in gaining objectives, which showed a slight improvement in doctrine. However, they were mostly unable to hold these positions from being recaptured by rapid Axis counterattacks. Operationally the series of battles contributed to the wearing down of Axis forces who now struggled to make a decisive breakthrough when British forces were in retreat.

The historiography is more prolific on this engagement as it forms part of the trilogy of Alamein battles fought between July and November 1942. Niall Barr's study argues that the Eighth Army failed to gain a decisive victory because of poor command, doctrine and equipment, though for once the tactical importance of the terrain features in this battle are noted.[17] Kippenberger provides excellent detail in his memoir on the 2nd NZ Divisional operations whilst Peter Bates gives another useful narrative about the July battles in which he fought.[18] Barrie Pitt does not show the real importance of why the ridges were being assaulted whilst Alexander McKee only briefly notes the problems of fighting amongst the depressions.[19] Whilst the terrain may have been noted in terms of the overall narrative the impact of the landscape on the tactical battle has been largely ignored by other commentators, as they focus on the issues of failures in command, equipment and execution of the July battles which most refer to as First Alamein.

First Alamein: Terrain

The capture of key positions remained the priority of operations for both sides. They needed tactical control of the various ridges and depressions which made up the

17   Barr, *Pendulum of War,* pp.13-68 and p.83.
18   Kippenburger, *Infantry Brigadier* and Bates, *Dance of War,*
19   Pitt, *Crucible of War, Vol II*, pp.306-323, and Alexander McKee, *El Alamein. Ultra and the Three Battles* (London: Souvenir, 1991), p.78.

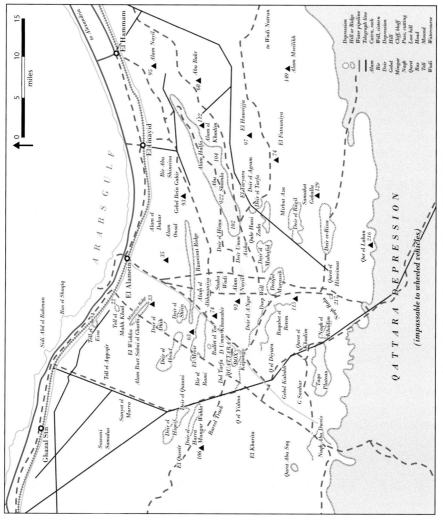

Map 8:2 First Alamein, 30 June–27 July 1942.

sector, with the most crucial being the Ruweisat ridge in the centre of the Eighth Army's defensive position. The Eighth Army stabilized a temporary line or very loose group of positions initially, from the Tel-el-Eissa ridge near the coast, across a series of ridges and depressions southwards for 35 miles to the Himeimat feature on the edge of the Qattara Depression.

The Ruweisat ridge in the centre of this line runs east-west for fifteen miles and dominates the central area. It is surrounded by some shallow depressions on either side which had to be captured before the ridge itself could be assaulted. There was more open ground south of Ruweisat which contained the El Mrier depression and beyond this the smaller Alam Nyal ridge and the much larger Munassib depression. East of Alam Nyal was Alam Halfa which at 132m was one of the highest points in the area and dominated the ground east of Alamein. The terrain south of Alam Nyal became more fragmented as it developed into various wadis, depressions and the Himeimat feature which overlooked the impassable Qattara salt marshes. This protected the desert flank meaning that any Axis offensive would take place in the coastal area.

First Alamein: preparations

Alamein had been selected as a possible defensive line as early as 1941 when Wavell ordered that some defensive preparations should be made there.[20] A Year late the Eighth Army halted on the position and gradually increased in strength as the troops were consolidated. The 1st South African Division which was weak in infantry was deployed in the Alamein box on the coast but powerfully supported by four regiments of artillery. Further south were more defensive boxes spaced at intervals up to 15 miles. In the centre, the weak 18th Indian Brigade held the Dier-el-Shein depression in front of the Ruweisat ridge. In the south, elements of the 50th Division were deployed in Jock Columns and the 2nd NZ Division was divided between the Bab-el-Qattara and Dier-el-Munassib features. The Eighth Army began this phase of operations with remnants of the Gazala Armoured Brigades but it was fairly rapidly reinforced with fresh tanks throughout July.

First Alamein: Battle summary

This battle is far too complex to provide more than a brief summary of the month long series of battles which occurred. When the Panzerarmee reached the Alamein line, Rommel planned to advance between the boxes and cut off Alamein from the coast road and 13th Corps from the rest of Eighth Army. In the event the flank move made by 90th Light Division was halted south of the box by concentrated artillery fire whilst further south a weak battlegroup ran into 18th Indian Brigade at the Deir-el-Shein depression.

20   TNA PREM 3/285. Auchinleck's Despatch, October 1941.

Once halted Panzerarmee was quickly forced onto the defensive for the remainder of the month, and Axis doctrine utilized rapid and determined counter-attacks to undermine British gains and to ensure the key heights were recaptured or disputed. Auchinleck directed further attacks on the static Axis position throughout July. By the 10 July, operations included joint attacks by the 9th Australian and 1st SA Divisions to capture the high ground at Tel-el-Eissa near the coast. These continued for three days but gained little ground and only added to the attrition of men and tanks.

In the centre the Ruweisat ridge became the focus for much of the Eighth Army's operations for the rest of July. On the 14 and 15 July two New Zealand Brigades and elements of 1st Armoured Division made an assault on the ridge, however it ended on 17 July, having failed to secure Pt 63 on the ridge. The NZ 5th Brigade's two leading battalions had rapidly overrun enemy strong points and one unit had secured its objective with the other halted just below the ridge. However, a typically swift Axis counter-attack captured left the forward units too weak and exposed to hold the ridge. The 2nd NZ Division made two major assaults to capture the Ruweisat ridge in July, but both failed due to a lack of Infantry manpower and poor coopera-tion from supporting armour, during Operation Bacon, 2nd NZ Division delivered a two battalion assault with just 500 men.[21] These operations further weakened crucial Infantry strengths as the repeated assaults and battles to defend newly captured posi-tions on the ridge highlighted the manpower shortages.

Auchinleck's plan for the subsequent 'Operation Splendour' included another attack west along the Ruweisat ridge by the 5th Indian Division. This was supported by a second attack from the south by 2nd NZ Division, supported by two Armoured Brigades onto the Ruweisat ridge. To reach the ridge it had to cross the El Meir depression held by the DAK. The newly arrived 23rd Armoured Brigade made an advance just south of the ridge which ended in bloody ruin for the newly arrived regiments.

First Alamein: Impact of terrain and doctrine

Rommel initially planned a rapid advance between the British defensive boxes in order to cut them off from the rest of the Eighth Army. However, the rough ground and deep sand slowed the DAK's approach as they moved towards the Ruweisat ridge. Consequently General Nehring ordered an attack on the British units which he realized were deployed in the Deir-el-Shein depression instead of manoeuvring around them.[22] Further south the 2nd NZ Division had been pulled back from the two depressions which were well forward of the 'line'. The withdrawal from El-Mreir straightened out the British line but the move had abandoned an important feature

---

21   TNA WO 201/390.The Battle for Egypt: Operational Reports.1942 May-Sept 1942. Operations of 5 NZ Inf Bde on Ruweisat Ridge Night 14/15 Jul and 15 Jul 42.
22   Mellenthin, *Panzer Battles*, pp.124-125

which protected the southern flank of the Ruweisat ridge. This made the later British attempts to recapture the ridge more problematic. British operations continued to be directed to capture the high ground; one later attack on the Miteiriya ridge, was a hasty combined assault using armour and Australian Infantry which fell short of the objective and left units weakened and unable to progress.

The first action showed how Eighth Army was improving its defensive doctrine. The 1st SA Division used concentrated artillery fire from numerous Regiments to halt the advance by 90th Light Division. The boxes and defended localities were still vulnerable though; further south at the Deir-el-Shein depression, the 18th Indian Brigade managed to slow down a powerful attack by the DAK before being finally overrun. This stubborn defence prevented a breakthrough in the centre of the line and contributed to the Panzerarmee being forced onto the defensive.[23] The Brigade had just two days to dig-in, and had little support from others despite a brief counter-attack by 1st Armoured Division which remained weakened from earlier battles. Eighth Army benefitted from the more numerous landscape features on which to create a more effective line, as they provided good defensible positions. They also forced Panzerarmee to divide its attacks when in a weakened state, almost the polar opposite of Eighth Army's experience at Gazala. The later attacks on Tel-El-Eissa highlighted how the coastal high ground was important to both sides but this area limited vehicle movement and defensive operations because of the salt marshes and narrow frontages to good going sectors.

There were continuing problems with command which included a lack of communication between armour and Infantry. The most quoted example being of the clash between Lumsden as CO of 1st Armoured Division, which resulted in the failure of supporting tanks to get through a minefield. The New Zealand Infantry was forced to withdraw from the Ruweisat ridge despite holding their positions for much of the day.[24] The attacks showed that the ridge objectives were attainable, but the limestone nature of the ridge made subsequent digging-in difficult. Operation Splendour highlighted the on-going problems of British doctrine and how the tactical focus was on the need to capture key terrain positions.

In other attacks, old problems re-occurred as inexperienced units were committed to battle before they had an opportunity to become used to desert conditions and combat. The newly arrived 23rd Armoured Brigade was committed to battle, to support a renewed assault near Ruweisat. In the hastily organized attack, two slow moving Regiments of the Brigade were committed to capture the El Mrier depression. Their line of assault caused them to run into a minefield and they were stopped by heavy anti-tank fire, from which only 6 tanks returned to the start-line.[25] Newly

23 Carver, *Dilemmas of the Desert War,* p.133.
24 TNA WO 201/390.The Battle for Egypt: Operational Reports.1942 May-Sept 1942. Operations of 5 NZ Inf Bde on Ruweisat Ridge Night 14/15 Jul and 15 Jul 42.
25 Bovington Archives 50th RTR Diary, From the History of the 23 Armd Bde.

arrived Infantry were also inexperienced and thrown into hasty combat. At the Miteiriya ridge the Australian Infantry were criticized for not working correctly with the supporting armour which caused unnecessary casualties.[26] Commanders had not learnt from previous errors in planning, coordination and doctrine and new formations were showing their lack of specific training.

British doctrine was also improving as much stronger tactical use was made of direct RAF support which averaged 570 per day throughout most of July. This also helped to delay Panzerarmee by inflicting heavy vehicle losses, caused unit disruption and shortages in fuel and equipment. At the same time the Axis defences and tactics were also strengthening so that even when units made progress, it was nearly impossible to hold onto the gains. The attacks made by the British 69th Brigade took ground within Axis defences and penetrated their minefields only to falter with heavy casualties after the initial break-in.

The effect of these continuous operations to capture key high ground was that they caused the Eighth Army to become exhausted in men and equipment once again. The 8th Hussars had lost all their tanks many times over since the 27 May and were left with just one third of their original personnel by August.[27] The heavy attrition also occurred amongst the Infantry with the 69th Brigade and 24th Australian Brigades suffering over 1,000 casualties between them. British Intelligence analysis also improved dramatically as Corps HQs intelligence now provided the majority of details of Axis formations to assist tactical operations more readily. In addition to Ultra, the 'Y' service provided information on targets and expected Luftwaffe attacks.[28] As the line became more static, some of the best intelligence came from the Forward Observers of the Royal Artillery who provided the most accurate information of enemy movements.[29] These regular reports contributed to an improving overall doctrine for Eighth Army operations which culminated in success at Second Alamein.

The operations during First Alamein had focussed on the capture and retention of the significant terrain of the battlefield which included the Ruweisat ridge and its adjacent depressions, as well the Miteiriya ridge. Despite some successes in a series of operations, all of these attacks had been driven off by swift counter-attacks or became bogged down in attritional battles. The Ruweisat ridge was too large for the battalions assigned to capture them, as the Infantry became as weak in company strength just as the armoured regiments became weaker in squadron strengths to carry out their assignments. Brigades also became too dispersed again trying to cover these numerous features, which weakened their fighting power and left individual battalions to be

26   Bovington Archives 44th RTR Diary. C Squadron unofficial Diary, 17 July 1942.
27   TNA WO 169/4486.8 King's Royal Irish Hussars, Diary.1941 Nov- 1942 Dec. 1 July 1942.
28   TNA WO 201/540.Weekly Desert Reviews: Intelligence Reports. June-Aug 1942.Review 9.7.42, p.3.
29   TNA WO 201/538.Lessons on Operations. 14 Sept 41-25 Aug 42. 50th Division Lessons, 20 July 42. Intelligence.

captured or overrun. There were also continuing failures in command, planning and problems with doctrine especially cooperation between armour and infantry.

Although the Infantry proved they could capture an enemy position, the difficulty was retaining it after the inevitable Axis counterattack. There were some improvements in the better use of concentrated artillery fire and intelligence analysis, but these were not yet fully developed. The inconclusive nature of the fighting at Alamein led to Churchill to order changes in Middle East command in early August and both sides regrouped for the further operations in later in the month.

9

Alam Halfa and Second Alamein, 30 August-4 November 1942

The battles of Alam Halfa and Second Alamein represent the first period of new command at the Eighth Army and Middle East Command.[1] They also represent the progression of tactics firstly in defence and secondly in assault doctrine. They also show the continuing impact of terrain on planning and objective setting by commanders which is seen alongside the steady development of Army doctrines in defence at Alam Halfa and in an improved level of assault at Second Alamein. The brevity of assessment of Second Alamein, is not to suggest that it was a major victory for the Army and a huge turning point in the British war effort. However the vast array of histories of the battle do not need to be replicated here, only those points which relate to the impact of the terrain and ongoing problems with doctrine are considered.

Alam Halfa

This battle was a successful defence by the Eighth Army which made full use of a key ridge in the defensive line and where fresh tactics were used to halt another powerful offensive by Panzerarmee. It also showed the development of air and ground units working more closely in cooperation to defeat the Axis thrust.

The historiography has often concentrated on the controversy over the plans for the defence of the Alam Halfa sector.[2] Niall Barr believes Eighth Army used just a 'fraction' of its strength in the battle which Panzerarmee lost due to the petrol crisis and the strike power of the Desert Air Force.[3] John Connell and Corelli Barnett argued that Montgomery used former plans drawn up by Eric Dorman-Smith for the defence. They continue to emphasize the importance of command, fresh troops

---

1   Churchill had appointed Lieutenant-General Montgomery to Eighth Army and General Harold Alexander as his new CinC at Middle East Command, as well as numerous other changes in GHQ in early August.
2   Barnett, *Desert Generals*, p.263.
3   Barr, *Pendulum of War*, p.250.

on the battle and the discussion of terrain remains part of the narrative. Michael Carver notes the armoured deployment along Bare ridge and the battle for Pt 102, and discusses the reasons why the Panzerarmee halted on the 31 August.[4] In a later work he concentrates on the debate surrounding whose plan the battle was based on.[5] Barrie Pitt emphasizes the problems caused by soft sand in the southern depressions which seriously delayed the Panzerarmee whereas John Strawson fails to mention the impact of the terrain at all.[6]

Alam Halfa: Terrain 30 August- 5 September 1942

Earlier British assessments of the terrain selected the Alam Halfa ridge to defend against an Axis thrust from the southern sector of the Alamein line. It was the highest feature in the rear of the line and south of the it, there was difficult-going through a series of depressions with deep sand, which would slow any eastward movement by vehicles. In the centre, one possible avenue for a motorised advance was across the open ground south of Ruweisat ridge and the El-Mrier depression before it reached the smaller Alam Nayal, although this area was subsequently mined by the Axis. East of Alam Nyal ridge was Alam Halfa, which reached 132 metres and dominated the southern sector of the Eighth Army defences. It provided a strong defendable position from an attack from the south, along its length, which enabled the British to prepare for attack from there.

Alam Halfa: Preparations

This battle was Montgomery's first operation as Commander of Eighth Army. The Army was still weakened from the month long battles of First Alamein, with August being a quiet period which allowed both sides to re-group and replenish for the next round of operations. Intelligence reports noted a, 'quiet week with enemy attention devoted to reorganisation of forces and consolidation of defences. Whole Axis front now believed covered by minefields.' It was a period, 'of positional warfare with heavy shelling by both sides.'[7] Intelligence from Ultra showed Panzerarmee was expected to begin a new offensive towards the end of the month aimed at breaking through the southern minefields and an outflanking move south of the Alam Halfa ridge.

British preparations for the defence were rapid and thorough thanks to the Ultra on Axis plans which enabled Montgomery to move up some formations. The 13th Corps was given the task of preparing a defensive position on the ridge but not to incur

4   Carver, *Alamein*, p.60.
5   Carver, *Dilemmas of the Desert War*, pp.135-137.
6   Pitt, *Crucible, Vol.III*, pp.25-26, and Strawson, *Battle for North Africa*, pp.149-150.
7   TNA WO 201/540.Weekly Desert reviews: Intelligence Reports. June-Aug 1942. 4 Aug 42.

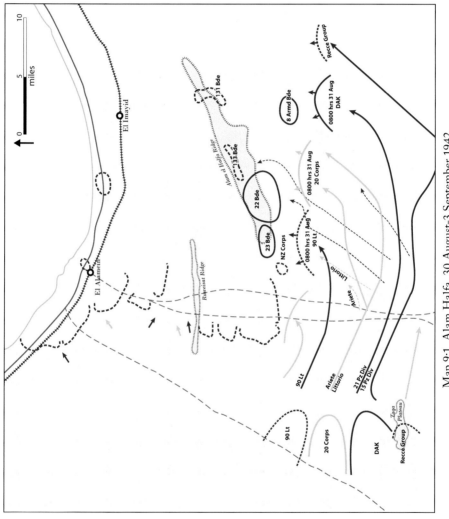

Map 9:1 Alam Halfa, 30 August–3 September 1942.

excessive casualties.[8] He requested and was given the newly arrived 44th Division which consisted of two Infantry Brigades to hold the ridge and this was supported by the 22nd Armoured Brigade which was dug-in around the western end, near Pt 102. The 23rd Armoured Brigade moved south to support them in reserve and to cover the gap along Bare ridge where a breakthroughs might be possible. The two Armoured Brigades totalled nearly 150 tanks with 90 of these being Grants.

Despite the problems of an over-extended supply line the Axis forces made an impressive effort to build up for this offensive logistically throughout August and they provided the frontline units with 234 German and 281 Italian tanks and plenty of ammunition. However they were still desperately short of petrol, thanks to RAF and naval targeting Italian fuel tankers using Ultra decrypts. The Panzer Divisions totalled some 200 tanks with a higher number of the Panzer 'Specials' used than previously, whose more powerful guns outranged the Grant tanks facing them.

Alam Halfa: Summary and impact of terrain

This attack began on the 30 August, with a night time approach march through the British minefields. The Panzerarmee was monitored continuously and its vehicle columns pounded by RAF bombers. The Axis force worked its way across the depressions south of the ridge, but was under constant bombardment and observed by observers on Alam Halfa. Panzerarmee commanders turned towards the ridge sooner when they realized the Eighth Army was prepared for them and made a series of assaults on the ridge. Axis forces had problems moving over the soft ground south of the Bare ridge and were unable to made the rapid moves of previous battles. They were also slowed down by natural dust storms and the effects of continual bombing by the RAF. The Panzerarmee remained in front of the ridge making various assaults until the 3 September, when the lack of progress finally forced it to retreat. There was a belated counter-attack by Eighth Army to cut off the retreating Battlegroups, however this was halted by effective Axis firepower. The Army, as many commentators have noted was not quite ready to successfully assault Axis positions just yet.

British defence tactics were better coordinated during Alam Halfa and contributed to the victory. The 7th Motor Brigade delayed the initial Axis advance through the minefields, and the heavy and continuous attacks by the RAF destroyed many Axis vehicles, disrupted their movement and exhausted enemy personnel. The anti-tank guns of 1st Rifle Brigade halted the attacks on the ridge by the 21st Panzer Division. They were supported by the two armoured Brigades who fought from hull-down defensive positions near Pt 102. The British armour had held its position and was supported by large concentrations of artillery deployed behind the ridge, as well as the noted RAF attacks.

---

8   TNA WO 201/424. The October Battle of Alamein and the advance to Tripolitania. Nov-Dec 42. Report Brief Notes on "El Alamein" battle, 23 Oct – 4 Nov 42, p.1.

British forces still had some issues with poor planning and problems in their assault doctrine. One Brigade from the newly arrived 44th Division made an obvious approach march for the counter-attack, which gave Axis forces time to prepare and repel the subsequent assault that night.[9] The 132nd Brigade also attacked southwards to block the retreat by 90th Light Division, only to suffer heavy casualties. It became clear that errors were still being made even in set-piece attacks; in the north a diversionary raid crippled the 2/15th Australian Infantry near Tel-el-Eissa. Despite the improving picture and better intelligence analysis which allowed Montgomery to prepare for the assault, not all units received the correct warning of Axis intentions, the CO of the 8th Hussars was not informed an attack had begun and found his Light squadron in observation and under severe air attack on the first day of the offensive.[10]

Alam Halfa: Conclusion

Alam Halfa was the first successful tactical defensive battle for Eighth Army. It had become more effective in using the terrain to its best advantage, then altering doctrine to maintain a defensive stance and combined this with an improved tactical flexibility and use of all arms to maximize firepower. Army HQ now received high quality intelligence which enabled it to make a strong deployment across the suitable Alam Halfa ridge, which proved to be an ideal defensive site from which to try new defensive tactics. Lieutenant-General Montgomery had insisted on fresh tactics at the ridge, with the armour remaining mostly hull-down, supported by strong anti-tank and supported by heavy concentrations of artillery to increase firepower against the expected Panzer attacks. Alam Halfa clearly demonstrated the Eighth Army's progress in doctrine.

This combination of anti-tank and heavy artillery fire was a highly effective tactic which would be repeated in future battles. The RAF made a significant contribution to the British defence by the constant round the clock bombing and strafing missions. These destroyed huge numbers of the Panzerarmee's vehicles, men and equipment and prevented it re-supplying frontline troops.[11] A heavy Khamsin storm caused problems for both sides and slowed movement by the Panzerarmee, which was already struggling through the soft sand in the depressions south of the ridge. Therefore, despite the success of improving doctrine, tactical success for the Eighth Army resulted from using the terrain to the best advantage.

9   Barr, *Pendulum*, pp.243-245.
10   TNA WO 169/4486. 8 King's Royal Irish Hussars, Diary.1941 Nov. – 1942 Dec. 31 August 1942.
11   Gladman, *Intelligence and Anglo-American Air Support*, pp.109-111.

Second Alamein Introduction

This battle was important to the British war effort at a political, strategic and operational level. Montgomery was determined to push for an October offensive which would coincide with the Allied Torch landings due in early November in Algeria and Morocco. The Eighth Army was then committed to an intense period of training, new doctrines, rebuilding and receiving new equipment designed to break the Axis line and defeat Panzerarmee. British planning was focussed on capturing two key ridges in the northern sector of the battlefield, so although providing two obvious objectives, key terrain, as in previous engagements, was to contribute to the outcome of this battle. The battle also developed to show the importance of other terrain features, which heavily influenced the fighting.

In the campaign historiography, this battle remains the foremost combat of the campaign, De Guingand's immediate post-war memoir noted Montgomery's close control of the battle and planning, which he believed was the key to the victory.[12] Michael Carver blames command planning whilst Corelli Barnett's revisionist polemic argued that the battle could largely have been avoided if Montgomery had been more aggressive at Alam Halfa.[13] Niall Barr's more recent study shows the Army was still developing into a confident and battle hardened force which won the day, despite losing some of its experienced Divisions to other theatres. Artillery and Engineer doctrines were becoming ever more complex but flexible and a force multiplier at last for future battles, whilst the armour and Infantry still had problems which depended on training.[14] Jon Latimer meanwhile, notes the tactical importance of the artillery support and the doggedness of the Infantry in maintaining the battle over the thirteen days.[15] Jonathan Fennell contends that the recovery of morale in the autumn, following a crisis within the Eighth Army in the late summer, made a decisive contribution to the victory.[16] The latest study by Bryn Hammond argues that it was a 'special case' in terms of assault doctrine which required weeks of planning, training and new specialised equipment, all of which was designed to breakthrough exceptionally deep Axis defences and minefields.[17] The domination of Second Alamein in the historiography tends to undermine the importance and relevance of other battles in the campaign.

12 De Guingand, *Operation Victory*, p.193.
13 Barnett, *Desert Generals*, p.265, and Carver, *Dilemmas*, pp.138-139.
14 Barr, *Pendulum*, pp.409-412.
15 Latimer, *Alamein*, pp.317-318.
16 Fennell, *Combat and Morale*, p.283.
17 Bryn Hammond, *El Alamein: The Battle that Turned the Tide of the Second World War* (Oxford: Osprey, 2012) pp.159-161.

Second Alamein: Terrain

The British objectives for Second Alamein included capturing the Miteiriya ridge and Aqqaqir hill beyond it. The key feature of the battle was the Miteiriya ridge which runs on a north-west alignment. The area around the ridge was noted as, 'featureless, but with slight undulations and ridges which when captured gave fair observation.'[18] Beyond it was the low hillock, Tel-el-Aqqaqir, a low hill in the centre-rear of the Axis line and this became the main objective for the later revised plan, codenamed 'Supercharge'. It dominated the ground in the rear area and its capture would lead to the break out by British armour. In the north, the ridge at Tel-el-Eissa was also an objective for the 9th Australian Division and was designed to draw Axis forces away from Tel-el- Aqqaqir.

The assault plan was focussed on securing these key terrain features. They also included the 'good-going' ground which ran parallel with the coast road and six miles to the south. Army HQ wanted to thrust the Armoured Corps through the Axis defences and along this faster ground to strike for the air bases at Daba and Fuka. This would push back the Luftwaffe and also cut of the static Axis Infantry lying to the south of the Mitieriya ridge. The ridge was an objective despite British forces already controlling good observation heights near Alamein. The approaches to the ridge was an area of restricted ground which meant the deployment for the six Divisions to be used in the attack was quite restricted and this had an impact on the British advance, (see Fig.9.2).[19]

Second Alamein: Preparations

The initial planning for Operation Lightfoot began in August with the main objective to destroy the enemy's forces in their current defences. To achieve this, the plan targeted the capture of the Miteiriya ridge, by the Infantry, which would then provide the Eighth Army with suitable ground from which to defend against the expected Axis counter-attack. It was hoped that the armour would make a break-out to cut off the Axis from their landing grounds near Daba and Fuka and their supply lines. There was a major administrative supply problem when two Corps were deployed in the same area of ground, which created a cramped space for so many Divisions.[20] The Eighth Army had 30th Corps providing the Infantry for the main assault supported by a new 10th Armoured Corps and other Independent Armoured Brigades. Further south the 13th Corps would make diversionary assaults using elements of two Divisions. The administrative and logistical preparations for such a major assault were huge, and the

18   TNA WO 201/424. The October Battle. RA Notes on the offensive by Eighth Army.
19   TNA WO 201/424. The October Battle. Appreciation and Plan of Lightfoot; Ground.
20   TNA WO 201/432. Operation `Lightfoot': planning. August 1942.

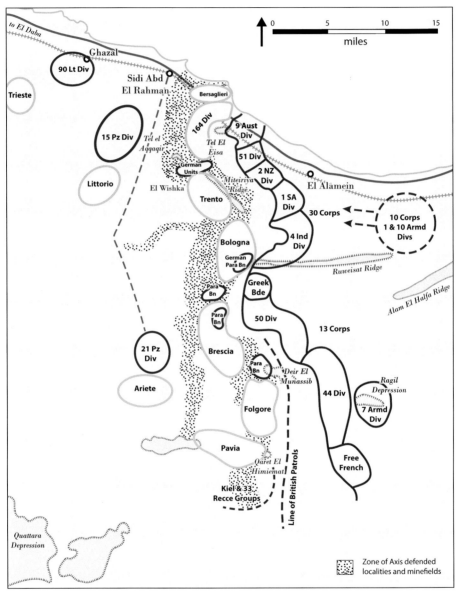

Map 9:2 Second Alamein, 23 October-4 November 1942.

air support was equally impressive, ensuring that the RAF dominated the battlefield in the first few days.

The new assault doctrine focussed on firepower from concentrated batteries of artillery to enable the Infantry and engineers to break-through the deep minefields and capture enemy positions across the ridge. This was a defining feature of the initial assault and was a significant new tactic for the Eighth Army. The break-in process was to be made in the north by four Divisions supported by over 800 guns over a frontage of 7,000 yards. They were to advance to a depth of 4,000 yards in the first phase. The use of photo reconnaissance enabled the mapping of defence positions and the Artillery fire-plan concentrated on these. The barrage included a 20 minute concentration on each location and a steady lifting of the barrage of 100 yards every three minutes. The 51st Highland Division had a more locational barrage and used 'flash-spotting' and air reconnaissance targeted the estimated 454 Axis guns in the frontline sector. These were noted in readiness for a counter-battery programme, which aimed to neutralize them within the bombardment phase.[21]

The British Signals organisation and planning was made more complicated due to the close proximity of a large number of Headquarters for different formations, but close control of signals kept communications running smoothly. The Engineers developed new tactics to make gaps in the minefields and widen them to allow the armour to advance onto the ridge.[22] Operation Bertram, which was the deception plan, enabled the Eighth Army to deploy in the forward areas without giving away any information to the Axis intelligence.[23] The six weeks of preparations had allowed the Eighth Army to train for the assault but it had also allowed the Panzerarmee to establish minefields. These were five to nine thousand yards deep across the area, covered by numerous linked areas of anti-tank and artillery positions.[24] Axis forces held the line with six Divisions and kept the Armoured DAK in reserve. German forces were spread amongst the weaker Italian formations and had reached 75% of their full strength.

Second Alamein: Battle summary and the impact of terrain and doctrine

The attack commenced on 23 October, with a large artillery bombardment followed by an Infantry assault. Over the next two days, the Infantry continued the 'crumbling phase' which gradually reduced the Axis defences. Montgomery noted that the 25 October for him, was the crisis point of the battle, where he forced his hesitant

---

21   TNA WO 201/424. The October Battle. RA Notes on the offensive by Eighth Army, p.9. The Axis artillery was estimated at 200 field, 40 medium and 14 heavy guns.
22   METM No.7. Lessons from Operations Oct and Nov.1942, (Buxton: MLRS, undated), p.4.
23   Latimer, *Alamein*, pp.160-162.
24   TNA WO 201/424. The October Battle. Nov-Dec 42. RA Notes on the offensive by Eighth Army.

Armoured Commanders to push their Regiments out into the 'open' as he called it.[25] There followed a series of Axis counter-attacks in the centre area which were halted in hard-fought actions. The Australian 9th Division also attacked northwards towards Tel-el-Eissa, prior to the renewed Operation Supercharge which became the final phase of attacks and breakout through the Axis lines. Eighth Army had achieved a decisive victory but at the high cost in Infantry, Engineers and some armoured Regiments. These phases of the battle have all been well studied and analysed to provide detailed battle narratives, whilst this study is more concerned with the direct impact of the terrain and notable changes in doctrine.

The Axis defences took advantage of the landscape features by using the undulating ridges to conceal the density and depth of the minefields. Their numerous defensive positions made best use of each fold across the ridge and created major problems for the Eighth Army's assault. Eighth Army's Infantry experienced mixed success in reaching their objectives due to the combination of the ground conditions and fighting through the complexity of the Axis defences. The supporting Armoured Regiments came forward to drive through the gaps in the minefields but came under heavy fire when attempting to cross the ridgeline. The tanks were silhouetted against the crest-line and became easy targets for Axis Self-Propelled and anti-tank guns on the reverse slopes. The 3rd Hussars had this experience on the Miteiriya ridge where they lost a high number of tanks and officers which crippled the leadership of the regiment.[26] The terrain conditions served to slow down the British advance, and forced Montgomery to rethink his plans.

Despite the intense planning and training, this battle demonstrated the old issues for British doctrine had not been fully resolved. Regiments became dispersed again during operations while trying to capture too many objectives. The Regiments of 23rd Armoured Brigade was assigned to different attacks, which dispersed their firepower and effectiveness as a unit. The complexity of the defences also caused confusion and heavy losses to both armour and Infantry. The 40th and 46th RTR lost many tanks to mines and anti-tank fire when they supported the 9th Australian Division during its assault near Tel-el-Eissa. The Infantry was forced to dig-in short of the objectives whilst the Brigade artillery was hampered by continuous re-deployments within the mined areas and failed to give adequate fire support.[27] Even the improved and more mobile artillery support had problems coping with the complexity of the Axis positions. The Infantry assaults in the north continued the offensive whilst the armour re-grouped for Operation Supercharge. However they were important in drawing Axis reserves away from Tel-el-Aqqaqir sector. The multiple objectives made it more

---

25   B.L. Montgomery, *The Memoirs of Field Marshal Montgomery* (London: Collins, 1958) pp.129-130.
26   TNA WO 201/424. The October Battle. 3rd KOH, Action at Tel el Aqqaqir 2 Nov 1942, p.1.
27   TNA WO 201/471. 23rd Armoured Brigade: operations `Lightfoot' and `Supercharge'.

difficult to provide rapid and effective artillery support to the front line and this made each attack more attritional and inconclusive.

One successful British defensive tactic made good use of low hummocky ground and contributed to one of the turning points of the battle. This occurred during the 'Snipe Action' on the 26 October and took place in the central sector of the battlefield. A Motor Rifle Brigade was pushed forward to extend the bridgehead and draw out the Axis armour onto the Brigade position. This included two features consisting of low, hummocky dunes, which were code-named Snipe and Kidney ridge. The position was occupied by 2nd Rifle Brigade and an additional anti-tank battery normally equipped with nearly thirty 6pdr anti-tank guns. Unfortunately only nineteen guns reached Snipe as the remainder became stuck in the soft sand in the advance. The Artillery support for the unit was confused again when there were problems in locating the correct position from map references. Despite this the Rifle Brigade fought off numerous attacks by the Axis armour and received some fire support from the nearby 24thArmoured Brigade.[28] Axis forces were thought to have lost between thirty and fifty tanks over two days, which dramatically weakened their Panzer Divisions for the final phases of the battle. This was thought to have been one of the turning points of the battle, in which the Axis armour exhausted itself trying to pinch-out British advances. As in previous and later battles, low profile anti-tank guns in difficult ground proved to be a highly effective tactic in neutralizing armoured attacks.

The armoured battles held many examples of both progressive doctrine and some issues of old, re-occurring problems. In the later phase of the battle, the 23rd Armoured Brigade was parcelled out by regiment or squadron to different attacks but managed retained near its strength up to the night of 28/29 October. Then both 40th and 46th RTR were gathered in to support the 9th Australian Division for its assault near the coast. Unfortunately the situation became confused for the Regiments soon after crossing start line. The Infantry dug in by dawn, but were only half a mile forward and many tanks were soon lost on mines or to anti-tank fire. The 46th RTR had lost their CO and all their squadron commanders, experienced officers who the Regiment relied on, along with many other crews, the Regiment was left with just eight tanks left. The 8th RTR re-joined the Brigade and 46th RTR was moved to the rear to reorganize. The Artillery supporting the Brigade was a Regiment of self-propelled Priests, 105mm guns mounted on tracked vehicles, yet even this mobile unit felt hampered by continuous re-deployments within the narrow lanes amongst mined areas.[29] Therefore even close fire support was still proving to be problematic because of the narrow sectors of terrain in which the Brigade was attempting to manoeuvre in.

Axis defences proved to be difficult to crack, even with an improving assault technique being used. In the final phase of the battle, 8th RTR was to support the 152

---

28   TNA WO 201/424. The October Battle. Account of the action by 2RB at Snipe, 26/27 Oct 42, p.3.

29   TNA WO 201/471. 23rd Armoured Brigade: operations `Lightfoot' and `Supercharge'.

Brigade in their attack by the 5/7th Gordons Infantry, to capture a section of the Sidi Rahman track. This attack appears to have been less successful, with heavy tank losses and the Infantry ordered to dig in just 1500 yards from the start line. A smoke barrage had been used instead of an HE barrage because of false intelligence, but the barrage also created dustclouds which added to the confusion.

During Supercharge, the 9th Armoured Brigade made the crucial assault which cracked the last Axis anti-gun line along the Rahman track behind the Axis line. The 3rd Hussars advanced as a Regimental Group, supported by a Company of Infantry, an anti-tank unit and a Recce squadron, in two mixed columns. During the initial advance through the minefield gaps, the whole formation was heavily shelled which eliminated all the supporting troops moving in trucks, Bren-carriers and anti-tank guns. One objective 'Skinflint', was gained by 0450 hours by the 2 November, but with only 23 tanks remaining. The advance to the objective Rahman track continued by armour alone, and with no supporting barrage. The Regiment was quickly engaged by a mass of close range anti-tank weapons was quickly and reduced to just seven tanks. Broken communications forced the CO to move between tanks to convey orders. The 3rd Hussars held a temporary line, using smoke as cover, until a fresh unit, the Queen's Bays Regiment, came up on their right. The Hussars appeared to have overrun a large anti-tank position and although it was left crippled in tanks and crews, it had destroyed numerous Axis guns. The whole action then enabled the supporting 2nd Armoured Brigade to continue the break out and force Rommel to make the decision to retreat from the Alamein line. Each Regiment had targeted a separate tactical feature as an objective and each one had been badly mauled in the process, but had continued on regardless of losses, and the Brigade was later praised by Montgomery for its heroism, of the ninety tanks which began the assault, only nineteen remained.[30]

Second Alamein: Conclusion

The battle was an important stage in the development of new doctrines for the Eighth Army. Fighting during each stage of the operation had been affected by the key features of the landscape. These had increased the complexity of the Axis defences, which had taken full advantage of the ground. Eighth Army used the build-up phase to practice specific tactics to break-in and 'crumble' the defences, using combined arms of Infantry, Engineers and armour to capture a succession of defensive lines. They were now fully supported by a programme of massive Artillery bombardments and RAF ground attacks, thorough Intelligence analysis and deception operations which was a noted improvement from earlier offensives. Montgomery had maintained a strong grip over the planning, and command of the operation, which had enabled him to alter the original assault when it became stalled within the deep Axis defences. Armour expert Richard McCreery believed he materially contributed to advising

---

30   Bierman & Smith, *Alamein,* p.326.

Montgomery to adapt his plans to Supercharge, which became more decisive than the days of heavy but inconclusive combat waged until that point.[31] This led to the renewed armoured assault (Supercharge) which broke through the rear of the Axis line and forced the Panzerarmee to begin the long Axis retreat into Tunisia.

Second Alamein was a turning point for the Eighth Army in improving its tactical doctrine and for showing that terrain was a key consideration of its operations now. Following the long Axis retreat, the British would fight their next major battles in Tunisia in early 1943 and prove themselves adept at both attack and defence. The British victory led to the Axis fighting more defensively for much of the remainder of the campaign in North Africa.

31   Richard Mead, *The Last Great Cavalryman. The Life of Richard McCreery, Commander Eighth Army* (Barnsley: Pen & Sword Military, 2012) p.227.

10

The final battles – Medenine, Mareth, Wadi Akirit and Tunis, March-13 May 1943

This series of four final battles for the Eighth Army show the greater impact of terrain on British operations in the Tunisian landscape than earlier planning and the development of its offensive and defensive doctrines. The outcome of each battle also showed how well Eighth Army had developed its offensive tactics to overcome increasingly complex Axis defences, but they still highlighted some ongoing problems of intelligence or training with some inexperienced units. Eighth Army planning across all arms now meant that the preparation phase was a major part of all operations and that the analysis of the terrain to be crossed was an essential part of the process. Studies were now made about the terrain ahead of the Army, whilst at the tactical level, assaults were made in less obvious sectors; at Mareth, attacks were targeted across low ground, away from heights, but despite supporting massed firepower units were still halted by heavily defended dominating features within the wadis, from which Axis firepower controlled the surrounding terrain. The fighting in Tunisia also highlighted the increasing tenacity of Axis units and their methods of making the best use of the terrain to improve the defences. By the end of the campaign the Eighth Army was able to adapt its operations and be flexible in manoeuvre to outflank and undermine these defences which in earlier periods of the campaign would have halted attacks.

Tunisia: The impact of terrain on British operational movement

The Tunisian landscape had more major relief than either Libya or Egypt, so that its influence on operations became even greater. The Axis command made best use of the key heights to defencd central Tunisia, Kesselring wanted a larger Axis 'bridgehead' and reinforcements were continually rushed from Italy to build up a strong defensive line across the high ground. The Tunisian hills and relief features gave them more opportunities to develop powerful defensive positions which used multiple heavy machine-guns, backed by mortars and artillery to sweep the steep slopes, which only Infantry could assault.[1] The technical weakness of such a static defensive line of positions was that as each one was captured it weakened or outflanked the adjacent positions which gradually made them untenable. Combined with problems of bad winter weather and supply issues added to the slow advance of the Allied Armies in Tunisia. In the south, the continuing plan for the Eighth Army was a step-by-step capture of the heights which dominated the terrain and the ports en route to Tunis. It would then break out into the Kairouan plain to exploit the rear of the northern Axis defences and overrun the all-weather airfields located there. Each stage of ground, which overlooked a valley or plain, had to be captured in order to continue.[2]

Introduction: Medenine 6 March 1943

Following Alamein, the Eighth Army advanced 1,400 miles in three months as Panzerarmee conducted a model withdrawal despite being badly weakened. There has been much debate on whether Eighth Army might have crushed the Axis rear guard and reduced Axis troop numbers for the final phases of the campaign. Montgomery considered the Eighth Army to be 'unbalanced' as there were only a few formations near the front, including 7th Armoured Division, and for the Infantry, 2nd New Zealand and 51st Highland Divisions, so that he made only cautious advances fearing the potential for a swift Axis riposte. Although Eighth Army was suffering too, from supply issues, it also became clear that in doctrinal terms, the advance was cautious and sluggish at first. Rommel decided not to make a serious defence at any of the most feasible positions along the coastal route of the retreat, such as El Agheila, Homs or even near the main port of Tripoli. However Panzerarmee continued the Axis retreat across Libya and into southern Tunisia, against the wishes of his superiors at Comando Supremo, he had continued the retreat into southern Tunisia and only halted along the French built Mareth line, designed to protect the southern approach towards the main Tunisian ports.

There are few histories of this particular battle, which has been largely overlooked until recently, Bruce Watson notes Rommel's plan to choose the unlikely approach and cross soft ground to confuse Allied watchers, but fails to emphasize the impact of the Eighth Army's deployment in the low Metameur hills.[3] Equally David Rolf's detailed work only mentions the impact of Ultra which enabled the Eighth Army to deploy effectively.[4]

1   John Frost, *A Drop too Many* (London: Sphere, 1983) p.127, and John D'Arcy-Dawson, *Tunisian Battle* (London: Macdonald & Co, 1943) pp.59-60.
2   TNA WO 201/598. 8th Army operations in Tunisia. Feb.-May 1943, p.16.
3   Bruce A. Watson, *Exit Rommel. The Tunisian Campaign 1942-43* (Mechanicsburg: Stackpole, 1999), pp.112-117.
4   David Rolf, *The Bloody Road*, pp.160-161.

Medenine: Terrain

The principle of controlling key high ground for artillery observation purposes remained vital to both sides. The Eighth Army's line of approach was north-west towards southern Tunisian across ground which was semi-desert and contained fewer populated centres. Any possible outflanking routes were to the west contained difficult or impassable ground for vehicles and so the coast plain remained the main area of operations. Tactically the landscape was a significant factor at Medenine where, thanks to Ultra, the expected Axis spoiling attack was halted. Eighth army made good use of low hills to deploy massed anti-tank guns along with armour, in front of a larger hill feature used by observers who called in concentrated artillery fire. The position was selected operationally as the optimum site to halt the axis advance.

Medenine was a small town with a vital road junction for routes into southern Tunisia along with a useful landing ground. The best defensive position was east of the town. Here, Lieutenant-Colonel M.E. Parker, noted that forward units, 'arrived in the plain looking towards the Matmata hills with a very splendid observation post behind us, the Tajera Shrir, renamed for convenience as, 'Edinburgh Castle.' At the top of this height all the gunner [Observation Posts] were installed and all had telephone lines laid to their guns [batteries] behind our positions.'[5]

Medenine: Preparations

After earlier offensives against the Allied First Army, Axis forces had re-grouped and Rommel was given the Panzer Divisions to make a spoiling attack to further delay the Eighth Army's approach towards the Mareth line. Rommel used his veteran 15th and 21st Panzer Divisions, along with the the newly arrived 10th Panzer Division, plus elements of the 90th Light and 164th Infantry Divisions, to make the assault.

Eighth Army plans for Medenine used Intelligence from Ultra which gave Montgomery clear details of the Axis approach. He later admitted to some misgivings about receiving an assault by these three veteran Panzer Divisions,[6] but his message to the troops reminded them to, 'hold firm in their defended localities,' and that there would be no retreat.[7] The Eighth Army had limited forces available near the front, although they were well supported by the massed guns of 5th AGRA and the tactical support of the RAF. Montgomery deployed elements of 5th NZ Brigade with numerous anti-tank guns which were well sited and the whole position was well camouflaged by these experienced troops. It was an ideal defensive position for the

5   IWM, Cat no.479.Papers of Lieutenant Colonel M E Parker, CO of 257 AT Battery, p.166.

6   Bennett, *Ultra and Mediterranean Strategy*, p.210.

7   IWM, Montgomery Papers, Manuscript Draft of Field Marshal Viscount Montgomery of Alamein's Personal Message on the Eve of the Battle of Medenine, March 1943, http://www.iwm.org.uk/collections/item/object/1030002496. Accessed 12 May 2012.

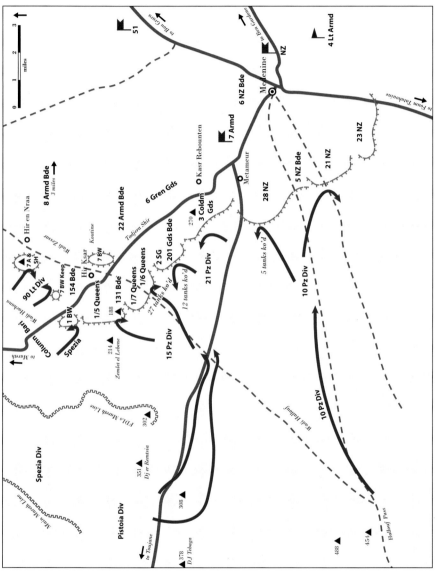

Map 10:1 Medenine, 6 March 1943.

New Zealanders, because the ground fell away in front of the Brigade position and commanders were confident that the Artillery had, 'mastered the technique of quickly putting down massive concentrations [of fire].'[8]

Other formations on the frontline included the 201st Guards Brigade, with 8th Armoured Brigade supporting the 131st Infantry Brigade. Eighth Army deployed some 600 anti-tank guns and 400 tanks – sited in a series of hull down positions overlooking the approaching plain. The commander of one Anti-tank Gun Regiment, Colonel Parker advised the Guards Brigade, 'to pull back a good mile into broken ground that lay at the foot of the Edinburgh Castle.'[9] Behind the hill feature, the Eighth Army deployed a full Artillery Group with their Forward OPs used Edinburgh Castle heights to overlook the whole area.

Medenine: Battle summary and impact of terrain and doctrine

The Axis battlegroups also used the terrain to disguise their approach, which was made across difficult low ground in an attempt to confuse Eighth Army about their direction. From the 3 to the 5 March they began with minor probing attacks which confirmed the reports from Ultra that a large scale armoured assault was imminent. As the main assault began, Colonel Parker watched, 'the Germans drove blindly onto the anti-tank screen and lost 52 tanks without ours being engaged…the cryptanalysts had told us what was coming and when.'[10] Two Panzer Divisions advanced up to the Guards Brigade anti-tank guns and appeared to wander vaguely about in front of their position for sometime. Brigadier Kippenberger thought the Axis made a very badly coordinated attack as 10th Panzer Division approached his units and they appeared undecided about where to attack. The confusion of the German units was compounded by the New Zealander's use of the tactical terrain to create a concealed defensive position which was later praised as a model deployment.[11] The Guards and Highland Brigades had a more testing battle however all the Axis attacks were repulsed and 5th AGRA was personally thanked by the 7th Armoured Division for their fire support.[12]

British tactics were clearly improving as the Artillery support was well directed and planned, for example 64th Medium Artillery Regiment had a large number of defensive fire plans arranged and as the attacks intensified many concentrations of fire were put down including one regimental bombardment. It was noted that, 'the enemy did

8   Kippenberger, *Infantry Brigadier*, pp.271-272 and p.276.
9   IWM, Papers of Lieutenant Colonel M.E. Parker, CO of 257 AT Battery, Cat no. 479 p.167.
10   IWM, Papers of Lieutenant Colonel M.E. Parker.
11   Kippenberger, *Infantry Brigadier*, pp.273-274.
12   Denis Falvey, *A Well Known Excellence*, p.145.

not like the attention he was receiving from our guns,' and the attacks were directed at Pt 270 which, 'affords us some excellent observation.'[13]

Medenine: Conclusion

The terrain was significant in deciding how the Brigades deployed. They had made best use of the low hills for anti-tank and Infantry; while the Tajera Shrir hill behind provided the ideal observation post for artillery Ops.[14] The latter had registered defensive fire plans which were used extensively on the day. The 5th AGRA was praised for its vital support in bringing down large concentrations of fire where needed. The success of this battle boosted Eighth Army morale and their confidence in Montgomery, that he would always deliver a victory.[15] He had planned and dictated control of two defensive battles and an offensive one at Second Alamein, which increased his own confidence enormously.

The Eighth Army now received timely intelligence which had enabled it to deploy in suitable defensive terrain. The battle clearly demonstrated the progress in defensive doctrine, combining hull-down tank positions with well deployed anti-tank guns, all supported by heavy concentrations of artillery. At Medenine the Panzer assault had been decisively defeated in just one day, and was a clear defeat for the veteran Axis Divisions. Rommel ordered an immediate retreat after Axis forces lost 52 tanks out of 135, most of them the invaluable 'Specials', and 600 casualties for no gain. In comparison Eighth Army losses were said to be trifling.[16]

Mareth: Introduction

The battle for the Mareth line in late March 1943 was the first major offensive battle for the Eighth Army since Second Alamein. Codename Operation 'Pugilist', the planning for it was heavily influenced by the terrain features which dominated the defences. The strength of defences along the inland hill features, made Eighth Army HQ opt for an assault across the low ground near the coast. There are fewer studies about this latter part of the campaign, Rick Atkinson's recent study mostly focusses on the First Army's campaign from the Torch landings and is one of the most detailed. He argues that the final victory at Tunis was a strategic one which opened up the Mediterranean to the Allies but also useful for the tactical experience gained by the

---

13   TNA WO 201/2156. 8th Army Intelligence Summaries, Jan-Mar 1943. No.448, 6 Mar 1943.

14   This study is the first to note the importance of this feature within the Eighth Army's defence line.

15   Doherty, *A Noble Crusade*, p.125.

16   TNA WO 201/2156. 8th Army Intelligence Summaries, Jan-Mar 1943. No.450, 8 Mar 1943.

First Army.[17] Geoffrey Blaxland offers a dual assessment of the final campaign – of both the First and the Eighth armies as does David Rolf's more recent operational study.[18] As with earlier battles, Kippenberger's memoir provides some of the best details on New Zealand Corps operations, showing how they became highly skilled at combined arms assaults.[19] Two wartime accounts give some excellent details of the main battles; John D'Arcy Dawson's account defends the First Army operations, which have suffered some criticism,[20] while A.D. Devine provides similar aspects of American experiences towards Tunis.[21] Both are wartime published memoirs which note the terrain more readily than many post-war studies.

Montgomery now believed Eighth Army was 'balanced' and able to switch attacks quickly; it was growing in confidence in its doctrines. It had successfully advanced 1,400 miles in three months and had just defeated the last thrust to be commanded by Rommel before his departure from Africa. It was now ready to take on the ever strengthening defences in Tunisia. The Army arrived in front of Mareth on the 20 February.

From the west, First Army under General Anderson, was pushing into Tunisia along the few viable routes from the coast down into the central mountains. Both armies now operated under General Alexander's command as 18th Army Group.[22] First Army units had their own problems of fighting with in-experienced units, long supply lines whilst facing a determined enemy. On the northern flank, V Corps was being blocked by strong defences along the few usable approach routes.

Mareth: Terrain

The Tunisian landscape was a very different type of terrain for which Eighth Army had been used to in operations. The principle of capturing and controlling the high ground for artillery observation purposes remained a key objective. The landscape in the southern sector was semi-desert and contained fewer populated centres or passable routes, so Eighth Army clung to the coast for ease of re-supply. Any potential desert outflanking routes here were blocked by difficult or impassable terrain inland. The frontline was already nearly 200 miles from Tripoli, so the coastal plain remained ideal as the main area for operations. Further north the Tunisian coastal sector also

17   Rick Atkinson, *An Army at Dawn. The War in North Africa, 1942-1943* (London: Abacus, 2004), pp.537-540.
18   Gregory Blaxland, *The Plain Cook and the Showman. The First and Eighth Armies in North Africa* (Abingdon: Book Club Associates, 1977).
19   Kippenberger, *Infantry Brigadier.*
20   John D'Arcy-Dawson, *Tunisian Battle* (London: Macdonald & Co, 1943).
21   A.D. Devine, *Road To Tunis* (London: Collins, 1944).
22   TNA WO 201/598. 8th Army operations in Tunisia under 18th Army Group. Feb.-May 1943.

had to be occupied to capture the supply ports such as Sousse, the third largest of all the ports in Tunisia. The advance had to be maintained in this sector.

The southern Tunisia plain provided good going across mostly undulating or featureless ground which was frequently cut by deep wadis. The inland route was blocked by the Djebel Dahar hills through which there were few tracks. West of this line of hills was the Great Erg desert region, with twenty miles of shifting sand dunes which was impassable for most formations.[23] Southern Tunisia was divided from the central plains by a series of salt marshes or Chotts which left only one passable gap of twenty miles from the sea at the Wadi Akirit, and Gabes Gap. These salt marshes dried up quickly after May, but Alexander could not wait for the summer heat, and wanted operations to pass north of Gabes more quickly than this.

The Mareth line was sited between the coast and the dominating Matmata hills which were noted as, 'impassable for any large force [and which] ran back at right angles to the Mareth line, and more or less parallel to the coast for more than a hundred miles to the narrow Tebega gap.'[24] Axis Engineers had developed the old French defensive works which were sited behind two wide wadis. They had scarped the banks of the wadis into steep-sided anti-tank ditches. Above these the defences consisted of a series of strongly fortified positions running for twelve miles inland, from the northern end of the hills, across the plain to Mareth and Zarat near the coast.[25] They had added newly entrenched features consisting of concrete blockhouses, often lined with armour plate, although because of their larger calibre guns many new gun positions, were made to the rear of the concrete bunkers.

The two wadis made ideal natural anti-tank obstacles; the wadi Zeuss facing the British and behind the main wadi Zigzaou, had mostly rock slopes which had been scarped up to 20 feet deep. The wadis were up to sixty feet across, the heavy rains had waterlogged them and created streams eight feet deep, all of which created a formidable anti-tank obstacle. There were 19 miles of minefields and wire entanglements around nests of strongpoints each of which held up to half a battalion and were sited in defiladed areas to break up any advance across the wadis.[26] These fortifications were considered to be so strong by Alexander that only a full scale assault would breakthrough them.[27]

Axis commanders were also fully aware that behind the Mareth defences there was a possible inland route via the Tebaga Gap which outflanked the line and led to El-Hamma in the rear. The changes in terrain from mainly desert to much more hill country, also created a tactical change in Army reconnaissance, so that one of the LRDG's final tasks was to find a passable route to Tebaga and then to lead the New

23   TNA WO 201/578. Topography of Tunisia. Report by Eighth Army. March 1943.
24   Kippenberger, *Infantry Brigadier*, p.276.
25   TNA WO 201/598. 8th Army operations. Feb.-May 1943, p.2.
26   Playfair, *Mediterranean and Middle East. Vol IV*, p.332.
27   Barnes, *Operation Scipio*, p.6.

Zealand Corps around Mareth and enable it to drive in the Axis defence from this rear approach march.[28]

Mareth: Preparations

Eighth Army by this time, was described as being in 'peak condition, with a sick rate of only one in a thousand.' It was ordered to break through the Mareth defences, and destroy as much of Panzerarmee before it retreated to the Gabes gap which was considered to be another strong defensive position further back.[29] Preparations for the assault took a month because three Corps were involved and each required a large amount of supplies and ammunition to be brought forward from Tripoli which was just being re-established as a supply port. Half the troops planned for the assault were still 600 miles to the rear in Cyrenaica.[30] The Infantry divisions were also low on manpower, such as the 50th Division, which had received no reinforcements since Alamein whilst General Freyberg was cautious because the New Zealand reinforcements were limited by his Government and the 4th Indian Division only had two brigades. To limit the expected casualties, the initial attacks targeted the defences in the low lying sections near the coast to avoid being overlooked.

The plan, was codenamed Operation 'Pugilist', included a series of assaults along the line of defences, one by the 50th Division was supported by Valentine tanks. The attacks were preceded by a series of night attacks, Operations 'Walk' and 'Canter', to clear the advance positions, and these began on the 16 March, followed by the main assault in better weather on the 20 March. For this 151st Brigade would cross the wadi Zigzaou, supported by 50th RTR tanks. Further east the 69th Brigade would capture a position called the 'bastion' and 4th Indian Division would follow through and exploit beyond the bridgehead.[31] The whole attack was supported by sixteen regiments of Artillery with Engineers were brought up to clear the extensive minefields and deploy fascines to make an artificial causeway across the flooded wadi.[32]

Montgomery's strict methodology was to carefully build-up ammunition and supplies for the assault to support the elements of three Infantry Divisions for the frontal assault. At the same time he increased the forces available to 27,000 troops to form a separate New Zealand Corps. This formation had strong Armoured and Artillery support and was to move around the Matmata hills range, through a gap reconnoitred by the LRDG, and breakthrough to the Tebaga Gap to the coast, ideally

28   David Lloyd Owen, *Providence Their Guide. The Long Range Desert Group 1940-1945* (Barnsley: Leo Cooper, 2003), p.121.
29   Barnes, *Operation Scipio*, p.5.
30   TNA WO 201/598. 8th Army operations in Tunisia. Feb.-May 1943, p.2.
31   Richard Doherty, *A Noble Crusade. The History of Eighth Army 1941-45* (Staplehurst: Spellmount, 1999), p.126.
32   Large bundles of branches designed to fill ditches and take the weight of a tank rolling over them.

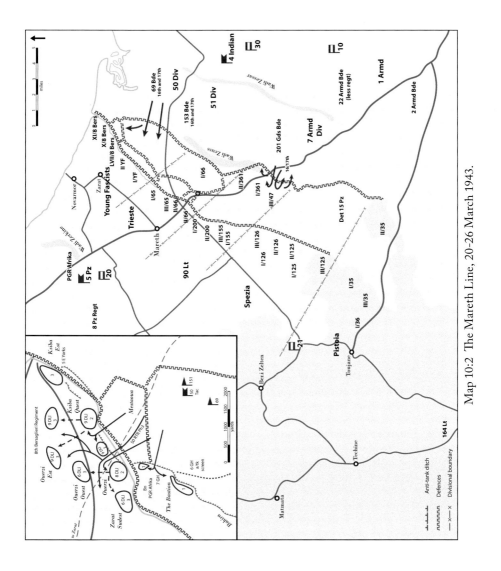

Map 10:2 The Mareth Line, 20-26 March 1943.

to block the retreat to the Gabes gap.[33] Alexander had moved some Free French units from First Army to west of the hills, but Montgomery stubbornly refused to acknowledge their usefulness in combat. Eighteenth Army Group was slowly linking up to shrink the Axis Bridgehead.

Mareth: Battle summary

The main assault included two Brigades assaulting different sectors of the defences. The 201st Guards Brigade assaulted the 'Horseshoe' feature with two battalions but suffered 40% casualties for almost no gain because of weak intelligence. The 69th Brigade made more headway and reached the wadi Zigzoau, but heavy rain prevented much of the supporting armour from crossing the waterlogged wadi. The artillery support was impressive but could not prevent the Axis firepower from crippling both armour and Infantry, struggling to cross the wadis. Fighting continued for two days and the Eighth Army was forced to withdraw after suffering heavy casualties for little gain.

Many of the failures were blamed by the Divisional commander Nichols, who went forward to urge on his troops and lost control of the battle. Manpower shortages had forced the old problem of committing an inexperienced unit to combat whilst there was a dearth of any detailed intelligence on the strength of the Axis position it was to attack. For the main assault the 50th Division crossed the broad Zigzaou, despite it being waterlogged and deep in mud, but was supported by a heavy barrage. Many men from one new unit, the 8th Durham Light Infantry, thought the assault would be 'a picnic', and took their objectives but with heavy casualties which left their morale shattered.[34] There were further delays with the assault because the Engineers had to clear gaps under heavy enfilade fire, while the tanks of 50th RTR and other support units were unable to get through because the only causeway became blocked by a sunken Valentine tank leaving the weakened Durhams isolated on the far side.[35]

The terrain delayed attempts to reinforce the main battle, the better Sherman tanks were too heavy for the causeway which left the weaker Valentines facing a determined, localised counter-attack by 15th Panzer Division, which heavily defeated 50th RTR and pushed the Durhams back to the edge of the wadi.[36] The wadi feature also delayed a fresh attack by British units trying to relieve the pressure on the beleaguered 151st Brigade. The Division spent the next two days in mopping up operations which were equally costly.

---

33   Playfair, *Mediterranean and Middle East. Vol IV*, p.320.
34   Ronald Lewin, *The Life and Death of the Afrika Korps*, (Barnsley: Pen & Sword, 2003), p.191.
35   Richard Doherty, *A Noble Crusade*, p.127.
36   The Regiment lost 30 tanks which left the Infantry with little support.

Montgomery was forced to revise his plans from the 23 March, and halted the main assault. The New Zealand Corps later turned the Axis line by its flanking move. It fought a separate battle to break-through the Tebaga gap and then El-Hamma to block the Axis position. [37] The long flank march had been dictated by the difficult terrain and by the its Commander, General Freyberg, being sure the Axis armour was committed to the Mareth line, leaving him free to deal with lighter forces at Tebaga. His attack was timed for a daylight assault because of the expected heavy air support from the RAF.[38] Further key heights at Tebaga were captured by the 25 March, again using constant heavy fighter-bomber support.

The British assault doctrine had developed into a successful combination of Infantry and supporting Armour where passable, clearing the high ground and hill features of enemy anti-tank guns, which allowed fresh Armoured Regiments to advance across the plain. Each hill position, once captured, enabled the Corps to 'unlock' the next position, though additional firepower being brought to bear on it. One of the combined assaults was made by 3rd RTR and 6th NZ Brigade, who captured the key Pt 201 which enabled the New Zealanders to outflank and capture Hill 184, which in turn undermined the defences on Pt 209.[39] This final height held out in a tougher battle and its subsequent capture finally broke through the Axis defences, 'We had seen the awe-inspiring sight of the hundreds of tanks of the 1st Armoured Division rolling in masses past the left of Pt 201 and on through the gap made by the attack.'[40] As the 1st Armoured Division advanced through the Gap, Axis units retreated under cover of a dust storm, and the smoke created by a heavy RAF bombardment. This assault had successfully outflanked the difficult Mareth line and this forced Panzerarmee to retreat to the next defensive position at the Gabes gap using the Wadi Akirit as its next important defensive position.[41]

Mareth: Conclusion

The assaults on the Mareth line proved that Eighth Army's doctrines were becoming well established in preparations, coordination with the tactical Air Forces and nearly always in combined arms. However, carefully sited Axis defences could still cause problems. At Mareth the attacks on the 'Horseshoe' position caused heavy casualties to two battalions of Guards.[42] Higher terrain features overlooked or enfiladed the wadis with well sited anti-tank and MG positions, which caused severe delays

37   Lewin, *Life and Death*, p.193.
38   Air Historical Branch, *Air Support*, (London: Air Ministry, 1955) p.78.
39   Patrick Delaforce, *Taming the Panzers. Monty's Tank Battalions, 3rd RTR at War* (Stroud: Sutton, 2003) p.146.
40   Kippenberger, *Infantry Brigadier*, p.274.
41   Barnes, *Operation Scipio*, p.8.
42   The Brigade suffered over 300 casualties mostly from the newly arrived 6th Grenadier Guards.

and heavy casualties to the assault units. The waterlogged wadi Zigzaou proved too much for either trucks or tanks to cross, leaving the forward infantry cut-off when counter-attacks occurred. Here then, localized Axis counter-attacks worked well in stopping the British advance. Terrain problems also affected the flank march, where deep sand made the going slow and difficult. The 27,000 strong column was also delayed by its sheer size and number of vehicles following a difficult route. Later on, positions on the Djebel Melab and Pt.209 delayed armour, but these were overcome when the experienced Maori Battalion captured them.[43] The New Zealand Division suffered fewer casualties at Tebaga, but its rifle companies were already understrength and they could ill-afford to lose men. The Italians suffered many losses and many fresh German troops quickly surrendered once they had received a taste of the heavy bombardments made by the concentrated artillery fire. The German 164th Division lost many killed in the heavy bombardments and a whole battalion which surrendered when cut off.[44]

Intelligence was also improving rapidly with Ultra being fed more quickly through to the 18th Army Group. However, in western Tunisia, there were still errors in interpretation by First Army commanders and their HQs.[45] Yet the Eighth Army also still made errors in planning and using poor intelligence, the frontal assault on the 'Horseshoe' was made in bright moonlight against a position protected by masses anti-personnel mines which crippled the attacking Guards Battalions, despite this they achieved their objectives but were too weak to hold them. The later, main assault also suffered from a lack of reconnaissance. The preparatory attacks were made during a period of heavy rain in which little air or ground reconnaissance was made or analysis conducted of the key defences.[46] The heavy spring rains were unfortunate and certainly created major problems maintaining the causeway across the wadi and left units cut off in the bridgehead.

The Eighth Army was seen as being more audacious in the offensive now and Montgomery made a bold move by switching to a left flank thrust. The Eighth Army commander was now considered a flexible and daring commander, but there were also errors in command which influenced the battle. The Corps commander, Oliver Leese, left the detailed planning to the more inexperienced Major-General Nichols at 50th Division. Following the breakthrough there was a confusion of orders between Horrocks and Montgomery which delayed the advance by the 10th Corps. When the delays were sorted out, an Axis rearguard defence prevented the leading units from exploiting the advance.

Doctrines were also gradually improving, with the heavier weight of the artillery bombardment providing close and timely barrages to cover the infantry assaults. The

43   Doherty, *A Noble Crusade,* p.130.
44   Kippenberger, *Infantry Brigadier,* p.289.
45   Gladman, *Intelligence and Anglo-American Air Support,* p.159.
46   Neillands, *Eighth Army,* p.197.

continuing heavy fire support contributed to the decline in morale of the defending Italian units who began to surrender in numbers after the 21 March. Similar mass surrenders later took place at the Wadi Akirit. The British Armour began fighting alongside new and more powerful 17pdr anti-tank guns which defeated a German counter-attack near El Hamma. This method of quick defence had been learnt from earlier German doctrine used since 1941. The 2nd NZ Corps now attacked on a narrow front towards El Hamma and was also heavily supported by an RAF bombardment of relays of medium bomber squadrons, who targeting the enemy defences and armour.[47] One onlooker noted, 'at 1600 hours…waves of Fighters – Kittyhawks, Hurricanes and Spitfires came in from the west, so that the Axis had the sun in their eyes'.[48] The RAF had become a more flexible fire-support option, to be called in as needed by a Ground Liaison Officer located within 8th Armoured Brigade, who directed the waiting fighter-bombers onto the Axis positions.

The assaults at Mareth and Tebaga represented a new phase in Eighth Army operations. Frontline units were depleted but had become highly experienced and who maintained good morale overall. They had improved equipment and doctrines for both attack and defence. The army had developed quite far since the retreats in 1941, and had learnt many lessons since Second Alamein. There was still a need to capture and hold key heights and this remained a significant issue on all operations. The breakthrough at Tebaga ensured the Mareth line was untenable and Axis forces retreated to the Gabes gap.

The Wadi Akirit, 6 April 1943

Operationally, General Alexander took direct control of the US II Corps to work more closely with the British to aid the breakthrough of the Gabes Gap onto the plains south of Tunis. This would enable the Allies to capture the vital airfields there. These would provide bases to give air support for the final capture of the Tunis-Bizerta bridgehead and threaten the ever narrowing Axis sea supply lines to Sicily.

The terrain defined the parameters of the battle for the Wadi Akirit. This feature ran the length of the Gabes Gap which was eighteen miles wide and was dominated by high ground behind the wadi. Five miles along the wadi was the 500 feet high Djebel Roumana, which was considered a superb artillery position and the Germans considered the wadi to be the strongest in North Africa. However Eighth Army's assault was still able to overrun within 24 hours.[49] Montgomery's noted, 'the enemy position was extremely strong, and he held all the observation areas.'[50] The Djebel

47   TNA WO 201/598. 8th Army Operations in Tunisia. Feb.-May 1943, p.8.
48   Falvey, *A Well Known Excellence*, p.148. Again using Axis tactics of having the sun behind the attacking units.
49   Falvey, *A Well Known Excellence*, p.149.
50   Brooks, (ed), *Montgomery and the Eighth Army*, p.197.

Roumana dominated the central sector, overlooking the flat plain on the British side of the wadi. This became a key objective against which both Armour and Infantry was committed. One of the attacking units was the 7th Argyll & Sutherland Highlanders, its CO described the ridge and Pt 112 as '… a huge brier of a hill, which…rose into an enormous, steep sided rocky lump, which was Roumana itself.'[51] Next there was more low ground before the desert left flank was dominated by a high,'massif' feature which needed to be taken. This reached 900 feet and was a complicated mass of gullies, escarpments from Pt 275 on the forward edges to the Djebel Fatnassa behind it.[52]

General Tuker noted that his plans for the 4th Indian Division pre-empted the main assault by, 'seize[ing] this area by first light, El Meida, Pt 275, El Aligh, and the scarps south-west of Pt 275…to enable us to reach out to the enemy's rear positions…and open up the whole position for exploitation by 10th Corps.'[53] He feared the attacks across the central plain by 51st Division and 50th Division would be overlooked and halted by Axis artillery observing from these heights if they were not captured quickly by daylight.

Akirit: Preparation

General Alexander wanted the Eighth Army to make the frontal assault on the wadi Akirit to clear the Gabes Gap whilst the First Army applied pressure in the rear of the Axis bridgehead. Some commanders thought a rapid assault might capture the position but Montgomery ordered 30th Corps to make a set-piece assault, and noted, 'I must attack quickly, before he[the enemy] has time to make the position too strong.'[54] Montgomery wanted two Divisions for the assault, the 51st and 4th Indian Divisions, with 2nd NZ Division and 8th Armoured Brigade exploiting afterwards, but Lieutenant-General Oliver Leese later inserted the 69th Brigade from 50th Division, to attack the centre low ground also.

The battle plan was heavily influenced by the terrain, when a reconnaissance by the two Divisional commanders forced the original plan to be altered so that 4th Indian Division would make a silent assault on the left flank high ground, before the main assault by the 50th Division went in. Christopher Mann has argued that this was an example of improved command decisions as the more experienced Divisional commanders were allowed to adapt the set-piece plan provided by Lieutenant-General Leese at 30th Corps HQ.[55] Eighth Army was becoming ever more flexible in its plan-

---

51   Barnes, *Operation Scipio,* Appendix G, Account of the 7th Bn Argyll & Sutherland Highlanders' part in the Battle of the Wadi Akirit. p320.
52   Rolf, *Bloody Road to Tunis*, p.200.
53   Tuker, *Approach to Battle*, p.320.
54   Brooks, (ed.), *Montgomery and the Eighth Army*, p.197.
55   Conference paper given by Dr. C. Mann (RMAS), *'Not what Pugilists call "good finishers": The Eighth Army's Command and conduct of operations in Tunisia March–May 1943.'* Symposium at Birmingham University, 14 November 2012.

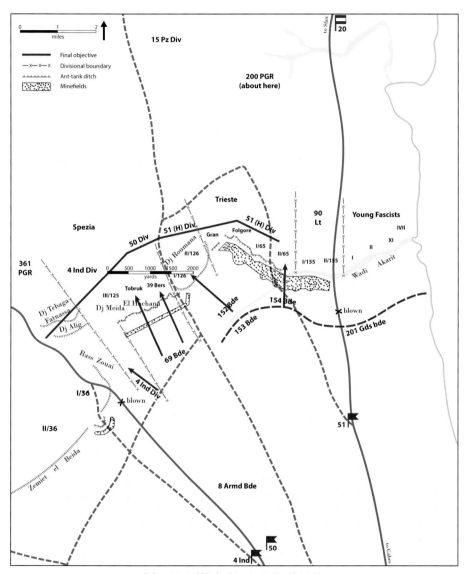

Map 10:3 Wadi Akirit, 6 April 1943.

ning and operations, also the Divisions were supported by much greater heavy artillery and air cover than before.

Montgomery thought that a different type of assault, using the no-moon period, would catch the Axis out, as it had not done before by Eighth Army.[56] A three Divisional assault appeared to be large scale, but the reality was that 4th Indian would assault the difficult hill positions on the left flank with elements of two Brigades while 50th Division used three Infantry battalions to attack the low ground. The 51st Division would attack both the Djebel Roumana and further east across the plain with just five battalions directly supported by two Armoured Regiments, the 22nd Armoured Brigade and the 5th AGRA. The combined Allied Air Forces continued to provide support against Axis ground targets.

The Axis defences were prepared quite quickly from the end of March, despite growing problems. The new CinC, General von Arnim had become dispirited by the growing lack of supplies getting through to Africa and thought the Italian units were, 'tired of war' with little remaining combat value.[57] The position itself was strengthened by 4,000 mines and wire entanglements and was held by three German battalions and elements of two Italian Divisions. Most of 15th Panzer Division was in reserve behind the position despite being weak in tanks and 88mm guns.[58]

Wadi Akirit: Battle summary

The attack opened with the 4th Indian Division's 1/2nd Gurkhas making a silent, night assault, which secured the key eastern high ground and enabled the 5th Indian Brigade to pass through and capture the vital El Meida height. In the centre, Medium Artillery Regiments fired an exceptionally heavy programme against enemy batteries and infantry strongpoints. In return the Axis defensive fire was thought to be very weak considering the excellent observation they had from the high ground.[59] The scale of the bombardment awed onlookers and supported the infantry attacks all day. The 51st Division Infantry made continued assaults on Roumana, despite extremely tough Axis fire captured Pt 112 by early morning which created two gaps for armour. The 69th Brigade assault suffered heavy casualties and was pinned down, but achieved some objectives with armoured support from 4th CLY.[60] Alistair Borthwick, a subaltern who went in with the 5th Seaforth Highlanders onto Roumana, noted how the crest-line was the vital objective, if the Army was to hold the southern side of the wadi in more security. His battalion had the difficult task of taking Pt. 198, considered to

56   Brooks, (ed.), *Montgomery and the Eighth Army*, diary entry for 5 April 1943, p.197.
57   Rolf, *Bloody Road to Tunis*, p.200.
58   Playfair, *Mediterranean & Middle East, Vol IV*, p.363.
59   Falvey, *A Well Known Excellence*, p.150.
60   Playfair, *Mediterranean & Middle East, Vol IV*, p.370.

be the key to the whole hill feature.[61] The unit lost 32 killed and 96 wounded from an already weak Infantry strength.

The Axis counter-attacked and committed their Panzer reserves to hold onto the Roumana heights with more infantry and pushed the 152nd Brigade off Pt 112 also so that the battle dissolved here into one of attrition for the heights. As the day wore on a units from the 69th Brigade and 5th Indian Brigade made breakthroughs on the lower hills, capturing El Hachana hill and 1,000 prisoners, which broke the Italian defences on the centre left, but the German commanders could do little and were frustrated because their reserves had been committed against the Roumana hills in the centre.

British doctrine now showed its ability to counter Axis moves with large numbers of RAF bombers and fighters, who disrupted any concentrations of enemy armour or troops moving against Eighth Army.[62] The failure of the Axis counter-attack, combined with 4th Indian Division capturing the high ground, forced the Axis commanders to consider whether to withdraw and by 7pm, 90th Light Division summarized that, 'The enemy has captured all the commanding features of the Akirit Line and thus brought about its collapse.'[63] General Messe, commander of First Italian Army, ordered his forces to retreat back to Enfidaville, the next dominant set of heights beyond the Goubellat plain, the Axis had at least 5,300 POWs taken whilst the Eighth Army lost some 1,289 casualties.

Wadi Akirit: Conclusion

The Army had shown flexibility in tactics and was able now to alter its doctrine, even at a late stage of the planning. The moon-less night aided the 4th Indian Division's silent assault on the massif, rather than waiting for the next full moon, when Axis forces expected the next assault. The high ground facing 4th Indian Division was the key to the main position, while the Djebel Roumana dominated the central sector and was also captured quickly or contested, as local counter-attacks forced 51st Highland Division off the crest-line in places and the Infantry suffered heavily fighting for these hill-top positions. The German commanders dutifully committed all their reserves to this point and so were unable to block further British moves by fresh battalions in the left-centre across the low ground.[64] The greater command controversy remains why Lieutenant-General Horrocks did not take advantage of the breakthrough created by 4th Indian Division and order his 10th Corps armour forward more quickly to trap the retreating Axis units.[65] First Italian Army was able to retreat across the

61   Alistair Borthwick, *Battalion. A British Infantry Unit's Actions from El Alamein to the Elbe, 1942-1945* (London: Bâton Wicks, 1994, first published in 1946) pp.85-87.
62   Barnes, *Operation Scipio*, p.246.
63   Playfair, *Mediterranean & Middle East, Vol IV*, p.374.
64   Barnes, *Operation Scipio*, pp.244-245.
65   Playfair, *Mediterranean & Middle East, Vol IV*, p.363.

Goubellat plain to the Enfidaville heights to participate in the final battles for the Tunis bridgehead.

Tunis: The final phase of the campaign

During the final phases of the campaign the Eighth Army had rapidly crossed the central Goubellat plain, to be halted by further Axis defences amongst mountainous features above Enfidaville. In the west it was dominated by the twin-peaked Kournine height, which was noted as being, 'too good an observation post to remain in enemy hands…Kournine was absolutely bare and after several attempts had been made to hold it we had to [retreat]. From adjacent hills artillery and mortar fire could be brought to bear on the crest…and under fire from guns further back.'[66] Many accounts have failed to note the significance of the ground and how it impacted on operations to such a degree. It was now an integral part of planning, objectives and doctrinal methods of overcoming difficult Axis defences. Nearby, the equally impressive sheer Takrouna heights were captured by a small platoon of veteran Maori troops who defeated a German force of nearly 200 men.[67] It dominated the plain from near Enfidaville, overall though the heights blocked further advances by Eighth Army.

Tunis: Preparation

The final Allied plans to break the Axis line were altered by terrain and also impacted on the doctrine of the final assault. The strength of the defences in the Kournine hills, made attacks by the New Zealand Division only partially successful, so Montgomery halted these having failed to secure the high eastern point of the Enfidaville ridge. This meant the Eighth Army could not thrust through the defile to Bou-Ficha, so Alexander switched fronts to make the final assault in the First Army sector, across more accessible ground.[68]

However this showed how flexible British forces were now quite formidable, under General Alexander's firm leadership, The 18th Army Group transferred 7th Armoured and 4th Indian Divisions over 100 miles across difficult terrain. This was achieved by these veteran units through good navigation across difficult lateral routes using 'wireless silence' they only needed just four days to prepare for the assault.[69]

The final assault represented an Army which now had confidence in its doctrines. It had the full support from the Allied Air Forces who added a powerful force multiplier in firepower and were able to neutralize enemy positions allowing Armour and

66   D'Arcy-Dawson, *Tunisian Battle*, pp.218-219.
67   Brian Horrocks, *A Full Life* (London: Collins, 1960) pp.162-163.
68   TNA WO 201/598.EIGHTH ARMY.8th Army Operations in Tunisia. 01 February 1943 – 31 May 1943, pp.16-17.
69   TNA WO 201/467.Seventh Armoured Division: operations leading to the capture of Tunis, 1 May-13 May 1943.

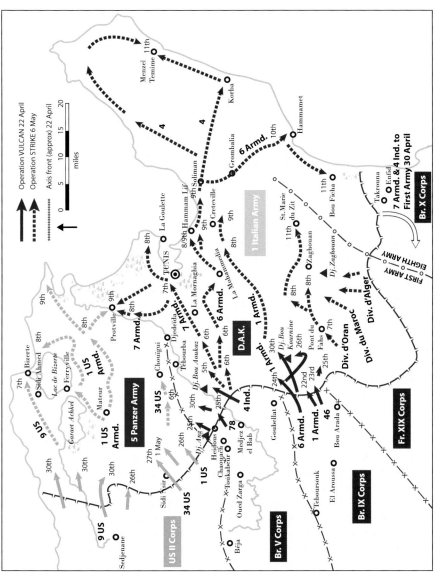

Map 10:4 The final assault on Tunis, 6-13 May 1943.

Infantry to reach and capture them quickly. The two Divisions combined with two experienced First Army Divisions for the final breakthrough assault into the Tunis-Bizerta bridgehead. 'Operation Strike' targeted Tunis itself rather than just capturing Axis hill positions on the outskirts.[70]

The plans were influenced by the terrain to be traversed, 'on May 2 all cmds [commands]…spent the day getting to know the country and gleaning as much information from it.' There was also a lack of time so the objectives were selected from maps, which highlighted that the, 'two dominating areas of high ground,' were the Djebel Achour and St Cyprien, which covered the main road into Tunis.[71] Typical of how efficient and experienced the HQs and commanders had only one day to prepare as the orders were issued on the 4 May and the assault began on the 6 May. The commanders were also confident as the first objectives were to be captured by 5am and two further ones by 7am, Horrocks said if they had been gained by the end of the day and the armour was at least forward on either flank, 'we shall have done well.' Yet both he and General Alfrey from the First Army remained confident they had the support and numbers to breakthrough.[72]

The doctrine was a repeat of the Tebaga Gap assault adapted to develop an attack with a two Divisional front with new heavy armour supporting each Infantry Divisions on a 3,000 yard frontage. This needed heavy fire support from over 400 guns because both Infantry Divisions had only two Brigades and the whole of the RAF resources were made available for the assault.[73] The superiority of the supply situation also showed how the First Army's supply situation had coped with additional units added to its operations. Other tactics used since Second Alamein also included a deception plan which used dummy tanks to confuse the Axis as to where the Armoured thrust would come from.

Tunis: Battle summary

The British forces now had a formidable and impressive assault doctrine and this was aided by the clearer weather from 5 May, which brought in waves of fighter-bombers who targeted any Axis defence positions. Allied bombers added weight to the Artillery bombardment and the Infantry had captured the high ground by mid-morning the following day. In a subsidiary assault, American forces finally opened up

---

70   Blaxland, *The Plain Cook*, p.248.
71   TNA WO 201/467.Seventh Armoured Division: operations, 1 May-13 May 1943, p.2-4. The 7th Armoured supported 4th Indian Division on the left and 6th Armoured supported British 4th Infantry Division on the right flank.
72   D'Arcy-Dawson, *Tunisian Battle*, p.231.
73   TNA WO 201/467.Seventh Armoured Division: operations, 1 May-13 May 1943.

the northern coastal route to Bizerte when they captured the twin positions – Green and Bald hills – by outflanking them.[74]

The British also had the flexibility to hold off weak Axis forces and not be deflected from the main assault. The Axis made insignificant counter-attacks which needlessly used up the latest powerful Tiger tanks (MkVIs) and other armour. The 81st Anti-Tank Regiment's new 17pdr anti-tank guns held them off and a further assault by just twenty Panzers, whilst 6th Armoured Division continued its main thrust towards Tunis. The main Axis counter-attack towards the 1st Armoured Division was also 'smashed' by waiting artillery.[75] The 15th Panzer Division was crushed by the weight of firepower and overwhelmed by the assault on the Masicault ridge. Their command structure crumpled and units withdrew towards Tunis.

There were still some issues though as the 4th Indian Division complained the armour was too slow in exploiting their success, but their advance remained a measured one for a time.[76] In comparison the 6th Armoured Division moved quickly forward some 20 miles ahead of the supporting Infantry, towards St-Cyprien which was another naturally strong defensive height. The tactical assaults were directed at the ridgelines as 1st RTR assaulted a final hill defence and overcame a few Panzers and numerous 88mm guns, the German forces now became demoralized and heavily outnumbered by British armour.

The final phases of the assault highlighted the combination of tactics being used by British forces; Scout cars moved from ridge to ridge, followed by armour on each flank, checking all likely defensive sites. Infantry in armoured carriers moved up steadily and more infantry in trucks occupied the hill positions.[77] When armour was stopped by enemy fire, medium artillery batteries were brought up which soon eliminated them, allowing the armour to move again. The Allied Divisions made their final dash into the city. The advance took two days with any sectors of stiff opposition being by-passed and left for units coming up behind.[78] The final operations continued with feint attacks which contained Axis units behind the frontline, directly contributed to the final surrender.[79] On the 7 May British Armour swept into Tunis just as US Forces entered a flattened Bizerte and Axis forces formally surrendered on the 13 May. They lost over 250,000 men as POWs, going into captivity. It was a greater defeat than Stalingrad had been five months earlier.

74   Blaxland, *The Plain Cook,* p.250. These two hill positions had blocked First Army for five months.
75   D'Arcy-Dawson, *Tunisian Battle,* p.233.
76   Rolf, *Bloody Road to Tunis,* p.261.
77   Blaxland, *The Plain Cook,* p.253.
78   D'Arcy-Dawson, *Tunisian Battle,* p.236.
79   TNA WO 201/598. Eighth Army Operations in Tunisia. 01 February 1943 – 31 May 1943, p.17.

Tunis: Conclusion

British doctrines had evolved into a formidable combination of attack and defensive tactics. They were complemented as both the Eighth and the First Army Divisions became more experienced in battle and were able to work together. The 18th Army Group had evolved to become a powerful fighting force in attack or defence with RAF fighter-bombers and Heavy Corps Artillery fire being called down onto the slightest opposition, which enabled the heavily armoured Churchill tanks to support the Infantry right into the Axis defensive positions.

The four battles discussed clearly show the increasing impact of the tactical terrain had on each battle and how doctrines were altered to take account of it. They enabled Eighth Army Divisions to develop their battle doctrines in attack and defence. Medenine was a clear improvement on tactics which had been first used at Alam Halfa, where good use had been made of defensive ridges and low hills, to deploy powerful combinations of anti-tank guns and armour, backed by massed artillery. The Mareth Line proved to be a tough frontal battle for the Eighth Army in poor weather conditions which contributed to the difficulties created by the tactical terrain and more powerful defences. The flexibility of the Army was shown by the successful flanking Corps which made a telling daylight assault on tactical hilltop positions using massed waves of bombers and heavy Artillery and Armour. The Wadi Akirit highlighted the flexibility of experienced units such as 4th Indian to alter from Montgomery's usual form of heavy assault to making a silent assault to ensure the capture of key heights. The main Infantry assaults were also directed at the central hill ridgeline and drew in the expected Axis counter-attacks which enabled fresh British Armour to break-through and outflank the defensive positions. The final assaults into Tunis specifically targeted high ground with combinations of tanks and infantry, heavy artillery and waves of bombers, all of which crushed Axis defences.

11

Other factors: British doctrine, training, equipment, command, and Intelligence

---

During the campaign in North Africa, British forces were also affected by factors including major changes to their doctrine; command and intelligence issues; supply problems and the difficulties of maintaining support from both the RAF and Royal Navy. British units made improvisations in both attack and defence doctrine between 1940 and 1943 and these were significant in deciding the outcome of operations. Command and intelligence issues were a key factor in the campaign and they remain a dominant feature within many studies. Supply influenced RAF and Royal Naval operations as they targeted the destruction of Axis supply routes, as being a more effective use of aircraft while the Mediterranean Fleet targeted the Libyan bound convoys. This chapter will look briefly at these issues and discuss some examples of their influence on the campaign.

The major changes in doctrine occurred at the tactical level, where tactics were developed on the battlefield through a series of improvisation due to the nature of the terrain, and operational need. The most striking example of this is the development and overuse of Jock Columns. The Motorised Battalions within each Armoured Brigade were meant to provide close support for the armour, and to act as a 'pivot group' on which the armoured regiments could manoeuvre. From March 1941 to October 1942, they nearly always fought separately as Jock Columns. This was an all-arms formation designed by the commander of 3rd RHA, Lieutenant-Colonel, (later Brigadier) J.C. 'Jock' Campbell. They were designed for both for reconnaissance and to harass enemy positions, and became a standard doctrine for the Infantry Brigades holding the line and often within major operations up to late 1942. The formation provided intelligence, weakened enemy positions and enabled to overcome the need to disperse units often along a front line which was too long to hold by the available units.

They commonly consisted of a company of Infantry, one battery or troop of artillery and platoons of three Bofors AA and 2pdr AT guns for defence. The dispersal of Artillery batteries deployed amongst Jock columns quickly resulted in an equal dispersal of their firepower, rather than retaining them for larger Regimental firing. Even when batteries fired at high rates, they could not replicate the density of shelling a regiment of twenty-four guns could produce. This formation was assumed to be effective in engaging the enemy. However, the experience of some columns highlighted weaknesses in relentlessly using this formation. Lieut-Colonel Roscoe from 1st Rifle Brigade clearly warned about their lack of effectiveness when the column lost 40% of its vehicle strength due to the near impassable going and a lack of petrol.[1] The dunes and soft going near the Wadi Feragh ruined truck engines and suspensions, leaving Jock Columns short of vehicles. Signalling problems caused them to lose contact their supply echelons and so they also lost fuel and ammunition. When these occurred at times of enemy pressure these problems quickly emasculated the Columns and left them with little option but to retreat.

In the summer of 1941 the 7th Support Group used Jock columns continuously and during the Battleaxe offensive they were assigned a flank role. In November during Crusader, the Group later deployed Jock columns against the flanks of the Panzergruppe, where their attacks influenced Rommel's decision to retreat from the battle.[2] Auchinleck believed they were the way forward for offensive tactics, although he was also influenced by the mixed performance of the Armoured Brigades, which had suffered tremendous losses for little gain during Crusader. The Artillery's 25pdr gun proved to be a weapon capable of knocking out Axis armour at a longer range than the tank's 2pdr could engage at, so that Jock Columns were used throughout the Spring of 1942 as the Eighth Army sought to dominate 'no-man's land' in front of Gazala.

The limited success of some Jock Column activity masked their inherent weakness. In March, the newly arrived 50th Division targeted two airfields at Martuba and Tmimi which successfully diverted Luftwaffe operations away from a vital Malta convoy. At Gazala after the British armoured defeat, the Free French Brigade Jock Columns still attacked Axis supply units and harassed the Panzerarmee as it approached Tobruk. Despite the defeat at Gazala, Auchinleck's advisor, Major-General Eric Dorman-Smith, still emphasized his ideal 'battlegroup' which consisted of two companies of Infantry, one battery of artillery and supporting AA and anti-tank guns, in other words another Jock Column. He wanted an Infantry division of three brigades, to deploy into nine of these new 'battle groups'. He had effectively discounted armour as the primary strike force.[3]

A few days later at Matruh, the British centre was held by just two Jock Columns, which were quickly overrun and enabled the Axis battlegroups to drive onto Alamein. During First Alamein, one enterprising New Zealand commander deployed a more powerful column based around a full Regiment of Artillery with four troops of

1   IWM, Papers of General Briggs. RB2/5. Roscoe to 2ndArmd HQ, April 1941.
2   Clifford, *Crusader,* p.109.
3   National Army Museum. 2009-17-12-01. Report by E.Dorman-Smith, June 1942.

anti-tank guns for defence which trebled its offensive firepower.[4] Montgomery finally ended their use a month later, as he imposed his new Divisional doctrine and training programme upon the Eighth Army, in readiness for Operation Lightfoot.

At the tactical level, armoured units were influenced by key terrain features which affected their doctrinal planning, training and operations. The threat of air attack and a lack of cover also caused vehicles to be more dispersed whilst moving and operating in units, and led to demands for improved equipment, such as tanks with better guns and improved armour. Consequently the Army received successive deliveries of new equipment which brought its own problems of coordination and re-supply of parts and ammunition which also altered the way armour, infantry and the artillery fought the enemy. The lack of armour forced commanders to use their artillery and infantry more offensively from the beginning of hostilities. The improvised new tactic of Jock columns, combined with the practice of dispersion created a different mind-set amongst many commanders.

From late 1942 onwards the new commander General Montgomery made the first successful reorganisation of the Eighth Army, which contributed to its improved operational performance from Second Alamein to the end of the campaign. He gave the Army a renewed focus in training and operations which contributed to an improved morale and confidence in its abilities so that by February 1943, the Eighth Army assaults were fully backed by massive Air support and concentrated Artillery fire support, which commanders recognized as a vital part of the assault and break-in phases. Combined arms became a standard again and the tactics of attack and defence were more focussed and supported by better weaponry were concentrated into standard doctrines, but with elements of flexibility needed for changing situations. This finally overcame issues of too much dispersal of units or firepower, which had been prevalent for so long. These new tactics would continue to develop and be used by the British Army in future campaigns.

Attack and defence doctrine

During early engagements, individual Armoured Regiments developed their own improvised methods of operating to overcome the dispersed nature of desert warfare. Cyril Joly noted how, in five weeks on patrol, his troop, 'evolved certain simple drills which covered most of the troop's tactics…We all acquired a great deal of confidence in…and made ourselves into a really effective fighting unit.'[5] Following this, armoured assaults became more separated and consisted of closing with the enemy, in order to bring their 2pdr main gun into effective range. A lack of HE shell for this main gun also affected the ability of tank crews to deal with enemy artillery

---

4   http://nzetc.victoria.ac.nz/tm/scholarly/tei-WH2Arti-c10-1.html. NZ Official History online version, accessed 12 March 2011.
5   Joly, *Take These Men*, p.25.

and anti-tank weapons at longer ranges. By the end of 1941, during Crusader, the Cruiser armoured experience was a mixture of separate Brigade actions which highlighted their doctrine. Typical of this was 3rd RTR, who in one action 'formed line for an attack which went in...the sqn was then encircled and it became a race to escape the circle.'[6] In the immediate aftermath of Crusader, armoured combat was accepted as, 'largely a matter of columns of all arms...over large distances... widely separated.'[7] Yet in reality the use of combined arms was rare, but actions by Regiments or Brigades had become more widely dispersed, and so they lacked the ability to support each other.

Some effective assault doctrines were practiced during Operation Compass. Here the Infantry made prepared assaults either led by or followed up by support 'I' tanks and artillery, which worked well. Yet by the summer of 1941, during Battleaxe, assaults were being directed at too many terrain features as objectives, which were spread over too wide an area. The armour should have co-operated more closely with attached artillery but this was viewed as an 'area weapon' and assumed to be not effective against well dug-in gun positions.[8] In the same period of build-up towards Crusader, the Armoured Brigades received the new training manual, *Middle East Training Pamphlet 2* (or METP No.2), which confirmed that the key Armoured Regimental doctrine was to attack.

Another problem was the suggested best practice versus the reality of combat; Lieutenant-Colonel 'Pip' Roberts of 3rd RTR, noted that great stress had been placed upon fighting as a Brigade, 'but when it came to operations each Regiment was sent off to conduct its own battle.[9] Even the Armoured Brigades were being dispersed into individual Regimental battles. Before Gazala in May 1942, he noted that, 'Days [were] spent selecting Brigade hull down positions from which they would fight.'[10] However, when the Axis finally advanced on the 27 May, 3rd RTR just failed to reach its allotted position in time and was forced to fight isolated from its fellow Regiments and in the open, with predictable casualties. His fellow regiments also suffered with 5th RTR and 8th Hussars being caught moving out of their night-time leaguers and were both heavily mauled. The result of the actions were that the Armoured Brigades were quickly reduced in strength and suffered serious losses of tanks and experienced crews.

During the middle phases of the campaign, some attempts were made at combined arms assaults once again. At Gazala, during Operation Aberdeen, the assault by the

6   Bovington. 3rd RTR Diary, *'Account of C Squadron's action received from Capt. C.B. Joly.'* 17 Dec 41.
7   TNA WO 201/450. Cyrenaica: Lessons from Operations. Nov.1941- Mar 1942, No.2, Armoured Tactical Notes, 10 Dec 41.
8   Joly, *Take These Men*, p.45.
9   Bovington Archives. 3rd RTR Diary. *'Some notes on Knightsbridge battles after conversation with General Roberts (who commanded 3rd RTR there)*, p.2.
10   Bovington. *'Some experiences of an Armoured Regimental Commander.'* Pip Roberts, p.2.

32nd Army Tank Brigade on the Sidra Ridge was a complete failure. Major Tatum of 42nd RTR, noted, 'we came first under enemy artillery fire which had no effect on the tanks but a considerable effect on the lorry-borne infantry.'[11] Elsewhere the main assault took place south-east of the Sidra Ridge when the 22nd Armoured advanced with two Indian Infantry Brigades from 5th Division into the Axis held 'Cauldron'. The armour was quickly separated from the Infantry, suffered heavy losses and retired leaving two dispersed Infantry Brigades across the depression and adjacent ridgeline with its artillery spread across the whole area, but unable to give effective supporting fire. These separated Brigades and Regiments were all overrun by rapid Axis counter-attacks, because they were divided and unable to support each other.

By the autumn of 1942, the new Eighth Army Commander, General Montgomery ordered a large scale training programme for Operation Lightfoot. Battle drills became more standardized and there was a strong combined arms approach, utilizing massed artillery support.[12] During First Alamein Infantry, such as the 2nd NZ Division had suffered from poor cooperation with supporting armour so that Freyberg demanded that an Armoured Brigade was now directly attached to the Division for Lightfoot. By 1943, the Eighth Army was much more confident of its battle doctrines against difficult Axis positions. One of the main developments was its flexibility and the capacity to try a different approach. At the operational level, the flank move around the Mareth line was a good example, quickly flowed by tactical changes further north.[13] Equally at the Wadi Akirit, some variations in tactics were used, including attacking under a 'no-moon' period, but the build up still took six days to stockpile the necessary artillery ammunition for the other assaults. Here training was considered unnecessary as, 'the plan of attack was simple and after the customary fashion.'[14] The Army had developed a well versed doctrine of assault, the full development which as seen during the final operation on the Tunis bridgehead in May 1943. The plan of attack was designed by General Alexander and made full use of an Artillery Corps and nearly 1,200 aircraft in direct ground support to a four Division assault. British doctrine had developed a long way from the modest Regimental and Brigade levels of 1941.

Early commentary in local training and procedural orders on defensive doctrine called for the importance of keeping dispersed formations cohesive as defensive positions became over extended while trying to block off the open desert flank. By May 1942 Infantry Brigades were deployed separately in Brigade box defences. The Eighth Army commander General Ritchie re-defined defensive doctrine using a combination

---

11   Bovington Archives. 42nd RTR Diary. Letter by Major J.W.G. Tatum.
12   Bovington Archives. 3rd RTR Diary. '3 R.Tanks. Directive No. 5. Battle Drill'.
13   TNA WO 201/598. Eighth Army Operations in Tunisia under 18th Army Group. Feb.-May 1943.
14   TNA WO 201/598. Eighth Army Operations in Tunisia under 18th Army Group. Feb.-May 1943.

of fortified positions and armoured counter-attacks.[15] An interesting view on this desert tactic was made by the newly arrived 50th Division who noted that the Brigade box frontages were very wide and had to be held irrespective of an Axis breakthrough.[16] In theory these boxes should have been self-sufficient for three weeks, however the experience of the Gazala battle proved that very few Brigades could hold out for more than a few days or perhaps ten days with re-supply.

The boxes proved to be too weak because they were often sited too far apart and became vulnerable when Axis units seized high ground which overlooked them; the position held by 150th Brigade near the Trigh Capuzzo, was overlooked by higher ground, 'with a perimeter of twenty miles [and] was isolated from its fellow 69th Brigade by a gap of six miles. The position was too big for three battalions, uncompleted and very hard to defend in the rear. Yet it was obvious that the Germans would cut off this position and attack it in the rear.'[17] The defensive posts would be systematically targeted by artillery and anti-tank guns, which undermined the British defence and made a longer fight almost impossible to carry on. The expected counter-attacks by Cruiser Armoured Regiments were either too weak, or were held off at a distance, whilst the Box was steadily destroyed. Ritchie's tactic needed some re-thinking.

Training

Recent studies on British Army training during the Second World War have highlighted different aspects which affected the Army's performance. These include the conservative nature of the military hierarchy and the different backgrounds of the men who made up the 'citizen army' from 1941.[18] Tim Moreman notes the rapid expansion of forces which created a 'training deficit' in the Middle East. GHQ issued training pamphlets from autumn 1941 which emphasized that mobile warfare needed specialized training.[19] New Training Schools were established to aid the new personnel and Regiments arriving in the desert, but despite the expanded numbers of Schools by GHQ, for different arms, Regiments noted there was a lack of actual training actually carried out.

Therefore it was still quite common for fresh units, with higher proportions of inexperienced troops, to be committed to operations without sufficient training or knowledge of how best to operate. The huge increase in citizen-soldiers created

---

15   TNA WO 201/538. Eighth Army: Lessons from Operations, Sept 1941-Aug 1942. GHQ. Fixed Defences and the Defensive Battle, 26 May 42, p.1.
16   Clay, *The Path of the 50th*, p.50.
17   Clay, *The Path of the 50th*, p.51. It was also 10 miles south to the Free French Box at Bir Hacheim.
18   Tim Harrison Place, *Military Training in the British Army 1940-1944. From Dunkirk to D-Day* (London: Frank Cass, 2000), French, *Raising Churchill's Army*.
19   Moreman, *Desert Rats*, pp.36-37.

high numbers of in-adequately prepared units being sent out to the Middle East.[20] Individual Brigades and Regiments were committed with no time to practice local doctrines for combat or any sort of best practice. This left a succession of new units who either would 'sink or swim' once thrust into combat. During Crusader, the 22nd Armoured Brigade was rushed into action at Bir-el-Gubi, and quickly suffered heavy losses, whilst at Gazala, the newly arrived 5th Indian Division commander had to plan Operation Aberdeen in one afternoon and the Division was committed to the assault the following day. Most infamously at First Alamein, the recently arrived 23rd Armoured Brigade was committed hastily to an advance which failed with terrible losses.

For Operation Compass, the more experienced 4th Indian Division still trained hard for the impending assaults and practiced attacks against full scale replicas of the camps at Tummar and Nibeiwa to maximize success.[21] This training method does not appear to have been fully repeated until the six weeks training implemented by Montgomery before Second Alamein in the autumn of 1942. GHQ tried to pass on the lessons of combat for newly arrived formations but these documents took time to come through. The Lessons about the first Cyrenaican campaign were written by General O'Connor before his capture in April 1941, but the Training pamphlet, *Notes from the Theatre of War (NTW)*, on Libya, did not appear until early 1942, with NTW No.6 relating to armoured experiences during Crusader against German forces. During Gazala, General Ritchie thought that newly arrived Armoured Regiments did not have the training to be effective in combat and so the crews were forced to hand over their fresh tanks to exhausted crews from the depleted frontline units. He appears to have lost confidence in the ability of untried Armoured Regiments to win against the more experienced Axis battlegroups.

Auchinleck made an assessment of the Army following his arrival in July 1941 and laid down some principles of training and doctrine before any further offensive was undertaken.[22] By September the same year, GHQ had issued the first Middle East Training Pamphlets or METPs, with titles including, *'Tactical Handling of Armoured Divisions'* which became the basis for future doctrine.[23] They provided officers with details on how to operate in the desert, but whether they were actually used is more difficult to ascertain. The *METP No.2*, for Army Tank Brigades stipulated the use of combined arms assaults with Infantry, but the notes on defence practice was a much lower priority, with far fewer comments.

By May 1942 Auchinleck again reiterated that training was of the first importance and his report defined areas in need of training. However, the Axis offensive began

20   Fennell, *Combat and Morale in the North African Campaign,* pp.220-221.
21   TNA WO 201/2691. Operational reports: First Cyrenaican Campaign. Sept 1940-Feb 1941, p.3.
22   TNA PREM 3/285 Auchinleck's Despatch covering the period 5th July to 31st October 1941
23   MLRS, *Middle East Training Pamplets*, Vol I, (Buxton, Derbyshire, 2011).

two weeks later and only relatively low numbers of troops had been processed through the new Training Schools.[24] Experienced formations returned to the Eighth Army in the autumn of 1942, including the 9th Australian Division which had undergone intense training in Lebanon and was considered 'battle-ready' by October.[25] The experienced 2nd NZ Division also continued full scale rehearsals, training over similar ground and using live minefields and ammunition to make the practice as realistic as possible. The Engineers were a vital part of the break-in assault now and trained to clear gaps in the deep mine-belts, to enable the Armour and Infantry to pass through.

In the latter stages of the campaign, the advance to Tripoli left little time for training for the Army. As it drew close to the Axis defences along the Mareth line, Montgomery held a study week for new officers to learn from the more experienced frontline units. General Patton attended but many other Divisional Commanding Officers sent their Staff Officers instead.[26] This may have showed that they felt more confident of their new doctrines, even though later combat experience would develop these further in the final assaults in Tunisia.

Command and Intelligence

Command – either the abilities of different commanders in the field, or their key decisions and intelligence made available – were key factors which directly influenced operations for both sides in the campaign and some of the main issues will be discussed briefly here. The influence of Churchill on operations in North Africa has been widely noted and debated in numerous studies as he interfered in many aspects of operations. He often used raw decrypts from Ultra to make his decisions, pushed his commanders for action and sent them barrages of telegrams.[27] He sacked Wavell after the failure at Battleaxe and later on sacked Auchinleck for losing Tobruk, which was regarded as a political loss as well as a part of a heavy military defeat for Eighth Army.[28] Churchill's harassment and sacking of his successive Middle East Chiefs and other Generals has in some views, diverted a proper analysis of their command abilities in the field, but it contributed to command decisions then made during operations.[29]

The changes in commanders prevented good working relationships developing in HQs, whilst a cumbersome Command structure also contributed to problems in frontline operations, where multiple layers of bureaucracy often created slower reaction times. British commanders often operated from rear areas with patchy communications, which slowed down reactions to fast moving situations, In June 1941

---

24   TNA WO 201/532. Eighth Army: Commanders conferences. 1941 Dec.-1942 May. Notes on Training conference held at GHQ, 10 May 42.
25   Dornan, *The Last Man Standing*, p.60 and p.135.
26   Rolf, *The Bloody Road*, p.118.
27   Bernard Fergusson, *The Trumpet in the Hall* (London: Collins, 1970), p.98.
28   Victoria Schofield, *Wavell Soldier & Statesman* (London: John Murray, 2006) p.150.
29   Correlli Barnett, *The Desert Generals* (London: Castle Books, 2000) pp.78-79.

Beresford-Pierce commanded from sixty miles behind the lines using poor radio equipment. Other commentators have argued that British failures were caused by weak British Command methods combined with signalling failures, whilst David French argues that the British command structure was too cumbersome and this exacerbated operational and tactical errors.[30] These factors were obviously crucial at times, though also operational distances due to the scale of the desert theatre were having an impact adding to the technical problems which caused communication failures.

The impact of Intelligence

In North Africa intelligence had a direct impact on operations and good quality intelligence was crucial to success for all levels of command and planning. Most notably it successfully directed the RAF onto Axis supply routes and their battle against the convoys was a major victory for the analysts.[31] During the ground operations it contributed to tactical successes including the approach marches made during Compass and Crusader, the defensive preparations at Alam Halfa and Medenine and the preparations for Second Alamein. As Intelligence improved analysis of terrain became a standard part of all weekly reports to Army HQ.

Ultra Intelligence provided partial information on Axis movements and unit strengths and was more useful for analysis as it was often out of date which meant some Army commanders were often reluctant to use it.[32] The reports confirmed what actions had recently taken place rather than what was about to happen along with analysis of aircraft numbers and types.[33] It was most effective in targeting Luftwaffe enigma, and by late March 1941 it had a breakdown of strengths and deployment of the Fliegerkorps in Libya.[34] Delays were common because of the time taken to make an appreciation or analysis of the data from London. The volume of messages decoded daily averaged around 50 and increased to 250 per day by April 1941, meant there was a delay in getting information out to the Middle East.[35] Army intelligence was being read effectively by May 1942, but as this coincided with the crisis following Gazala, better use was not made of it until First Alamein and after.

Some operations were influenced by tactical intelligence failures and Commanders made errors because they lacked time to analyse the reports. Wavell admitted an error in his appreciation about Axis forces arriving in Cyrenaica, whilst shortly after

30   John Robert Ferris, *Intelligence and Strategy, Selected Essays* (Oxford: Routledge, 2005) pp.200-238, and French, *Churchill's Army*, p.239.
31   Gladman, *Intelligence and Anglo-American Air Support*, p.180.
32   Hinsley, *British Intelligence. Vol I*, p.398.
33   TNA HW 13/1, G.A.F. Intelligence summaries. Summary of Naval Intelligence, CX/JQ, 10.4.41
34   TNA HW 13/1, Intelligence summaries based on sigint: G.A.F. Activity in the Central Mediterranean, 31.3.41.
35   Hinsley, *British Intelligence. Vol I*, p.195.

2nd Armoured Division HQ wrongly interpreted RAF reports which contributed to confusion during the First retreat. Commanders failed to appreciate the arrival of 15th Panzer Division at the front during Battleaxe, and reasons for the Second Retreat from Cyrenaica in 1942 was famously blamed on Jock Whitely, the Eighth Army's Intelligence Chief, in his not allowing for the arrival of fresh tanks at Benghazi.

The arrival of the Germans in Libya created a sudden increase of material to de-cipher. Army codes relating to the Panzergruppe were broken occasionally from this time and not fully until later in May 1942. Analysts often needed time to develop the art of writing a coherent signal useful to commanders.[36] Decrypts of Axis armour strengths on the Libyan border also contributed to Wavell ordering Operation 'Brevity' in mid-May. Army enigma was initially broken in September 1941, and then read only intermittently until April 1942, which gave HQs an incomplete analysis of Axis plans up to the actual offensive began.[37]

Air reconnaissance concentrated on the Italian Air Force but later also provided intelligence for Operation Compass.[38] Signals listening or 'Y' services had problems of using different methods of interception, analysis and interpretation. In early 1941 the Army Y service was struggling to understand German signals which used enigma while Italian units had begun to improve their signals security.[39] During Crusader daily flights by the Strategic Reconnaissance Unit (SRU) carried out aircraft spotting tasks at each of the main Libyan airfields, along with ships at Benghazi and columns of motor transport (MET) on the main Cyrenaican routes. All of this information was sent back to the HQ as targets for fighter-bombers and Wellington night bombers.[40] It had limitations though, when in August 1942, despite good air superiority, the RAF could only offer reconnaissance flights for one Army Corps front because of limited RAF fighter protection.[41] By comparison in 1943, the Wadi Akirit was monitored from mid-March by photo reconnaissance on a daily basis which provided the Eighth Army with much more effective intelligence on the defensive positions.[42] As back in the UK for D-Day, it took time to develop good analysts of the intelligence received.

Reconnaissance units, principally the Long Range Desert Group (LRDG) mapped large areas of the desert and possible routes for future operations. They also carried out raids on Axis airfields and bases to contribute to the strategic war on Axis supply and air support, but their primary role was reconnaissance. From September 1941 they began the road-watch along the coast road west of El Agheila, which became one

36   Bennett, *Ultra and Mediterranean Strategy*, p.27.
37   Hinsley, *British Intelligence*, Vol I, pp.391.
38   Air Historical Branch, *The Middle East* Campaigns. *Vol I*, p.65.
39   Gladman, *Intelligence and Anglo-American Air Support*, p.43.
40   TNA WO 201/363. 'Air Operations. Operation Crusader.' 1942, p.5.
41   TNA Air 23/1751. War Diary Monthly, July-August 1942, 285 Wing to 211 Group, 27/8/42.
42   TNA WO 201/2156. Intelligence Summaries. Jan-March 1943; report No.456, 16 March 43, p.2.

of the most useful long term intelligence sources for GHQ.[43] Intelligence gathering was developed to include improving knowledge of the terrain as well as enemy units, so that it became a part of the weekly summaries at Army HQs. The local, tactical knowledge was better provided by the Y service, Reconnaissance and Forward OPs who constantly observed the Axis positions and noted their intentions more readily. Intelligence was vital but could not always guarantee success in battle, too often there were gaps in the knowledge, or delays in communication, so that units had little information about enemy positions or strengths.

Axis Command and Intelligence gathering was directly influenced by the dynamic leadership of General Erwin Rommel, the continuation of the campaign was clearly influenced by the decisions and plans of this able commander, which have been discussed in numerous biographies and studies of Axis forces, perhaps to the detriment of studies about Italian forces and commanders. Successive Italian commanders found that he soon dominated operational control of the fighting. Italy showed its commitment to the campaign by bringing in General E. Bastico, in July 1941, however Rommel largely continued to ignore Italian orders if they disagreed with his own plans and he remained in an almost constant state of disagreement with them.[44] Rommel was a maverick commander who often challenged the chain of command above him. In 1941 he convinced the Italian CinC General Gariboldi to give him full command of the frontline units and used his ambiguous orders to take advantage of the British halt at Agheila in 1941.[45] Ultra decrypts noted orders from two different higher HQs by the end of May 1941 but could not read and therefore appreciate how Rommel's continual by-passing of them to Hitler allowed him to carry on.[46]

At the operational level the doctrine of 'Command by directive' or Vollmacht, allowed commanders on the spot to use whatever forces were available to achieve their objectives. It was standard throughout the German Army and perhaps explained Rommel's style of command,[47] although, at least three of his extended advances are similar to his most successful advance which he made as an Infantry commander during the First World War.[48] In April 1941 Halder thought Rommel had 'gone mad' after his advance across Cyrenaica and the hasty attacks made on Tobruk and British intelligence was often misled when they assumed that Rommel would obey orders. Rommel was physically and mentally tough and believed a commander should set an example to his men, often taking command of Battle groups in action and

43   PRO, *Special Forces in the Desert War 1940-1943*(London: PRO Publications, 2001), pp.76-77.
44   TNA PREM 3/285. Gen. Auchinleck's Despatch, Jul.-Oct 1941, p.14.
45   Kitchen, *Rommel's Desert War*, p.55.
46   TNA HW 13/1, Intelligence summaries based on 'sigint': German Code names in Africa, 30.5.41, p.
47   Megargee, *Inside Hitler's High Command*, pp.7-8.
48   Erwin Rommel, *Infantry Attacks* (New York: Fall River Press, 1990).

making key decisions on the spot.[49] His appearance at key points of the fighting often converted difficult situations into localized successes or stabilized disordered units. Rommel was an expert operational commander who understood tactical situations and recognized defeat as well as success. He quickly called off the attacks at Alam Halfa and Medenine when he realized the strength of Allied forces opposing him. Barnett considers Rommel's major strategic success was to turn the campaign from minor defensive role into a major land campaign that absorbed much of the British war effort in the early years.[50] Questions may still remain about his abilities as a higher level commander, but his impact on the campaign was significant.

Supply

British strategy initially focussed on keeping Egypt as a base of operations to hold the Middle East.[51] Some argue that the huge resources committed by Britain and later the USA were a key factor in the final Allied victory compared to the limited resources committed by the Axis.[52] However, even during Crusader and Gazala when the army was very well equipped, British forces failed to decisively defeat the Axis.

The ports of Tobruk and Benghazi, along with their adjacent airfields, became the focus of British objectives in 1941 and 1942. After the first British advance across the province, however, planners realised that units should not over-reach themselves logistically by advancing too far.[53] Prior to Gazala, the Eighth Army assessed the coast road as the most viable route supply route forward saving over a day's journey on the desert route. However, air attacks meant that the Mechili/Msus route or a journey by sea became preferable. Although Benghazi had a capacity of 45,000 tons per month, Luftwaffe raids made it particularly untenable for British units in spring 1941 and January 1942. Tobruk had a capacity of about 40,000 tons per month, but realistically only unloaded 18-20,000 tons. It was noted by the British as being the best deep water anchorage between Alexandria and Tunisia although the port was found to be less than ideal because of the time lost by units collecting supplies from the scattered depots around the base.[54]

The railway line to Mersa Matruh was another vital British supply route. It was extended to Belhamed for the Crusader offensive where it significantly aided British operations and an improved water supply was extended adjacent to the railway to enable operations for up to two Corps,[55] which supplied water for both the locomotives

49   Lewin, *Rommel As Military Commander*, p.243.
50   Barnett, *Hitler's Generals*, p.315.
51   Butler, *Grand Strategy Volume II*, p.306.
52   Bungay, *Alamein*, p.42.
53   TNA WO201/2691. Operational reports: 13th report, p.15.
54   TNA WO 201/418. Crusader supply report, Admin. Nov 41, p.13.
55   TNA WO 201/156. Command Reorganisation, Nov 1940-July 1941. p.2.

and the troops.[56] From the base depots distribution was transported to Field Supply Depots which developed into larger supply centres by 1942.[57] Frontline units needed large numbers of vehicles to move supplies. Infantry Divisions needed 3,700 vehicles at full strength, which meant a large administrative 'tail' of men and equipment to keep them moving.

In the early phases of the campaign there was a lack of equipment, which reflected a delayed supply route from Britain and shortages at home. It took time to rebuild the depth of supplies required for British Forces to operate effectively.[58] In the autumn of 1940 the 7th Armoured Division received fresh deliveries of tanks when London made a bold move by supplying half the remaining British home tank strength for Operation Compass. In 1940, Operation Compass was planned as a five day raid due to a supply shortage, and Wavell's reluctance to start an offensive was partly because of a lack of equipment throughout the services.[59]

By August 1942 the Eighth Army received 400 tanks, 500 guns, 7,000 vehicles and thousands of tons of supplies. Again a huge increase in tanks and equipment re-armed divisions, with armoured strength increasing to 1,351 by the beginning of Operation Lightfoot. The Tunisian campaign was affected by the long supply routes which remained a problem until forward depots were built which enabled the Allies to complete the campaign. The numbers of troops and weight of material directly influenced operations in Tunisia, together with the stranglehold over the single supply route into Tunis. The Allied landings provided a new flow of equipment and reinforcements into North Africa. American planners chose ports further west to ensure safe supply ports but this arrangement added delays which impacted on the campaign for some months.

RAF support

Airpower ultimately provided an important role within the campaign but it took nearly three years to become fully effective. More information can be found in the detailed study of the effectiveness of the RAF by B.W. Gladman. However, his final conclusion, that RAF was the 'single greatest factor in land power' of victory is polemic to say the least and whilst acknowledging the importance of air power this assertion must be challenged, as armoured units quickly discovered, they could not hold ground once taken without Infantry and air units might have dominated ground but could retain

---

56   R. Micklem, *Transportation*, (London: The War Office, 1950), p.60, and Rainier, *Pipeline to Battle*, p.60. The railway facilitated the unloading of pipes en route.

57   TNA WO 201/370. Major operations Q (P) aspect, Dec 1941-Mar1942. DAQMG Office, 10 May 42.

58   TNA WO 201/2691, Operational reports: first Cyrenaican campaign, Sept 1940- Feb 1941. Appendix C, 20 Oct 1940.

59   Haglung, D.G., 'George C.Marshall and the Question of Military Aid to England, May-June 1940', *Journal of Contemporary History*, Vol.15,No.4, pp.745-760.

it.[60] In the early phases of the campaign, RAF 202 Group, under Air Commodore Collishaw, worked well with General O'Connor but Collishaw had a more simplistic approach to operations by insisting on squadrons making costly and repetitive daytime attacks, which reduced RAF strengths, however they inflicted damaging losses on the Italian Air Force, who lost over 1,200 aircraft in the first campaign into Libya.[61] Once In Cyrenaica, the Group focussed upon attacking airbases, ports and on supply convoys on the coast road.

In May 1941, Air Marshal Tedder became RAF CinC Middle East and he began a period of reorganising and re-building before the RAF could regain air superiority. Crusader was preceded by a massive air effort and during the offensive DAF commander Air Vice Marshal Coningham insisted that communications were targeted first, then enemy airfields and lastly to provide ground support for the Army, who still noted that the RAF was more visible over the battlefield, than previously.[62] By early 1942, the RAF was overstretched again covering the vulnerable forward position near Agedabia. Later during Gazala, Coningham wanted to concentrate on gaining air superiority and again on attacks against Axis supply columns, but direct ground support was not yet a tactic.

However within weeks, by June 1942, the RAF was committed to round the clock support of the Army. Cooperation remained poor as Coningham's HQ remained separate from Auchinleck's Army near Ruweisat Ridge. From late August sorties were better targeted and more effective because of improved intelligence, and the RAF gained air superiority again. The intensity of air operations was increased dramatically during Alam Halfa, the number of sorties doubled by the end of the battle. General Bayerlein noted how the, 'continuous and very heavy attacks of the RAF...pinned my troops to the ground and made impossible...any advance according to schedule'.[63] These continuous air attacks forced Panzerarmee to retreat.

From August 1942, the RAF became a central part of Eighth Army operations. The massed squadrons of medium bombers were a powerful force multiplier for the Eighth Army's firepower while the fighter squadrons secured air superiority.[64] Targeting and cooperation improved when Montgomery relocated his HQ adjacent to Coningham's HQ at Burg-el-Arab and they found that larger strikes committed by an Army level HQ were more effective.[65] Montgomery and Air Marshal Tedder differed on how the RAF would support the assault, Montgomery wanted it added to the preceding bombardment whilst Tedder wanted to 'hammer' the Axis positions

60   Gladman, *Intelligence and Anglo-American Air Support*, p.191.
61   Bickers, *The Desert Air War*, p.49. 58 shot down, 1,100 damaged and 91 captured intact.
62   Bungay, *Alamein*, p.104.
63   Richards & St George Saunders, *Royal Air Force. Vol II*, p.230. General Bayerlein, commander of *DAK*.
64   Chappell, *Wellington Wings*, p.103.
65   Mortensen, *Airpower and Ground Armies*, p.21.

for days beforehand.[66] Air superiority enabled the RAF to repeat its successful tactics of round the clock sorties on vehicle concentrations and the retreating Panzerarmee after Second Alamein, carrying out over 1,600 sorties, mostly on retreating columns and shipping.[67] By 1943 the Allied Mediterranean Air Forces were built up to achieve massive air superiority in Tunisia so that from then on Allied airpower became more effective in supporting ground forces and overwhelming the Luftwaffe. As more Allied Air Squadrons were deployed into Tunisia they impacted strongly on the final month of operations which was an important contribution to Allied victory.

The impact of Malta

The air battle for the control of the British base on Malta became one of the major, long term battles fought in the Mediterranean to 1943 and was also a major part of naval operations in this period. The island was a crucial forward base from which bombers, ships and submarines could damage the Axis supply route to Libya. It became protected with increasingly stronger anti-aircraft defences around the port and airbases, along with a growing air defence capability.[68] The Royal Navy's major role was to convoy supplies, personnel and aircraft to maintain it as a forward base for operations but its airspace was dominated by Axis planes bases in Sicily. The build-up of RAF strike forces in the autumn of 1941 caused Hitler to intervene again and he directed the Luftwaffe to reduce the island by air attack from January 1942. As the RAF Torpedo-bombers became more effective, Italian merchantmen called the route to Libya the, 'route of death'.[69] The battle for Malta influenced the North African campaign in terms of planning by the Prime Minister, the COS and GHQ Cairo, who became pre-occupied with preventing the island being totally neutralized.

The British attacks from Malta on Axis supply convoys certainly influenced the land campaign. The Axis responses to the attacks on a number of occasions affected decisions made during Crusader, Alam Halfa and Second Alamein and in Tunisia. In the spring of 1942 Churchill pushed Auchinleck for an immediate offensive to ease the pressure on Malta. Auchinleck and the Middle East Committee responded by questioning the how much Malta actually influenced Libyan supply routes and argued that even a limited offensive would not overcome the large numbers of Axis armour near the front.[70] The Navy and RAF re-built the offensive strength in aircraft and submarines so that Malta was resurgent from August, and took an increased toll of Axis shipping, which contributed to the defeat at Alamein. By 1943, the main

---

66   Richards & Saunders, *Royal Air Force. Vol II,* p.234.
67   TNA CAB 66/31/11. War Cabinet Weekly Resumè No.168. 12 Nov-19 Nov 1942, p.9.
68   Air Ministry, *The Air Battle Of Malta. The Official Account* (London: HMSO, 1944) p.60.
69   Lee Heide, *Whispering Death. My Wartime Adventures* (Oxford: Trafford Publishing, 2000) p.122.
70   TNA CAB 66/24/26. Telegram from ME Defence Committee to War Cabinet, 9 May 1942, pp.1-2.

target was the routes into Tunis-Bizerte, working with powerful Allied Air Forces they closed the supply routes which contributed to their final surrender in May.

The Mediterranean Fleet was mainly concerned with maintaining a strategic threat to the Italians, and dominating the Eastern Mediterranean, which protected British bases.[71] The CinC, Admiral A.B. Cunningham, believed Malta was a vital part of the war against Italian convoys and had to defend itself. He wanted Malta to be fully operational with submarines, destroyers and aircraft by April 1941.[72] The island became a key part of operations against the supply route to Tripoli. At first the island was still poorly equipped for air defence and vulnerable to blockade, despite its potential as a strike base.[73] The Royal Navy also developed a vital role supplying the Army along the coast, especially to Tobruk during the siege and when the Army advanced across Cyrenaica.

Conclusion

The British campaign in North Africa was influenced by terrain, but also by other military factors discussed here. These include the development of doctrinal improvisation, the effect of command and intelligence issues, the impact of supply issues and the growth of support from the RAF and Royal Navy. This chapter has discussed some examples of each of them on the campaign. All of these factors have been the focus of numerous studies which often argue that they were the major part of the reasons for British success and failure. The factors of supply, airpower and naval support influenced the campaign, and in some instances were indirectly influenced themselves by the terrain. The geography of the coastline dominated supply issues because the Army needed bases to advance or defend in Cyrenaica. RAF support for ground forces was overshadowed by the slower development of an effective airpower doctrine. Air power also influenced operational strategy because of the need to control airfields to give air-cover to naval operations, which again meant that ground forces were required to capture the area and this became much more apparent in the final Tunisian battles. Royal Naval support was essential to maintain the Army along the Libyan coastline and at Tobruk throughout 1941. However it too had additional separate roles to interdict the Axis supply routes and the maintenance of Malta to contribute to the British campaign.

---

71 Cunningham, *A Sailor's Odyssey*, p.241.
72 Playfair, *Mediterranean, Vol I*, pp.159-161.
73 Michael J. Budden, 'Defending the Indefensible? The Air Defence of Malta, *1936-1940.*' *War in History.* Volume 6 (4), pp.447-467, p.448.

12

Conclusion

This volume set out to determine the impact of terrain and its effect on improvisations of British tactical doctrine during operations in Egypt, Libya and Tunisia from 1940-1943. The evidence was provided from a range of primary source documents from numerous archives and a re-examination of the historiography. The primary battle reports, unit war diaries and soldiers' personal papers provided conclusive evidence about the impact of terrain features and details of changes in improvised doctrine, showing how much they affected British operations.

Any new study of the campaign should include an analysis of the geography and tactical terrain of the coastal sector in much greater detail now than previous works along with an assessment of Army operations. The analysis of the key terrain features at the tactical level and the development of doctrine, much of which was improvised, show they should be considered equally along with other military factors, which previous studies usually regard as the major influences on Army operations.

Much of the historiography has largely ignored the importance of the tactical terrain or assumed that it was of little importance and focussed on these other factors, including the impact of command and intelligence, equipment issues, supply problems and support from the RAF and Royal Navy. Other studies have considered topics such as morale, but only applied them to limited periods of the campaign, such as Jonathan Fennell's work.[1] Specific studies have been undertaken by Niall Barr, Jon Latimer and Bryn Hammond who all consider the Alamein battles in detail, while the impact of RAF operations and Command and Intelligence issues have been assessed by Gladman and Ferris. This study intends to contribute both the impact of terrain and about the development of doctrine which denotes the 'British way of fighting' during the Second World War.

At the operational level the geography of the coastal sector impacted on British forces as they made repeated attempts to capture and hold Cyrenaica in Libya during 1941-42. This approach logically aimed to safeguard the security of bases in Egypt

---

1   Which covers the related morale crisis of mid-1942.

around the Suez Canal and Alexandria, from air attacks and to keep Axis ground forces from threatening Middle East oil resources. British forces were unable to retain control of the province partially because the peninsula 'bulge' of land was too large an area to hold against a determined ground assault, and partially because it was too close to Axis air bases in Tripolitania and Sicily, the scale of Cyrenaica made it a hugely difficult region to defend, as was shown in 2010 by Libyan rebels, before NATO airstrikes stepped in to halt Qaddafi's armoured columns. At the tactical level there was a greater problem with the undulating plain offering so few suitable defensive sites that commanders chose to over-extend the frontlines in order to hold the area. This exacerbated the problems of having too few units to position along them and an over-extended supply position, noted in many other works. Behind the front, successive British commanders resorted to deploying their Brigade-Groups across widely separated sites in 1941 and 1942 as part of an overall defence, but this simply left them isolated and vulnerable to better coordinated Axis advances.

By mid-1942, the defence along the 'Gazala line' was flawed on two levels. Operationally it was in the wrong place, noted by some commanders such as Tuker, who argued for it to be further forward, away from the vulnerable Tobruk-Belhammed supply complex. Tactically the line was undermined by a series of low ridges many of which ran east-west rather than a more useful north-south alignment. The ridges became the focus of much of the fighting and against which the bulk of British armour was committed in piecemeal assaults, which highlighted poor British doctrine and only aided the equally stretched Axis defence. Cyrenaica was then lost for a second time which added to the summer crisis of 1942. The need to defend the peninsula's strategic airfields, which protected convoys to Malta, had overstretched the British forward positions of early Spring, whilst the later Gazala position was lost tactically, because it was still too large a area to defend by too few ground units. The key turning in the fighting was that four key defensive positions were lost at the southern end of the line, which forced Eighth Army back towards Tobruk.

The tactical terrain again showed its importance; in attempting to hold the Axis at Matruh in late June, turned out to be another mistaken British operation as the entire position was undermined by the better going along the higher plateau above the escarpment, so consequently Eighth Army was forced back to the Alamein sector. The confused series of battles which constituted First Alamein were fought over the Ruweisat and Miteiriya ridges and the surrounding vital terrain features. The British defensive position at El-Alamein has been the most well studied of the entire campaign, yet very few of accounts emphasize the importance of the terrain, apart from the secure flank provided by the Qattara Depression. At Second Alamein the key features were still a focal point for most British objectives and Eighth Army used new assault doctrines to target these key heights. The subsequent pursuit was also affected by the impact of terrain features along the way, complicated by adverse winter weather, a difficult supply situation and an over-cautious commander. Montgomery was hesitant and wanted to avoid repeating previous failures across the problematical Cyrenaica plain. He was also cautious when Axis forces halted at the stronger defensive sites, near Mersa Brega, Agheila and later sectors of high ground along the coast in Tripolitania.

During the final stages of the campaign the terrain on Tunisia had an even greater impact on British operations. The strength of the French built Mareth line forced other units to outflank the whole position in order to undermine the Axis defence. Then at the Wadi Akirit, considered by many to be one of the strongest defensive sites in North Africa, British plans were altered to capture the key high ground across the position. Finally the high Enfidaville sector was a series of mountainous hills which proved too difficult to retain and the British were forced to change their approach towards Tunis and switch Divisions to the First Army front for the final assault. Planning here made the terrain an integral part of the operation which targeted all the high ground positions along the route to Tunis.

The landscape impacted on tactical doctrinal with unit dispersion forcing them into more open formations. These were necessary and logical to minimize casualties but could perhaps have inflicted a different mind-set on commanders. The need to defend an extended frontline forced them to find new formations such as Jock Columns which best used the Artillery and Infantry. The improvised Jock Column tactics were undoubtedly successful at times, and caused attritional losses on Axis positions. They were used extensively from the early stages of the campaign and by Crusader, went onto the offensive after the British Armour had been depleted. Their widespread use on patrols continued well into 1942 but they remained weak and operated hit and run tactics which contributed to a 'scarper' mentality noted by some participants, which affected most British formations following Axis breakthroughs. With Infantry Brigades dispersed into numerous Jock columns, the firepower of the Artillery Regiments were also dispersed, whilst the Infantry companies were too weak to make a formed assault.

There were other problems with tactical doctrine, the battles at Gazala and during the retreats from Cyrenaica of 1941 and 1942, all showed the continued separation of Armour, Artillery and Infantry at the tactical level. Support Groups fought separately from the Armoured Brigades they were meant to assist. Later at Gazala, the Infantry Tank Brigades were often diverted away from the Infantry units they were protecting in order to make their own isolated attacks which smacked of desperation by Eighth Army. It took a lot more training time for armour to work well with Infantry battalions and there were still failures of coordination even by Second Alamein. British doctrine developed further under Montgomery from late 1942, where he developed a better-trained force for a specific operational assault to defeat the enemy.

Second Alamein highlighted the Army's new doctrine, which included night-time set-piece assaults supported by massive artillery bombardments and air power to break the Axis defences. This was combined with increased RAF and Naval targeting of Axis petrol supplies from June 1942 and contributed to the collapse of Axis forces and their long retreat back to Tunisia. The Eighth Army began to use these new assault doctrines which included concentrated artillery fire to support combined arms assaults. These became more effective at breaking into even stronger defences at Mareth, the Wadi

Akirit and the final attacks on Tunis. The defensive doctrine which had been used at Alam Halfa was successfully employed again at Medenine in March 1943. Here the Army took full advantage of a series of low hills to support their defensive Artillery defensive fire and had learnt to fight without massed RAF support. The breakthrough at the Tebaga Gap was the first major use of a planned assault supported by masses of ground attack aircraft and massed artillery to enable the armour to punch through the defensive positions. The Army doctrine now included a rapid assessment of the key terrain features which targeted the high ground and ensured they were captured first before the armour made a strong thrust along the main highway towards Tunis.

Churchill influenced events with his continuous interference of planning decisions and new command appointments, while Intelligence gathering became a fundamental part of the Army's planning process. HQs demanded increased knowledge of key terrain as the Army advanced into Tunisia and assault plans became flexible to adapt to the difficulties created by the more extreme landscape. The Naval attacks on Libyan supply routes and a new RAF doctrine affected the final stages of the campaign as the Allied Forces became highly effective in blocking supplies to Tunisia, and still provided massive air power to support 18th Army Group.

The main argument of this study is that the key terrain features across the North African coastal sector, had an important effect on British Army operations. The secondary theme has been to consider the changes in tactical doctrine, many of which were improvised, and these changes were also linked to the impact of the tactical features of the landscape. The Army developed its doctrine until it had become a more effective fighting force by 1943. One participant made the simple comment that, 'because the desert was so...open the least rise or promontory or ridge became of great importance.'[2] It was this overwhelming point that was a defining factor of British operations throughout the campaign.

2   Cox, *Tale of Two Battles*, p.135.

Appendix

British Army Unit Organisation

Infantry Battalions

Four Infantry companies of 80-120 men, and one HQ company with supporting Mortar and machinegun platoons.
Motor Infantry Battalions – Three Infantry Companies and one anti-tank company (16 guns).

Armour Regiments

Three line squadrons of 14-16 tanks each, and one HQ unit with Close Support vehicles.
Infantry or 'I' Tank Regiments – three squadrons of 17 tanks each and one HQ unit.

Artillery Regiments

Three batteries of 4-8 guns dependent on the calibre of the weapon.

Infantry / Motorised Infantry Brigades:

Three battalions, plus support units.
Support units included anti-tank, Engineer, Artillery, Signals and supply units.

Armoured Brigades

Three Armoured Regiments and one Motor battalion.

Armoured Divisions

Three Armoured Brigades, One Motor Infantry Brigade, plus support units of Artillery, Reconnaissance and Engineers.

Bibliography

PRIMARY SOURCES

The National Archives, Kew, London (TNA)
Air 23/1751. War Diary Monthly, July-August 1942.
AIR 27/1588. 274 Squadron Operations: Diary of events, May 1941.
HW 1/237. North Africa: Italy and Africa Air Operations, 21.11.41.
HW13/1, G.A.F. Intelligence summaries based on sigint.
WO 169/1185. 7 Armoured Division: Support Group, January – December 1941; February 1942.
WO 169/4486. 8th King's Royal Irish Hussars War Diary, 1941 November- 1942 December.
WO 169/5021. 5th Green Howards War Diary, January-November 1942.
WO 201/156. Command Reorganisation, Nov ember 1940-July 1941.
WO 201/349. Operation Compass, Reports.
WO 201/355. Action at Sidi Rezegh: 1st Kings Royal Rifle Corps, November 1941.
WO 201/357. Operation `Battleaxe': lessons of the campaign, June-November 1941.
WO 201/361. 7th Armoured Division: Account of Operations in Libya, November-December 1941.
WO 201/363. Operation `Crusader': air situation: diary of events. November-December 1941.
WO 201/. Major operations Q (P) aspect, December 1941-March 1942.
WO 201/371. Major operations `G' Planning: campaign. February-April 1942.
WO 201/372. 4th Indian Division Operations 1942.
WO 201/379. Operations in North Africa: General Ritchie's Report, May-June 1942.
WO 201/390. The Battle for Egypt: Operational Reports. 1942 May-September 1942.
WO 201/404. Operations: telegrams and reports, June 1942.
WO 201/405. Telegrams 12-16 June 1942.
WO 201/418. Crusader supply report, Admin. November 1941.
WO 201/419. Cyrenaica campaign: planning. March 1942.
WO 201/424. The October Battle of Alamein and the advance to Tripolitania. November-December 1942.

WO 201/432. Operation 'Lightfoot': planning. August 1942.

WO 201/450. Cyrenaica: Lessons from Operations. November 1941- March 1942.

WO 201/467. Seventh Armoured Division: operations leading to the capture of Tunis, 1 May-13 May 1943.

WO 201/471. 23rd Armoured Brigade: operations 'Lightfoot' and 'Supercharge'.

WO 201/493. Despatch by General Sir A.P. Wavell, July 1941.

WO 201/500. General Auchinleck's despatch on Operation 'Crusader'. Brief Survey of Operations between 21 Jan and 5 Feb 1942.

WO 201/511. 22nd Guards Brigade: operation instructions, March-September 1941.

WO 201/532. Eighth Army: Commanders conferences. December 1941-May 1942.

WO 201/538. Eighth Army: lessons from Operations, September 1941-August 1942.

WO 201/539. Eighth Army: intelligence matters. November 19 41-August 1942.

WO 201/540. Weekly Desert Reviews: Intelligence Reports. June-August 1942.

WO 201/578. Topography of Tunisia. Report by Eighth Army. March 1943.

WO 201/598. 8th Army Operations in Tunisia under 18th Army Group. February-May 1943.

WO 201/2156. Intelligence Summaries. January-March 1943.

WO 201/2357. Libya, Cyrenaica and Tripolitania planning, July 1941 – February 1942.

WO 201/2691. Operational reports: first Cyrenaican campaign, September 1940- February 1941.

WO 201/2692. Operational Reports: first Cyrenaican Campaign. METP No 10, Lessons of Cyrenaica.

WO 201/2692. Operational Reports: Western Desert. May-July 1942.

CAB 66/24/26. Telegram from ME Defence Committee to War Cabinet, 9 May 1942.

CAB 66/31/11. War Cabinet Weekly Resumè No.168. 12-19 November 1942.

CAB 106/379. Wavell's Despatch: Operations in the Western Desert.

PREM 3/285. Auchinleck's Despatch, July-October 1941.

Bovington Archives, Bovington Tank Museum, Dorset

2nd RTR War Diary. November 1941.

3rd RTR Diary.

6th RTR War Diary. November 1941.

7th RTR War Diary. Diary of events, June 1940-June 1941.

42nd RTR. Report by Major J.W.G. Tatum.

44th RTR Diary. 27 May – 1 June 1942.

50th RTR Diary. From the History of the 23 Armoured Brigade.

Breakout From Tobruk , 21 November 1941, by Brigadier Willison.

4th County of London Yeomanry Diary.

Liddell-Hart Centre For Military Archives (LHCMA), KCL, London
Rea Leakey papers.
G.P.B. Roberts papers.
Major Daniels paper.

Imperial War Museum (IWM), Lambeth, London
Papers of Maj. Gen. R. Briggs. 2nd Armd Bde.
Papers of Sgt W.R. Hill 2nd Gloucester Hussars Yeomanry and LRDG.
Papers of Lieutenant Colonel M E Parker.
Montgomery Papers.
Papers of Maj. J.M. Mc Swiney.

Imperial War Museum Duxford (IWM), Cambridgeshire
Papers of Deutsches Afrika Korps.

Churchill Archives Centre (CAC), Churchill College, Cambridge
Papers of Lieutenant-General Thomas Corbett.

John Rylands Library (JRL), Manchester University, Manchester
Auchinleck Papers. AUC/825, Note on Middle East Policy to the ME Defence
    Committee, 27 April 1942.

National Army Museum (NAM), Chelsea, London
NAM 2009-12-19-4-1, Report by Maj. Gen E. Dorman Smith. 27 May 1942.

Unpublished Primary Sources
Gerald Jackson, 'A Long Parting', Private Memoir, Undated, Unpublished.

Official Histories and Published Primary Documents
Air Ministry, *The Air Battle Of Malta. The Official Account* (London: H.M.S.O. 1944).
Butler, J.R.M, *Grand Strategy, Vol II.* Sept 1939- June 1941 (London: HMSO, 1957).
H.M.S.O., *The Tiger Kills. The Story of the Indian Divisions in the North African
    Campaign* (London: HMSO, 1944).
Hinsley, F.H. (ed.), *British Intelligence in the Second World War. Its Influence on Strategy
    and Operations. Vol I* (London: HMSO, 1979).
MLRS, *Middle East Training Pamplets, Vol I* (Buxton: Derbyshire, 2011).
Playfair, I.S.O, The Mediterranean and Middle East. *Vol I* (Uckfield: Naval &
    Military Press, 2004).
Playfair, I.S.O The Mediterranean and Middle East. *Vol II* (Uckfield: Naval &
    Military Press, 2004).
Playfair, I.S.O *The Mediterranean and Middle East. Vol III* (Uckfield: Naval & Military
    Press, 2004).

Playfair, I.S.O *The Mediterranean and Middle East. Vol IV* (Uckfield: Naval & Military Press, 2004).

SECONDARY SOURCES

Air Historical Branch, *Air Support* (London: Air Ministry, 1955).
Atkinson, R, *An Army at Dawn. The War in North Africa, 1942-1943* (London: Abacus, 2004).
Barr, N, *Pendulum of War. The Three Battles of Alamein* (Woodstock: Overlook Press, 2004).
Barnes, B.S, *Operation Scipio. The 8th Army at the Battle of the Wadi Akirit, 6th April 1943* (Market Weighton: Sentinel, 2007).
Barnett, C, *The Desert Generals* (London: Castle Books, 2004).
Bates, P, *Dance of War. The Story of the Battle For Egypt* (London: Leo Cooper, 1992).
Beaumont, J, *Australia's War 1939-1945* (Sydney: Allen & Unwin, 1996).
Bennett, R, *Ultra and Mediterranean Strategy,*(New York: William Morrow.1989),
Bickers, R.T, *The Desert Air War* (London: Leo Cooper, 1991).
Bidwell, S & Graham, D, *Firepower. The British Army Weapons & Theories of War 1904-1945* (London: Pen & Sword, 2004).
Billany, D, *The Trap* (London: Panther, 1964).
Birkby, C, *Uncle George. The Boer Boyhood, Letters and Battles of Lieutenant-General George Edwin Brink* (Johannesburg: Jonathan Ball, 1987).
Blaxland, G, *The Plain Cook and the Showman. The First and Eighth Armies in North Africa (*Abingdon: Book Club Associates, 1977).
Borthwick, A, *Battalion. A British Infantry Unit's Actions from El Alamein to the Elbe, 1942-1945* (London: Bâton Wicks, 1994, first published in 1946)
Brett-James, A, *Ball of Fire. The Fifth Indian Division in the Second World War* (Aldershot: Gale & Polden, 1951), From : http://www.ourstory.info/library/4-ww2/Ball/fire09.html.
Brooks, S, ed., *Montgomery and the Eighth Army* (London: The Bodley Head, 1991).
Buckingham, W.F, *Tobruk. The Great Siege 1941-2* (Stroud: Tempus, 2008).
Bungay, S, *Alamein* (London: Aurum Press, 2002).
Carver, M, *El Alamein* (London: B.T. Batsford, 1963).
Carver, M, *Tobruk* (London: B.T. Batsford, 1964).
Carver, M, *Dilemmas of the Desert War* (Staplehurst: Spellmount, 1986).
Chappell, F.R, *Wellington Wings. An RAF Intelligence Officer in the Western Desert* (Manchester: Crécy Books, 1992).
Clay, E.W, *The Path of the 50th. The Story of the 50th (Northumbrian) Division in the Second World War 1939-1945* (Aldershot: Gale & Polden, 1950).
Clayton, T & Craig, P, *End of the Beginning* (London: Hodder & Stoughton, 2002).
Clifford, A, *Crusader* (George Harrap, 1942).
Clifton, G, *The Happy Hunted* (London: Panther, 1952).

Cochrane, P, *Charlie Company. In Service with C Company 2nd Queen's Own Cameron Highlanders 1940-1944* (Stroud: Spellmount, 2007).

Connell, J, Auchinleck (London: Cassell, 1959).

Connell, J, *Wavell, Scholar & Soldier* (London: Collins, 1964).

Cooper, A, *Cairo In The War 1939-1945* (London: Penguin, 1995).

Cox, G, *A Tale of Two Battles. A Personal Memoir of Crete and the Western Desert 1941* (London: William Kimber, 1987).

Crimp, R.L, *The Diary of a Desert Rat* (London: Pan, 1974).

Crisp, R, *Brazen Chariots. An Account of tank warfare in the Western Desert, November-December 1941* (London: Frederick Muller, 1959).

D'Arcy Dawson, J, *Tunisian Battle* (London: Macdonald & Co, 1944).

D'Este, C, *Warlord. A Life of Churchill at War, 1874-1945* (London: Allen Lane, 2009).

De Guingand, F, *Operation Victory* (London: Hodder & Stoughton, 1947).

Delaforce, P, *Monty's Marauders. Black Rat & Red Fox: 4th and 8th Independent Armoured Brigades in WW2* (Brighton: Tom Donovan, 1997).

Delaforce, P, *Battles With Panzers, 1RTR & 2RTR at War* (Stroud: Sutton, 2003).

Delaforce, P, *Taming the Panzers. Monty's Tank Battalions, 3rd RTR at War* (Stroud: Sutton, 2003).

Devine, A.D, *Road To Tunis* (London: Collins, 1944).

Doherty, R, *A Noble Crusade. The History of Eighth Army 1941-45* (Staplehurst: Spellmount, 1999).

Doherty, R, *The Sound Of History. El Alamein 1942* (Staplehurst: Spellmount, 2002).

Doherty, R, *None Bolder. The History Of The 51st Highland Division In The Second World War* (Staplehurst: Spellmount, 2006).

Doherty, R, *Ubique. The Royal Artillery in the Second World War* (Stroud: History Press, 2008).

Dornan, P, *Last Man Standing, Herb Ashby and the Battle of El Alamein* (Crows Nest NSW: Allan & Unwin, 2006).

Douglas, K, *Alamein To Zem Zem* (London: Bantam Books, 1985).

Duffy, C, *Frederick the Great, A Military Life* (Oxford: Routledge, 1988).

Falvey, D, *A Well Known Excellence. British Artillery and an Artilleryman in World War Two* (London: Brassey's, 2002).

Farndale, M, *The Years of Defeat. 1939-1941. History of the Royal Regiment of Artillery* (London: Brassey's, 1996).

Farran, R, *Winged Dagger. Adventures on Special Service* (London: Cassell, 1999).

Fennell, J, *Combat and Morale in the North African Campaign* (Cambridge: Cambridge University Press, 2011).

Fergusson, B, *The Trumpet in the Hall* (London: Collins, 1970).

Ferris, J.R, *Intelligence and Strategy, selected essays* (Oxford: Routledge, 2005).

Fletcher, D, *The Great British Tank Scandal. British Armour in the Second World War. Part 1* (London: HMSO, 1999).

Ford, K, *Gazala 1942. Rommel's Greatest Victory* (Oxford: Osprey, 2008).

Ford, K, *The Mareth Line 1943* (Botley: Osprey, 2012).

Forty, G (ed.), *Tanks Across the Desert. The War Diary of Jake Wardrop* (London: William Kimber, 1981).

Forty, G *The First Victory General O'Connor's Desert Triumph Dec 1940-Feb 1941* (London: Guild, 1990).

Fraser, D, *And We Shall Shock Them. The British Army in the Second World War* (London: Cassell & Co, 2002).

French, D, *Raising Churchill's Army. The British Army and the War against Germany 1919-1945* (Oxford: Oxford University Press, 2001).

Frost, J, *A Drop Too Many* (London: Sphere Books, 1983).

Gat, A, *British Armour Theory and the Rise of the Panzer Arm. Revising the Revisionists* (London: Macmillan, 2000).

Gladman, B.W, *Intelligence and Anglo-American Air Support in World War Two. The Western Desert and Tunisia, 1940-1943* (Basingstoke: Palgrave Macmillan, 2009).

Graham, D, *Against Odds: reflections on the experiences of the British Army, 1914-45* (London: Macmillan, 1999).

Greenfield, G, *Desert Episode* (London: Panther, 1955).

Greenfield, G, *Chasing the Beast,* (London: Richard Cohen, 1998).

Griffin H.J, *An Eighth Army Odyssey* (Bishop Auckland: Pentland Press, 1997).

Griffiths, P, *Forward into Battle* (Chichester: Anthony Bird, 1981).

Griffiths, P, *World War II Desert Tactics* (Oxford: Osprey, 2008).

Gudmundsson, B, *Inside the Afrika Korps, The Crusader Battles, 1941-1942* (London: Greenhill, 1999).

Hamilton, S, *Armoured Odyssey. 8th Royal Tank Regiment in The Western desert 1941-1942. Palestine, Syria, Egypt 1943-1944. Italy 1944-1945* (London: Tom Donovan, 1995).

Hammond, B, *El Alamein: The Battle that Turned the Tide of the Second World War* (Oxford: Osprey, 2012).

Harris, J.P, & Toase, F.H (eds.), *Armoured Warfare* (London: Batsford, 1990).

Harrison, F, *Tobruk. The Birth of a Legend* (London: Cassell, 1996).

Hart, P, *The South Notts Hussars: The Western Desert 1940-1942* (Barnsley: Pen & Sword, 2010).

Heide, L, *Whispering Death. My Wartime Adventures* (Oxford: Trafford Publishing, 2000).

Holland, J, *Fortress Malta. An Island Under Siege 1940-1943* (London: Phoenix, 2004).

Holland, J, *Together We Stand. North Africa 1942-1943: Turning the Tide in the West* (London: Harper Collins, 2006).

Holmes, R, *Bir Hacheim. Desert Citadel* (London: Pan Ballantine, 1971).

Holmes, R, *Battlefields of the Second World War* (London: BBC, 2003).

Humble, R, *Crusader. The Eighth Army's Forgotten Victory, November 1941-January 1942* (London: Leo Cooper, 1987).

Horrocks, B, *A Full Life* (London: Collins, 1960).

Jentz, T.L, *Tank Combat in North Africa. The Opening Rounds. Operations Sonnenblume, Brevity, Skorpion and Battleaxe. February 1941-June 1941* (Atglen: Schiffer Publishing, 1998).

Joly, C, *Take These Men* (London: Constable, 1955).

Kelly, O, *Meeting the Fox. The Allied Invasion of Africa, from Operation Torch to Victory in Tunisia* (New York: John Wiley, 2002).

Kenneally, J, *The Honour And The Shame* (London: Headline Review, 2007).

Kippenberger, H, *Infantry Brigadier* (Oxford University Press: London, 1949)

Kitchen, M, *Rommel's Desert War. Waging World War Two in North Africa, 1941-1943* (Cambridge: Cambridge University Press, 2009).

Latimer, J, *Operation Compass 1940. Wavell's Whirlwind Offensive* (Oxford: Osprey, 2000).

Latimer, J, *Alamein* (London: John Murray, 2002).

Lawlor, S, *Churchill and the Politics of War, 1940-1941*(Cambridge: Cambridge University Press, 1994).

Leakey, R, *Leakey's Luck. A Tank Commander with nine lives* (Stroud: Sutton, 1999.

Levine, A.J, *The War Against Rommel's Supply Lines, 1942-1943* (Westport: Praeger, 1999).

Ronald Lewin, *The Life & Death Of The Afrika Korps,* (London: Pen & Sword, 2003).

Liddell-Hart, B.H, *The Rommel Papers* (London: Hamlyn, 1984).

Liddell-Hart, B.H, *The Other Side Of The Hill* (London: Pan Books, 1999).

Lloyd Owen, D, *Providence Their Guide. The Long Range Desert Group 1940-1945* (Barnsley: Leo Cooper, 2003).

Lucas, J, *Panzer Army Afrika* (London: Macdonald and Jane's, 1977).

Lyman, R, *The Longest Siege. Tobruk The Battle That saved North Africa* (London: Macmillan, 2009).

Majdalany, F, *The Battle of El Alamein. Fortress in the Sand* (University of Pennsylvania Press, 2003).

Masters, D, *With Pennants Flying, The Immortal Deeds of the Royal Armoured Corps* (London: Eyre & Spottiswoode, 1943).

McKee, A, *El Alamein. Ultra and the Three Battles* (London: Souvenir, 1991).

Mead, R, *The Last Great Cavalryman. The Life of Richard McCreery, Commander Eighth Army* (Barnsley: Pen & Sword Military, 2012)

Megargee, G.P, *Inside Hitler's High Command* (Lawrence: University Press of Kansas, 2000).

Mellenthin, F.W, *Panzer Battles* (Stroud: Tempus, 2001).

Micklem, R, *Transportation* (London: The War Office, 1950).

Montgomery, B.L., *El Alamein to the River Sangro* (London: Hutchinson & Co, 1948).

Montgomery, B.L., *The Memoirs of Field Marshal Montgomery* (London: Collins, 1958).

Moorehead, A, *African Trilogy* (London: Hamish Hamilton, 1946).

Moreman, T, *Desert Rats. British 8th Army in North Africa 1941-43* (Oxford: Osprey, 2007).

Morewood, S, *The British Defence of Egypt 1935-1940: Conflict and Crisis in the Eastern Mediterranean* (London: Frank Cass, 2005).

Mortensen, D.R, (ed.), *Airpower and Ground Armies. Essays on the Evolution of Anglo-American Air Doctrine 1940-1943* (Alabama: Air University Press, 1998).

Neillands, R, *The Desert Rats. 7th Armoured Division 1940-1945* (London: Weidenfeld & Nicolson, 1991).

Neillands, R, *Eighth Army. The Triumphant Desert Army that held the Axis at Bay from North Africa to the Alps, 1939-1945* (Woodstock: Overlook Press, 2004).

Parker, J, *Desert Rats. From El Alamein to Basra* (London: Bounty Books, 2004).

Pitt, B, *The Crucible of War. Wavell's Command. Vol I* (London: Cassell & Co, 2001).

Pitt, B, *The Crucible of War. Auchinleck's Command. Vol II* (London: Cassell & Co, 2001).

Pitt, B, The Crucible of War. Montgomery's Command. Vol III (London: Cassell & Co, 2001).

Place, T.H, *Military Training in the British Army 1940-1944. From Dunkirk to D-Day* (London: Frank Cass, 2000).

Porch, D, *Hitler's Mediterranean Gamble. The North African and Mediterranean in World War I,* (London: Weidenfeld & Nicholson, 2004).

PRO, *Special Forces in the Desert War 1940-1943*(London: PRO Publications, 2001).

Rainier, P.W, *Pipeline to Battle* (New York: Random House, 1943).

Richards, D. & St George-Saunders, H, *Royal Air Force 1939-1945, Vol II. The Fight Avails* (London: HMSO, 1954).

Rolf, D, *The Bloody Road To Tunis,* (London: Greenhill Books, 2001).

Rommel, E, *Infantry Attacks* (New York: Fall River Press, 1990).

Roy, K, *War and Society in Colonial India* (Oxford: OUP, 2006).

Salerno, R.M, *Vital Crossroads. Mediterranean Origins of the Second World War, 1935-1940,* (New York: Cornell University Press, 2002).

Sandford, K, *Mark of the Lion. The Story of Capt Charles Upham, V.C. and Bar* (London: Hutchinson, 1962).

Sawyer, R.D, *Sun Tzu. Art of War* (Oxford: Westview Press, 1994).

Schmidt, H.W, *With Rommel in the Desert* (New York: Bantam, 1979).

Schofield, V, *Wavell, Soldier & Statesmen* (London: John Murray, 2006).

Spooner, T, *Supreme Gallantry. Malta's Role in the Allied Victory 1939-1945* (London: John Murray, 1996)

Stainforth, P, *Wings Of The Wind. Active Service with the 1st Parachute Brigade* (London: Grafton Books, 1988).

Stevens, G.R, Fourth Indian Division (Uckfield: Naval & Military Press, 2011).

Stewart, A, *The Early Battles of Eighth Army, Crusader to the Alamein Line 1941-1942* (Barnsley: Leo Cooper, 2002).

Strawson, J, *The Battle for North Africa* (New York: Charles Scribner's Sons, 1969).

Strawson, J, *El Alamein. Desert Victory* (London: Sphere Books, 1982).

Lord Tedder, *With Prejudice* (London: Cassell, 1966).

Trevor-Roper, H, *Hitler's War Directives 1939-1945* (Edinburgh: Berlin, 2004).

Tuker, F, *Approach to Battle* (London: Cassell, 1963).

Urban, M, *The Tank War. The British band of Brothers – one tank regiment's World War II* (London: Abacus, 2013).

Verney, G.L, *The Desert Rats. The 7th Armoured Division in World War Two* (London: Greenhill, 1990).

Verney, J, *Going to the Wars* (London: The Reprint Society, 1955).

Watson, B.A, *Exit Rommel. The Tunisian Campaign, 1942-43* (Mechanicsburg: Stackpole, 2007).

Weldon, H.E.C, *Drama In Malta* (Uckfield: Naval & Military Press, 2008).

Wynn, H, *Desert Eagles* (Shrewsbury: AirLife, 2001).

Young, C.P.S, *Men of Alamein* (Stevenage: Spa Books, 1987).

Journals

R.A. Bagnold, 'Early Days of the Long Range Desert Group', *The Geographical Journal*, Vol.5, No.1/2, pp.30-42.

Buckley, J, 'Tackling the Tiger: The Development of British Armoured Doctrine for Normandy 1944'. *Journal of Military History*. Vol 74 (4). pp.1161-1184.

Michael J. Budden, 'Defending the Indefensible? The Air Defence of Malta, *1936-1940.*' *War in History*. Vol 6 (4), pp.447-467, p.448.

Hafiz, 'The Offensive in Libya: December 1940-February 1941,' *Journal of the Royal United Services Institute for Defence Studies*, Vol.101 (602), pp.206-216.

Haglung,D.G., 'George C.Marshall and the Question of Military Aid to England, May-June 1940', *Journal of Contemporary History*, Vol.15 (4), pp.745-760.

K.S. Sandford, 'Libyan Frontiers', *The Geographical Journal*, Vol.96, No.6, pp.377-388.

Conference Papers

Dr. C. Mann (RMAS), *'Not what Pugilists call "good finishers": The Eighth Army's Command and conduct of operations in Tunisia March–May 1943.*' Symposium at Birmingham University, 14 November 2012.

Electronic Sources

https://www.awm.gov.au/collection/records/awm52/subclass.asp?levelID=297. AWM 52 8/2/16/6. 16th Infantry Brigade, War Diary. January February 1941, pp.1-2. Accessed 7 February 2012.

http://www.bbc.co.uk/ww2peopleswar/stories/94/a2064494.shtml, Memoir of James Palmer, 2nd RTR. Article ID: A2064494. Accessed 17 June 2011.

http://www.desertrats.org.uk/battles1941.htm. Maps for Gazala, Alamein and Alam Halfa. Accessed 3 January 2014.

http://www.iwm.org.uk/collections/item/object/1030002496. IWM, Montgomery Papers, Manuscript Draft of Field Marshal Viscount Montgomery of Alamein's Personal Message on the Eve of the Battle of Medenine, March 1943, Accessed 12 May 2012.

http://www.nzetc.org/tm/scholarly/tei-WH2-21Ba-c5.html. 21 Battalion History, p.119, accessed 29 March2012.

http://nzetc.victoria.ac.nz/tm/scholarly/tei-WH2Arti-c10-1.html.   NZ   Official History online version, accessed 12 March 2011.

http://www.qdg.org.uk/pages/WW2-Part-2-73.php , Detailed History of the Kings Dragoon Guards, World War Two – Part 2, El Agheila, Msus, Tobruk, Bir Gubi 1941-1942, accessed 27 July 2012.

Index

INDEX OF PLACES

INDEX OF PEOPLE

INDEX OF BRITISH , COMMONWEALTH
& ALLIED MILITARY FORMATIONS

INDEX OF GERMAN MILITARY FORMATIONS

INDEX OF ITALIAN MILITARY FORMATIONS

INDEX OF GENERAL & MISCELLANEOUS TERMS

Wolverhampton Military Studies

www.helion.co.uk/wolverhamptonmilitarystudies

Editorial board

Professor Stephen Badsey
  Wolverhampton University

Professor Michael Bechthold
  Wilfred Laurier University

Professor John Buckley
  Wolverhampton University

Major General (Retired) John Drewienkiewicz

Ashley Ekins
  Australian War Memorial

Dr Howard Fuller
  Wolverhampton University

Dr Spencer Jones
  Wolverhampton University

Nigel de Lee
  Norwegian War Academy

Major General (Retired) Mungo Melvin
  British Commission for Military History

Dr Michael Neiberg
  US Army War College

Dr Eamonn O'Kane
  Wolverhampton University

Professor Fransjohan Pretorius
  University of Pretoria

Dr Simon Robbins
  Imperial War Museum

Professor Gary Sheffield
  Wolverhampton University

Commander Steve Tatham PhD
  Royal Navy
  The Influence Advisory Panel

Professor Malcolm Wanklyn
  Wolverhampton University

Professor Andrew Wiest
  University of Southern Mississippi

Submissions

The publishers would be pleased to receive submissions for this series. Please contact us via email (info@helion.co.uk), or in writing to Helion & Company Limited, Unit 8 Amherst Business Centre, Budbrooke Road, Warwick, CV34 5WE, England.

Titles

No.1 *Stemming the Tide. Officers and Leadership in the British Expeditionary Force 1914* Edited by Spencer Jones (ISBN 978-1-909384-45-3)

No.2 *'Theirs Not To Reason Why': Horsing the British Army 1875–1925* Graham Winton (ISBN 978-1-909384-48-4)

No.3 *A Military Transformed? Adaptation and Innovation in the British Military, 1792– 1945* Edited by Michael LoCicero, Ross Mahoney and Stuart Mitchell (ISBN 978-1-909384-46-0)

No.4 *Get Tough Stay Tough. Shaping the Canadian Corps, 1914–1918* Kenneth Radley (ISBN 978-1-909982-86-4)